Contents

Dedication   v

Special Thanks   vii

Chapter 1   Outward Bound   1

Chapter 2   House Hunting   15

Chapter 3   Just My Imagination   37

Chapter 4   Storm Chaser   53

Chapter 5   The Dilemma   63

Chapter 6   Mulling It Over   75

Chapter 7   Judgment Day   83

Chapter 8   Making the Deal and Dealing the Dosh!   97

Chapter 9   Shopping, Money, More Money, More Shopping   119

Chapter 10   Just a Few Bags   133

Chapter 11   Pool with a View   145

Chapter 12   From Synchronized Buzzing to Synchronized Swimming   157

Chapter 13   Pork and Plastic   169

Chapter 14   A Tale of Two Chickens   183

Chapter 15   'Bona Gent'   197

Chapter 16   The Bull Run   219

Chapter 17   The Melon Man   231

Chapter 18   A Little Snip Here!   243

Chapter 19   A Fantastic Day   257

Chapter 20   When the Orange Blossoms   267

CW01499002

Orange Blossom Beginnings

by

Angela Love

authorHOUSE®

AuthorHouse™ UK Ltd.
500 Avebury Boulevard
Central Milton Keynes, MK9 2BE
www.authorhouse.co.uk
Phone: 08001974150

This book is a work of non-fiction. Unless otherwise noted, the author and the publisher make no explicit guarantees as to the accuracy of the information contained in this book and in some cases, names of people and places have been altered to protect their privacy.

© 2007 Angela Love. All rights reserved.

No part of this book may be reproduced, stored in a retrieval system, or transmitted by any means without the written permission of the author.

First published by AuthorHouse 6/26/2007

ISBN: 978-1-4259-6589-1 (sc)

Printed in the United States of America
Bloomington, Indiana

This book is printed on acid-free paper.

Dedication

I dedicate this book to my parents, John and Marian Heslop. Dad, you always believed that I could be a poet or a writer. Mum, you brought me up to believe I could be anything I wanted to be. God bless you both in heaven.

Special Thanks

I give special thanks to my wonderful husband Colin, who tolerates all my moods and imperfections and to Blaise and Ryan, who brighten up my life. This book wouldn't exist without you. Thanks also to my wonderful friend and illustrator, Christina Kemp, whose skill as an artist needs no words.

Chapter 1
Outward Bound

A million thoughts flowed in and out of my befuddled brain, carried like flotsam, this way and that, twisting, spinning and heading in no particular direction but flowing with all speed to an ultimate destination. The thought 'what happens to flotsam when it gets to the sea?' entered my head. I for one really didn't know the answer but sought it for self-assurance. For just like the flotsam, my life had been carried along with a yearning.

I often asked myself 'what I was yearning for?' Was it some drop of gypsy blood that drove me or was I, (as I felt most of the time,) just floundering on the sea of menopausal mystery, misery and chaos? Well, I would normally laugh at myself. However, there were others in my household that were affected by my soul searching. I reflected how readily they followed me on my journey into the unknown. I must therefore, have had some degree of reason and logic to my search for a better life-style that struck a chord or two with them.

'Them' by the way, are my family. My dear husband Colin, a rock in my turmoil, Blaise-Lianne my bohemian ten year old blessing of a daughter, Ryan, my stepson, well grounded, pleasant and as happy go lucky as I have ever found a teenage boy and our very old cat Zoetje, pronounced Zoochie (Dutch for little sweetie!)

Did I mention the entourage of at least one hundred stuffed toys of varying form, making up the extended imaginative family of my daughter? No I thought perhaps I hadn't. After all, it was my daily quest to rid the house of as many of these as I possibly could, whilst Blaise was out of eye and earshot. As we started yet another venture into the unknown, my supportive family minus Ryan, was with me as we headed off in the direction of Gatwick Airport.

Our quest was to find a house in Spain. I had suffered a back injury, a slipped disc, which meant that it was very difficult for me to be in sitting position and better for me if I pottered about or lay down flat. Having endured several painful sessions at the physiotherapists, on my last visit, I was told that it would be a good idea for me to relax more.

"Take a holiday," she said, "bathe in the sun, do nothing except potter about a bit."

Colin had agreed with her. He thought it would be an excellent idea to combine our quest for a home abroad with a relaxing break. He thought it would cheer me up and be a welcome diversion from the excruciating pain I felt on a daily basis. I happily agreed and our quest to find a house in Spain began in earnest.

To be more precise, our quest was to view the area and houses in the Valencia region of Spain. Colin and I, having first looked in France and the commercial and not so commercial Costas of Spain, decided that our starting point would be Valencia and the Costa del Azahar. The area, unknown to both of us and by all accounts a place where a good bargain, within our budget, was still to be had, was featured in 'Living Spain' magazine and had captured my imagination. With cases packed, Poshie (Blaise's favourite stuffed toy, a brown fluffy dog with a ribbon tied around its neck) tucked firmly into Blaise's in-flight backpack, folders, directions, magazines and the necessary documents such as passports and driving licenses safely tucked in my handbag, we set off.

I had booked our car in a long-term car park, so our first port of call was BCP, Gatwick. This was an experience in itself for us. We were usually reliant upon the goodwill of friends for 'drop off' and 'pick up' at airports. But the price seemed very reasonable and so I thought we should try it out.

I glanced at my checklist, flights were booked, agents contacted, car hire arranged, accommodation booked, all tickets, passports and money were safe in my bag, everything needed was present and correct. Now all we needed to do was arrive in one piece in Valencia and preferably together and our adventure would begin.

Colin drove and with the directions to BCP held firmly in my hand, I navigated while Blaise held an imaginary conversation with Poshie. We looked like a fine happy-go-lucky family. All of us were in good spirits and looking forward to the trip. Five days was enough to combine serious property viewing with just enough relaxation to keep Blaise from boredom.

"Colin, we are definitely going in the wrong direction, you have to go back on yourself at that roundabout!" I said calmly, having studied the map intently.

"Yeah, I think you are right Ange. I'll turn around."

For once Colin agreed without fuss and turned the car around. Directions in hand, we picked up the correct road and from that point on found our way easily to BCP.

We followed the notice board instructions BCP had erected, which was to leave the car in the chevron box and make our way to the reception. We presented ourselves at reception and booked in. It was very straightforward. We were advised to board the coach that would take us directly to Gatwick North Terminal.

BCP's set up was impressive. There were drinks and snacks machines to hand. Friendly and courteous staff greeted you too and it was altogether a very pleasant experience. Just the sort of experience you want when embarking on your holiday.

Blaise and I paid a visit to the toilet while we had the chance. The toilets were spotlessly clean.

"I'll wait for you outside Blaise," I yelled over the sound of Blaise's enthusiastic singing.

"OK mum," Blaise yelled back and continued with her song.

Colin was waiting outside and was talking away merrily to the coach driver. The coach wasn't leaving for another ten minutes and we didn't have to rush. Suddenly as I stood in BCP's reception, I realized that you could hear Blaise singing in the toilet. Colin and I laughed quietly, noticing the amusement on other passengers' faces as they booked in. Blaise's singing could definitely be summed up in one word… ENTHUSIASTIC! Bless her; she had the ability to cheer up everyone around her without even knowing it. She sang in the bathroom, in public toilets, in restaurants, in airport lounges and in pub restaurants. Yes, just about anywhere there was a bathroom for her to visit; she had a song bursting forth.

Blaise eventually appeared, with a great big smile on her face and we boarded the coach. No more than five minutes later we disembarked the comfortable BCP coach and collected our luggage.

Once inside Gatwick, we made our way to the nearest departure screen and looked for our flight number. The flight to Valencia was a scheduled flight, so fortunately for us, it was not likely to suffer a delay. The flight was due out on time and we would have sufficient time for a quick browse in the shops before we would be called to board. This was most fortunate; as I noticed Blaise was wearing most of the hot chocolate bought from the BCP drinks machine, down the front of her new and once very white T-shirt! Ten minutes later, wearing another new T-shirt, a clean and tidy'ish Blaise was ready to board the plane with Colin and me.

As the aeroplane taxied down the runway and the engines roared, my thoughts were already in Spain. What if the place didn't suit us? What if we hadn't got enough money? I felt a sharp twinge in my back as I sat back and a sigh escaped me. Colin squeezed my hand.

"We'll be up in a minute," he said, smiling.

Colin, aware that I didn't like flying, mistook my 'what if and ouch' look for air fright. I smiled as the aeroplane lifted off. I took out my book, pushed my spectacles further up my nose and dived into the text. Two hours later, we descended into Valencia airport, with a perfect blue sky and a brilliant yellow sun to greet us. At last, we were here. I had butterflies in my stomach; we were a step nearer our dream. I smiled at Colin and Blaise, realizing what a truly wonderful family I had.

Colin headed towards passport control and Blaise trotted behind him, looking for a toilet and a chance to stretch her vocal chords once again. Since my back was giving me some considerable pain, I walked with a very awkward gait and some of my fellow passengers stared at me in the most peculiar way. Perhaps they thought I was practicing a sketch from 'Monty Python.' It certainly felt like I was. I sort of slid and shuffled my way along, as this was the most pain free way of walking and in so doing, I caught sight of myself in the airport wall mirror.

"Good Lord is that me?" I said aloud, "I look like grandfather out the comedy series Bread."

My hair had greyed terribly since my slipped disc and I, not wanting to dye it, had left it 'au natural,' since I figured it would only get bleached by the sun and chlorine.

The passports were examined carefully. The guard looked at my passport and pointed to me. I looked over at Colin, lines of anxiety creasing my face. The guard was saying something I didn't understand and I wondered what, if anything, I had done wrong. Perhaps my awkward shuffle had been mistaken for something else.

"Please Lord; don't let him think I have a bag of something illegal shoved up my anus!" I whispered to Colin.

Colin looked at the officer, then me. The guard pointed at my passport.

"Colin, what does he want, what's wrong?" I asked, panic struck.

Colin smiled and his eyes lit up.

"He's saying happy birthday Ange," Colin announced with a broad smile on his face.

The guard pointed to where my date of birth was written.

"Ah yes! It was yesterday," I replied, beaming at the guard, who was grinning from ear to ear at me.

"Colin isn't that just so sweet of him to wish me happy birthday?" I said excitedly, my anxiety totally forgotten.

"I think I am going to like this place just fine," I added jovially.

I searched for my phrase book to check that my interpretation was correct and Colin headed towards baggage reclaim.

It was so quiet at the airport, hardly any tourists at all. At least what they wrote about the area was true. It was not your usual tourist place. Most people were either here on business or lived here. But the lack of bustle and hassle was delightful, not at all like an arrivals hall in a holiday resort's main airport.

I headed off to find Hertz car rental whilst Colin and Blaise waited for our luggage. My past experience of Hertz car rental (in Alicante years ago) was not a particularly pleasant one. I was charged several extras when I didn't want them and although they refunded the costs some six months later, it made me very wary of them. Still, the car was booked. There were two men in the Hertz booth and both of them looked very busy.

Colin had collected the luggage, visited the gents toilet, waited whilst Blaise returned from the ladies toilet and joined me at the desk before either of the Hertz staff had raised their head to look up at me or acknowledge me in some way. Eventually, one of them came to the desk and completed our paperwork. He handed us the keys and told us where to find the car. An hour after we had collected our luggage, we collected our car.

I had rented a compact car and was pleased to find we had been allocated a Fiat Punto. The car was in good condition and the price had been reasonable. Colin loaded our luggage in the boot and we got in. With directions to our destination firmly grasped in my hand, we set off for Lliria and 'Sunny Ridge,' Craig and Helen Holden's place and our accommodation for the next five days.

We followed the directions Helen had sent us and found 'Sunny Ridge' quite easily. We pulled up outside double metal gates, got out of the car and peered through the gate bars. We were delighted to see the inviting, turquoise swimming pool, glistening in the sun. The air temperature had risen considerably since our arrival and it was now 31 degrees. Feeling the effects of the intense heat, Colin wiped his brow, Blaise squinted against the sun and I wiped the moisture that seemed to have accumulated above my top lip.

At that point we were unaware that Helen had two rather large dogs. We rang the buzzer on the gate and both dogs loped towards us, barking loudly. I had a terrible fear of dogs and didn't want to enter the premises unless Colin carried me on his back, as for some reason I thought this would protect me. I realized that whilst climbing on to Colin's back might be the solution for small dogs, it definitely wouldn't do the job with what I saw before me.

Colin persuaded me to stand behind him as we rang the buzzer again. Our hostess, Helen appeared, welcomed us and introduced us to her two large dogs, a Bouvier called Ben and a Mongrel called Moxy.

I had seen a Bouvier once before in my life. It was a guard dog and although well trained, I was always wary of it. It was allowed in the family home and considered the family pet. The fact that you could have placed a saddle on it and took small children for rides on it only served to add weight to my anxiety. So upon seeing Ben, who unlike Moxy was not particularly interested in sniffing us, or wagging his tail, I felt the familiar panic start to build up and my heart started to thud.

Moxy wore a red polka dot bandana around his neck. He looked slightly zany but happy as he wagged his tail back and forth. The bandana looked quite peculiar but very cute and I tried to imagine dogs in England sporting this new 'doggy' attire. Helen explained that he was still quite a young dog and that Ben was the eldest. I was just about to try and scale the 7' gates when Helen explained that there was a separate entrance from the road to our accommodation. After leading us down a path to our left, a tall ornamental metal gate separated the rental accommodation from the main house and its grounds. Helen gave us the key to the guests' gates and ushered us through the internal gate to our accommodation.

We had booked bed and breakfast but due to alterations in Helen's kitchen, this was not now possible. Nevertheless, there was a fridge in the room that we could use, together with a small kettle and coffee making facilities. I didn't have the inclination to tell Helen that none of us drank tea or coffee. My only inclination was to get on the other side of the gate to the dogs, unpack and take a dip in the very inviting pool. No more than quarter of an hour later and we had all unpacked, claimed a bed, enjoyed a cool drink and dressed in our swimsuits ready for a dip in the pool. It was only then that I realized that we would have to use the internal gate to get to the pool. And what was on the other side of that gate? Man-eaters!

I don't know where I summoned courage from but I unlocked the gate and stood behind Blaise, ready to follow her to the pool area. Moxy spotted us from the other side of the garden and came running towards us. The path was about thirteen good-sized strides from the gate to the pool steps. In my hurry to get to the safe haven of the water, I covered this distance in about four leaps and felt a sharp pain as my back went into spasm. I tripped over the wasp catcher situated at the top of the pool steps and plunged head first into the pool. I surfaced spluttering and coughing. Blaise waved her arms and pointed to the pool. Not having my spectacles on, I was convinced Moxy had followed me in and was going to eat me alive. Slowly the water drained from my eyes and ears.

"Wasps mum! Wasps!" Blaise called frantically.

I had no idea that wasps could swim and having knocked the wasp catcher into the pool, the wasps had made their dash for freedom and were desperately trying to fly in the general direction of the steps and the sanctuary of terra firma!

I laughed at my good fortune. There I was in the pool and there on the side stood Moxy, studying me intently. Heck, what were a few wasps compared to Moxy? Still, Moxy was not to be beaten. Having lost his first attempt to secure prey, he still had another possible chance. He must have thought Blaise was worth a try, perhaps as an appetizer and he proceeded to put his mouth around the calf of her leg.

"MUM, MUM!" Blaise shouted in panic.

Helen must have heard the commotion and appeared in the garden. Thank goodness Helen had come to Blaise's rescue because I was dreading it. And of course, I would have sacrificed myself for her sake. What mother wouldn't? After all, why would Moxy want a chicken leg when he could have rump of pork! Helen calmly explained that Moxy sometimes mouthed you in play and that it was his way of being friendly.

"Hmmm. I'm not sure how the feel of my teeth on skin would show people that I was friendly," I said in a flat tone.

However, Helen assured us that Moxy was a friendly dog and that he just wanted to play.

"Does he ever jump in the pool?" asked Blaise.

"Well he only did it once as a puppy and he couldn't get out. We had to pull him out. It must have really scared him, as he's never tried to go in the pool since that day," Helen answered.

"YES! YES! YES!" I shouted. "SANCTUARY!"

Helen laughed. Not waiting a second longer, Blaise dived headlong into the pool, while Moxy watched with a sad look in his eyes.

"No chicken leg or pork rump for you mate!" I shouted as Blaise and I laughed.

The pool was cool and refreshing. It was difficult to swim due to my slipped disc but the physiotherapist had given me pool exercises and was convinced they would really help me.

Blaise found a large rubber ball in the garden. She brought it into the pool and clutching it to her chest, bobbed around the water. I thought I might be able to use it too, since I couldn't really kick my legs too hard incase the disc came out again. Blaise took the opportunity to make up a song. There were very few words to the song and hardly any tune, but she sang heartily:

> *"I'm baby bobbing, bobbing along,*
> *Baby bobbing, bobbing along,*
> *Baby bobbing, bobbing along,*
> *Baby bobbing, bobbing along."*

Colin, who was in bed trying to rest, couldn't stand it any longer and after suffering several repetitions of 'baby bobbing,' abandoned sleep altogether. He appeared at the side of the pool just in time for Moxy to launch a further assault. Moxy grabbed Colin's hand, his eyes gleaming and tail wagging. Colin isn't one for taking nonsense from anyone or anything. He often told us the story of the horse that galloped off with him. Colin had fallen off it and unfortunately, his foot had got stuck in the saddle stirrup. The horse decided to run back to it's stable, dragging Colin along the floor. Suffice to say, when the horse finally stopped, Colin reprimanded it fairly and justly and apparently, it never galloped off again!

I was holding my breath waiting for Colin to deliver his 'don't mess with me' command, when he befriended the mutt! There he stood, roughing it with the enemy, playing tough, rubbing Moxy's back, while Moxy wagged his tail and made all sorts of playful sounds. I put the wasp catcher back on the pool step and waited for Colin to join us. Eventually, after several minutes of rough play, Colin stepped over the wasp catcher, (which I had accidentally put in the path of the steps to the pool) and eased into the water, dodging the wasps in his path. He let Blaise and I know in no uncertain terms that the song had driven him mad before expertly karate chopping several wasps that buzzed angrily around him.

Blaise quickly picked up on the fact that collecting dead wasps would make a jolly good game. Thankfully, it distracted her from singing and she proceeded to collect dead wasps from the pool, scooping them up in a plastic cup she had found at the poolside. Peace at last. Here we all were, me and the two people I loved most, in harmony with the world and having a jolly good time.

Colin and Blaise were excellent at ridding the pool of wasps. They worked well, exterminating them and then disposing of them. Colin karate chopped them and Blaise collected the dead and unconscious ones in her paper cup. I clung on to the floating ball Blaise had deserted and without realizing it, began to sing.

"Baby bobbing, bobbing along."

Both Colin and Blaise shot me a look of exasperation, which instantly silenced me. I turned away from their glances and walked slowly towards the deep end until I was fully immersed and blowing bubbles. I pushed up very gently from the pool bottom and surfaced just as a Palm tree coconut seed landed 'SPLAT' on my head. We all laughed, giddy on warmth, sunshine, cool water, blue skies and good humour.

After our dip in the pool, we decided to explore the nearest town, Lliria, about two miles away. Helen's husband Craig worked for an estate agency in the town centre and we had booked to view a couple of properties with him towards the end of our stay. It seemed silly not to take the opportunity to view as many properties as possible while we could. Craig had given us some good tips on what to look for and what to be wary of. He told us that quite often the same house would be for sale with two different agents and that prices between those agents could differ significantly.

The evening was very warm as we made our way around the small town of Lliria. We had a small colour map marked out with what we thought was the estate agent where Craig worked. Having discovered about four, we spent an hour peering through glass windows, our noses pushed up flat against the outside pane, straining to catch sight of a real bargain. However, none of the estate agents that we found gave any indication that they spoke English. We decided that if we saw a Union Jack displayed, it would be a good indication that the estate agent spoke English and with this in mind, we set off for yet another trek around the town, trying to find estate agents displaying a Union Jack.

"Eureka!" I shouted joyfully. "Look, here it is."

Sure enough there was a Union Jack displayed on the outside of the shop. It was situated on the main road through Lliria. We would easily find it when we had to meet up for viewing in a few days time. I looked at the map that Helen had given us. Helen had kindly marked Craig's office with a cross on our map, so it wouldn't be difficult to find again. We returned to our car and drove the length of the town high street.

Colin found a signpost for Villamarchante, where we were to meet a different estate agent, VSI, the very next day. We found a local BBQ chicken take-away, commonly known as 'Pollos Asados.' The food smelt wonderfully aromatic. Colin bought a cooked chicken and some paella and we headed back to our accommodation for the night. Tomorrow we would meet our estate agent, Sally Putman from VSI and start viewing properties.

After the excitement of the day, we fell onto our beds exhausted but happy. I looked over at Colin and Blaise. They were asleep within minutes. I turned off my bedside lamp and closed my eyes. The night was peaceful save for the odd bark of a dog in the distance. I reflected on the day and chuckled to myself. I would have to face the demon dogs again no doubt but for now I was safely locked away from them.

In the stillness of the evening, a sniffing sound caught my attention. On the wall behind the bedstead, there was a tiny little window, about 18" square. You had to stand on the bed to look through it but it looked out onto the pool and patio area. The window although fully fly screened, could still be opened and was protected by black, wrought iron security bars. The noise was coming from outside the window and there was definitely something moving around outside, perhaps a mouse or a hedgehog. There it was again, a sniffing sound. I rose from my bed, stood atop it and peered through the window. There I was, eye-to-eye and nose-to-nose with Moxy, his large brown eyes peering at me through the wrought iron bars. He sniffed at the ground outside the window. I laughed softly, thinking how frustrating it must have been for him to see his supper laid out ready to eat and not be able to eat it. I climbed off the bed and chuckled to myself, while Moxy, on the other side of the bars, slumped his large leggy body down to keep guard for the night.

Chapter 2
House Hunting

I awoke from a hot, sticky night's sleep with the sound of the room fan buzzing in my ears. Thankfully we each had a single bed. I couldn't imagine curling up in a double bed next to Colin in the intense heat. How did couples manage to sleep together at all here?

"Make sure you look for a villa with air conditioning," I muttered to myself before closing my eyes once more.

Daylight broke the sky, as I grabbed my watch from the bedside cabinet. I squinted at the watch face, trying to make out the time without the benefit of my reading glasses. It was very early. I looked at the floor. Our lightweight quilts, thrown off our beds during the night, lay crumpled in what looked like one massive quilt mountain in the middle of the floor.

Colin and Blaise awoke and padded in turn into the bathroom. Although I looked quite bleary eyed, I felt wide awake. The excitement and the anticipation of what the day ahead would bring gave me tummy butterflies.

"Today's the day," I said cheerfully.

I planned a light breakfast outside on our tiny narrow patio, which was to the front and right of our room. It was quite a pleasant patio with a Jasmine shrub and two large terracotta tubs, filled with vivid crimson Geraniums. The poor Geraniums looked a bit worse for wear, their dried leaves and shrivelled blooms spilling over the sides of their tubs. I plucked off some of the dead blooms before carrying breakfast to the patio table. We had bags of lightly toasted croissants, fruit, packets of cheese, packets of ham and a pat of butter that liquidized in the heat before my very own eyes.

Blaise and I waited for Colin to join us for breakfast. Boy was it hot! It was only nine o'clock and already we needed the shade of the parasol. I arranged the croissants, ham, cheese, fruit, jam and juice on the white plastic patio table.

"Lovely, just lovely," I remarked to myself, while staring at the table.

It all looked so pretty, even if it was a little haphazardly laid out. Moxy stood at the side gate wagging his tail. Colin appeared carrying bottles of cold water and fresh fruit juice.

"It's a good job we've got that fridge in the room," he said.

Moxy on hearing Colin's voice, barked playfully at the gate and his tail wagged frantically.

"He's probably hoping for one or two scraps," Colin said in a matter of fact tone.

I ignored Colin's remark and tried my best to ignore Moxy's presence at the gate.

"Aww doesn't he look cute mum?" Blaise cooed. "Just look at his cheeky face."

"Just look at his teeth," I snapped. "Now listen here you two, please don't be friendly to him or he will never leave us alone. I don't want him biting any of us."

"He doesn't bite, he just wants to play," replied Colin testily.

"Well I for one, would rather he didn't," I replied curtly.

"Well Angela, if he wanted to bite you, he could have done so very easily. I tell you, its just playfulness. He's just a bit of a pup."

"Puppy's by definition don't stand 2' high at the shoulder," I retorted, adding "And anyway, I really don't like dogs so please don't encourage any of them. Whatever you do, don't forget to lock that gate," I warned sternly.

"OK, OK!" Colin replied.

"We'll just ignore him mum," said Blaise patting my hand.

I knew what would happen if those dogs got anywhere near me, it would be me for breakfast not scraps and nothing could convince me otherwise.

We tucked into a delicious breakfast of Brie and croissants, washed down with fresh Valencia orange juice, enjoying the early morning sun and warmth. Half an hour later, we had eaten, cleared the table and bundled into the car ready for our journey to Villamarchante and VSI. I had seen an advertisement for VSI in the Spanish Property Magazine. It was only a small advertisement but I found their website easily on an Internet search. I had emailed back and forth for quite a few weeks. VSI had employed an English lady called Sally Putman, who was most helpful. Sally had a pleasant, straightforward and reassuring manner. She replied to my email promptly and in a way that was clearly understandable. There was nothing ambiguous in her dealings and I had struck up a good business relationship with her.

Our appointment with Sally was scheduled for ten o'clock at the VSI office in Villamarchante Square. We arrived half an hour early and parked the car in a dusty, pot-holed, car park. We walked through a stone archway that led to the main road. Just across from the car park was the main square. A faded zebra crossing could just be seen on a raised area in the road, what the English would refer to as a 'sleeping policeman.'

The small pavement cafes were setting out their tables and chairs. Men and women had gathered and were sat on the stone slab seating outside the town hall. They chatted happily to each other and passed the time of day. Perhaps they had business to conduct or perhaps they arrived early so they could enjoy a good old chinwag with each other. Whatever their reasons, they congregated in their little groups. I was contemplating this when Colin called me over. He had walked some way ahead, towards VSI's offices.

"It's not open yet Ange," Colin shouted.

"We're very early Colin," I said reassuringly, "let's sit down and have a drink."

We sat down at a pavement table and looked up at the sign above the café. It read 'Salon de Jamon.' It was the only café in the square that had its tables and chairs set out ready for business. A young waitress welcomed us with a friendly "Hola," placed menus on the table in front of us and asked what we wanted to drink. We ordered three bottles of Fanta orange and watched as she disappeared inside the café. She returned in minutes with the drinks and three glasses on a tray. She placed them on our table, popped a little slip of paper under the serviette holder and disappeared again.

The square filled up little by little, getting busier and busier. We heard an English accent and spun our heads to search for its source. It seemed strange hearing our mother tongue. One of the pre-requisites of finding a location in Spain was that it was not to have a large English community. Colin wanted Spanish neighbours and as few English people around us as possible. However, as the café filled up, we were relieved to find that the English were still definitely the minority.

As the time approached ten o'clock, we paid our bill and stood up ready to leave.

"Adios!" Colin said.

"Ta lluego," replied the cheerful waitress.

"I think that's short for hasta lluego," I said confidently. "It means see you later."

We smiled at her and waved goodbye before walking the few yards to the estate agent's office.

Sally greeted us warmly as we entered. The offices were painted pale grey and felt quite cool. There were three desks in the main office. To the right of the entrance reception stood a full size table with eight chairs.

Sally introduced us to Alfredo Blasco and Jose Antonio. Alfredo was the owner's son. We shook hands and sat down in front of the desk. Alfredo did not speak much English but fortunately Sally spoke fluent Spanish. We explained our requirements again and, most importantly, our budget. Alfredo said he had six houses for us to see and invited us to travel with him in his air-conditioned car to view them. We would view three in the morning, have lunch and then view three more in the afternoon.

"Fine," Colin and I agreed. "Shall we go then?"

Sally and Alfredo sat in the front of the car, Colin, Blaise and I sat in the back. Thankfully, the car was air-conditioned, although I was not sure what good it did us being sat so close together in the back. We set off, my heart beating rapidly with excitement.

"Off to view our first property," I said quietly to Colin.

We drove through grove after grove of oranges. They stretched as far as the eye could see, lush and green. I thought this very unusual because most of the areas in Spain we had already seen had been dusty and looked more 'spaghetti western' terrain than fertile agricultural land. In stark contrast, what we now saw around us was lovely. Vast Pine forests on the hills, orange groves interspersed with olive trees, almond trees and melon groves. We even spotted a couple of vineyards here and there. It was spectacular scenery, beautiful in its simplicity.

"Well, we've come from the garden of England to the garden of Spain," Colin remarked smugly.

The beauty of the place mesmerized me and I found it hard to listen to what was being said. It was as if time had stood still. Alfredo pulled onto a dusty road on the outskirts of Villamarchante and parked up in front of a set of large metal gates. He got out of the car, rang the bell and stood expectantly at the gated entrance to the property. We followed and waited anxiously for the owners to answer the bell, Colin's video camera poised at the ready.

The first house, Sally explained, was a traditional Spanish house. It had a salon (lounge) with the kitchen and bedrooms off it. It was a good size and within our budget. A friendly retired English couple owned the house and they were selling because they wanted to move nearer to their friends.

"At least they aren't leaving because they don't like it here," I whispered to Colin.

Colin asked the couple for permission to use the video recorder inside the house. They smiled and said it would be fine. Colin pointed the lens busily this way and that. Blaise was totally besotted by their little white dog, which was carefully tucked under the man's arm. It was a friendly little dog but the owners said it had sharp claws and jumped up all the time when it was excited. They didn't want us to get scratched. Blaise stroked the dog lovingly, desperate to cuddle it.

Colin and I toured the large garden at the back of the house. Tomatoes and grapes were growing profusely and the owners had put an irrigation system in to keep them watered. Although rustic, the system worked just fine. Colin's expression told me that he was taking it all in, just in case we needed the same sort of system for our own house.

Finally we looked at the swimming pool. It was a plunge pool, very common in the Valencia region. Most pools in the region were of this type, with very few sunken into the ground. The owners kindly offered to let

Blaise stay there with them and play in the pool. It was already blisteringly hot and had I known the couple better, or as friends, I might have taken up their offer. However, I felt uncomfortable leaving Blaise with someone I didn't really know. I also felt that it would be taking advantage and I didn't want to feel obliged into buying their property for any reason. We said farewell and got back into the car. The house was comfortable but the gardens, although well stocked, were far too large and we simply wouldn't be able to maintain them without incurring a lot of expense. Nevertheless, I was impressed by what we could get for our money. £80,000 would buy us a detached traditional Spanish villa, with four bedrooms and a plunge pool. It was marvellous news and although Sally had told me that it was possible, deep down, I hadn't really believed it. But witnessing it with my own eyes, I was sure we would get a bargain for our money.

As Alfredo drove us to the next villa, he received a call on his mobile phone from Jose Antonio at VSI's office. Jose Antonio said a gentleman had just called in the office and he had a property to sell. It was in our price bracket and the gentleman said he could meet us at the property in minutes if we wanted to view it. The villa had four bedrooms and a pool. Colin and I both nodded in agreement and Alfredo drove us to the property to meet the owner and view it.

The villa was situated just outside the village of Pedralba, off a main road that linked Pedralba to Lliria. I had already looked at the area on the map before we left England. The village of Pedralba was the furthest from Valencia in terms of distance that I thought we should consider.

We drove through the tiny village of Pedralba, marvelling at the rustic beauty of the town houses and streets. The roads were tiny, narrow and dusty. From the narrow road through the village, cul de sacs on either side led to a series of stone steps, which in turn led to more terraced houses.

"Surely a car couldn't get through those roads," I remarked to Sally.

"Oh yes they can but it can be a bit scary at times, particularly if you meet something coming the other way," she called over her shoulder.

We left the village and drove through more fields of almond, olives and orange trees. The oranges were small and green. The fruit hung like lime green baubles and you could see the branches bowing, heavy with fruit. I was lost in thought. It was amazing to think that by December, these fields would be a mass of green and orange.

The second property was situated off a good tarmac road between Pedralba and Lliria. Access to the villa was good and we parked up outside a very neat cypress hedge that had been expertly trimmed to reveal a lovely dark wooden fence nestled between terracotta coloured cement walls. Large black double metal gates nestled under a sloping tiled roof, with an old-fashioned black iron lamp light overhead.

Jose Antonio pulled up just behind us with whom I assumed was the owner. The owner was a small elderly gentleman, with a kind face and firm handshake. He proudly showed us around his villa. Colin pointed the video recorder this way and that, the owner pointing out what he thought were the most important features, those not to be missed. He pointed out the double-glazed windows and fly screens, the recently re-wired electrics throughout, the air conditioning in every room, the modern American kitchen and the beautifully co-ordinated bathroom with medium oak accessories (towel rails, toilet roll holder, bidet towel holder, under sink unit and framed mirror). A new white bath and a white and blue mosaic washbasin with matching mosaic mirror and tiles from floor to ceiling finished off the look. He ushered us into each of the four double bedrooms and highlighted their fitted wardrobes.

Outside, at the rear of the property, he showed us the store room, paellero, (an outdoor BBQ for cooking paella), which also housed a huge double gas hob and electric oven, a huge double sink of the old Armitage Shanks kind and a front load automatic washing machine.

There was a separate tool shed or storeroom that housed not only his tools but also all his odds and ends of DIY paraphernalia and more importantly for us, where the gas boiler was housed.

At the front of the house, he showed us how to wind out the massive Dutch awning he had installed to give extra shade to the patio.

He explained that he had put railings in to secure the pool area so he could lock it and prevent his grandchildren accidentally falling into the pool and drowning.

He was very proud of the orange tree which he said bore fruit every year. He said the sapling at the bottom of the pool area bore fruit indigenous to Valencia but he couldn't tell us the English name for it.

We were ushered to the pool 'under build' where Colin could see the workings of the pump for the pool. The pool worked on a filtration system and had two jets for water flow and skimming.

We were shown the huge fruiting fig tree and the fruit tree indigenous to Valencia. He said the fruit was a cross between a plum and an apple and was very good, we were told with a wink, for improving virility. Colin and I laughed as once again the old man winked at us.

We passed another small outbuilding and Sally told us it was the pool house.

"The pool house," I mouthed to Colin, accentuating my words, as I stretched my eyes wide adding emphasis.

Sally having overheard me, told me that it was common in Valencia for there to be a separate pool house. The people of Valencia did not like walking through the inside of their homes wet through in order to shower and dry off.

"Pool bathing is strictly an outdoor activity here. You shower and dry off in the pool house before you enter your home," Sally informed me.

"Of course, it makes perfect sense," I responded and followed the procession of people down the path along the side of the pool.

The pool was quite large, about 28' by 14' and was sunk into the ground. Its small turquoise tiles gleamed in the sun.

"That's a beautiful pool," I remarked to Colin.

Colin nodded his head and gave me a look that said I was not to appear too eager or the price would go up. We looked into the pool to try and judge its depth. It had a shallow end of about 3'6" with a gradual shelf into deeper water, ceasing at about 6'6" deep.

At the bottom of the pool was an outside working shower in its own concrete shower base. The owner explained that water ran into the shower base and the gap at the rear of the base allowed the water to run into the ground and soak away towards the roots of the fig tree.

Finally, at the bottom of the garden, we arrived at the pool house.

"Wow, mum it's a complete bathroom," said Blaise excitedly.

"It's got spiders in it mum but that's good isn't it?" Blaise enquired, squinting at me in the sunlight.

"Yes darling, that's perfectly OK because we like spiders don't we?" I replied waiting for her to nod her head in agreement.

Sally looked at us and screwed her nose up.

"Blaise, tell Sally why we like spiders," I commanded, while the men gathered at the doorway, their heads peering through the opened door.

"We like spiders because they eat all the other horrid things, like flies and creepy crawlies," said Blaise proudly.

Thank goodness all those years of playing with the hairy eight legged arachnoids had paid off. I had seen many children over the years, frightened of almost everything that crawled or crept and I vowed that I would try not to let my own child become afraid of insects like those shrieking children I had encountered.

From an early age Blaise was encouraged to look at nature as something necessary and beautiful and not something to be scared of. Blaise grew up playing with ladybirds, honeybees, spiders, snails, damselflies, frogs and wood lice. She was not scared of any of these things. Each of them had a use and a place in our lives. Spiders, particularly, because they ate all the things that we didn't like, especially bluebottle flies. The beauty of a spider's web on a dewy autumn morning with the sun shining on it was breathtaking, the dewdrops glistening like droplets on a crystal chandelier. It was one of our favourite sights. Of course, I was very proud of Blaise. She wouldn't be one of those children that went running and screaming around the place at the sight of a beetle. Little did I know at that time that our perseverance and endurance in those early years would stand her good stead for a life in Spain.

Having been suitably impressed with the villa, I knew it would be ideal for us. I saw good rental potential for it, especially as the pool area was secure. The gardens were laid to borders, which meant they would be easy to maintain. It was a Spanish style garden with ornamental iris 6' high. It was a truly delightful villa.

Unfortunately, Alfredo couldn't tell us the sale price, as this was the first time he too had seen it. He walked over to the owner and they spoke quietly to each other. After Alfredo spoke to the owner for a few minutes, he walked back over to us

"€159,000. That's what he wants for it," said Alfredo in good English.

"What a bargain," I mouthed to Colin through closed teeth like a ventriloquist.

We thanked the owner, shook his hand and walked back to Alfredo's car.

The day was heating up and I felt parched. We took cold drinks from our cool box that Colin had sensibly put in Alfredo's car boot. Blaise was especially hot and looked totally exhausted. I took a large mouthful of ice-cold water, rolling it around my mouth. I felt like I hadn't drunk for a week. Finally Alfredo got into the drivers seat and started the engine. It was time to see the next house and after that, lunch.

We headed off in the direction of Villamarchante again. Sally continued to give us a running commentary on where this road led or where that road led. To get to the next villa, Alfredo drove us through a different part of Pedralba to that we had previously driven through. We saw run down terraced houses, their burnt sienna coloured plaster walls alight in the sun. Some houses had a fresh spring running in front of them and tiny arched bridges led from their front door to the road.

"Mum, look at the stream running in front of the houses!" Blaise exclaimed. "It's so pretty!"

The village was old, quaint and beautiful and reminded me of Venice.

"If I had the money Colin, I would by one of those town houses and renovate it," I said dreamily.

"Hmmm," said Colin thoughtfully.

Alfredo informed us that Pedralba had its own natural spring and that people came from all around the Turia valley to fill up their water containers. He said the water was perfectly safe to drink and we should try it. He pointed to the tap on the side of a whitewashed wall, just after the bridge over the river Turia, on the road out of town towards Villamarchante.

There were cars and battered old jeeps parked up in front of the tap, all waiting to fill their empty water containers. People were chatting to one another seated on concrete bench seats that had been carved into the rocks in the wall. Tall Pine trees shaded the spring and everyone looked happy, after all it was free drinking water, ice cold and straight from the spring. I guessed that is what Tunbridge Wells must have been like years ago, as people came and went to take the waters. It was a fascinating sight.

We headed in the direction of Villamarchante once again and pulled off onto a dust track, which continued for quite a way. By now Colin, Blaise and I were hot, dusty, thirsty, hungry and tired. We pulled up in front of yet another set of iron gates, ready to view the third property. Chained on a long leash outside the villa was a lively beige and white puppy. It bounced up and down happily as Alfredo unlocked the gates. The owners were out at work. Alfredo said that the dog was friendly and once inside the gates, Blaise immediately ran to the puppy and made a huge fuss of it. Although chained on a long leash, it had plenty of shade, food and water in what appeared to be a covered outdoor open plan kitchen.

The gardens were lovely, with lots of shade and trees to the front and laid to stone and coloured gravel at the sides. Looking at the house from just inside the double gate, the house was side on, which meant that the entrance couldn't actually be seen from the dirt track. There was a stone walled balustrade and two 10" high statues of Laurel and Hardy had been firmly cemented onto the top edging stones.

The villa looked typically Spanish with red geraniums in colourful pots fixed on the patio walls, making a very traditional looking Spanish patio. The house seemed big enough for us too. There was one large salon with several other rooms off it. I found it rather strange that you would step out of your bathroom or your bedroom and be stood in your lounge. The house needed quite a bit of work doing on it, but Colin and Blaise fell in love with it immediately. I could tell from their faces that they really loved it, from the quirky Laurel and Hardy to the fruit trees that surrounded it. Even I had to admit, it was a very pretty villa. However, the gardens were huge and the swimming pool was placed very precariously at the side of the property, where access was poor if not downright dangerous.

"The pool would have to be relocated," I shouted to Colin who was down at the bottom end of the garden.

He was looking to see where he could relocate the pool. I sensed that Blaise and Colin were getting just a little bit carried away by this villa. I was sure Blaise thought the puppy came with it as well as the two lovebirds whose cage hung in the corner under the covered patio. Feeling a sharp pain in my right leg, I slapped my calf hard. The sound of the slap echoed around the patio.

"Ouch! Something bit me!" I shouted.

Sure enough a large red circle appeared on my right leg. I walked towards Colin.

"I really like this house Angela," he said.

I took a deep breath. Colin had used my full Christian name. It was serious. He only ever called me Angela if it was serious.

"I know you do Colin but it's going to take major work to get it how we want it. That means no rental potential for some time. If we were going to live here straight away, then that would be different and this is exactly the sort of house we would buy, but we are not moving here. The house will be rented out until such time as we can come over for good and that won't be until Blaise finishes big school Colin," I reminded him.

Colin and Blaise proceeded to fidget around me, extolling all the virtues of the house, pointing out this feature and pointing out that. I wondered to myself if it was just the fact that Laurel and Hardy were the first things you saw as you entered that had endeared this house to them. Certainly, the gardens were rich in fruit trees and shrubs. The garden paths were prettily laid in coloured gravel. The vivid colourings and vibrant singing of the lovebirds added to the ambience, as did the scarlet geraniums wafting gently in the breeze. The scene was indeed set and I knew that as far as Colin and Blaise were concerned, this was the house for them.

We walked around the interior of the house again. It was dark and old fashioned. It needed a new kitchen and bathroom. Was there anything I liked about the interior of the house? NO!

Blaise gave the puppy a farewell pat and we climbed into the car once more. We had one more house to view and then we were going to have lunch in Villamarchante. I wanted to get the memory of the last house out of Blaise and Colin's head and viewing another property would help.

Colin and Blaise both talked non-stop with Sally about the third house. Although Colin had agreed that we would not make any decision on the spur of the moment or in front of the estate agent, every word uttered from his and Blaise's mouth led me to believe that they had made their mind up, even though we had another four houses to see. I sat with a slight sense of melancholy in my mood all the way to the next property.

By now, I hadn't got a clue where we were, which town was where or who was who for that matter. Blaise too was getting very hot and fractious. I scratched at the bite on my leg as hard as I could, the intense itching driving me delirious.

Alfredo's car turned off a tarmac road onto another narrower one. I noticed some graffiti on the wall to the first property and wasn't sure if this would be a good area. Alfredo stopped the car a couple of villas further on. The property had a high walled garden.

"Wow, this is a huge plot," I said, getting out of the car as quickly as I could.

The grounds alone were gigantic. Alfredo unlocked the gates and drove in.

There were numerous Pine trees all around the property. Two massive Palm trees flanked the front door entrance and everything else was so overgrown, you couldn't tell what it was.

I walked around the entire circumference of the property. The grounds were magnificent. The plunge pool was situated at the back, up some rustic garden steps. There was also a small Pine wood at the very rear of the garden, where an ornate, round, stone table with matching curved stone bench seats, had been placed.

The pool was a standard size plunge pool, about 10' by 20' however, the garden and woods were so big, you could have had a 60' pool put in and it still wouldn't significantly diminish the amount of garden. The grounds reminded me of those surrounding a castle or a palace. Although the vegetation was completely overgrown, it would make a fine colonial style dwelling. Sally shouted loudly to get our attention; she was opening the door to the house. I was very excited and made my way down the steps from the pool to the house. I thought of all the hard work it would need to make it tidy, but mostly all that was needed was a good clean up and scrub down. With a light and cheery mood, I entered the house. It had been sadly neglected, so much so that one look was all it took for me to discount it. I was so taken in with the grounds that I had totally forgotten about the house itself. I felt gutted. The disappointment must have shown on my face.

"Too small inside eh Angela," said Colin.

"Yes, and too much work needed on the basics, for instance security and making safe. I can't believe how small this salon is. Why have all this land and such a huge covered patio outside that it makes your inside so small you can't swing a cat in it?"

I was bitterly disappointed.

"Come on, let's go," I said, dismayed. "I've seen enough."

All the way back to Villamarchante in the car, I found myself saying "What a shame. What a shame!"

Alfredo parked the car and we all bundled out into the street. I was ready to eat and desperate for an ice-cold drink.

The restaurant was in a quiet back street on the outskirt of Villamarchante. As we entered, it looked spotlessly clean. It was quite dark too, which meant it was probably very cool. We were shown into a room at the back of the public bar area and a large circular table had been laid with fresh linen, cutlery and wine glasses. The smell of freshly baked bread wafted through from the kitchen. Colin, Blaise and I sank into our seats. I ran my hands through my hair. We were all weary, hot, tired, hungry and thirsty. We looked a sorry sight. We were all in desperate need of refreshments. The patron seeing our discomfort nodded a friendly greeting and asked what we would like to drink. We ordered large coca colas with lots of ice and lemon. Within minutes, the patron had brought the drinks over to our table. Colin, Blaise and I drank them in an instant and Alfredo seeing our empty glasses, ordered the same again, as he and Sally sat down to join us.

I was wondering just how much the lunch was going to cost us when Alfredo's voice broke my concentration. He was pointing to the menu and encouraging us to take a look. Sally translated the three-course special of the day. There was salad to start with, pork steak in a peppercorn sauce as main course and ice cream or fruit for dessert. Colin, Blaise and I all ordered exactly the same, the meal of the day.

While the food was being prepared and cooked, Sally asked us to summarize our thoughts on the properties we had seen so far.

Colin began, "First property nice but they got better the more we saw."

I agreed with him.

"Second house very nice but not much land," he went on.

I was flabbergasted! Just how much land did Colin want I wondered? We couldn't maintain a lot of land; you need gardeners and landscapers for that sort of thing.

"I like the third property best of all, typically Spanish, lots of potential, lots of land, the kind of house I would like to live in," he added.

"Me too," said Blaise and Sally smiled and nodded her head in agreement.

That was it! The pair of them conspired against me. I knew it. That blooming puppy! Dogs! Always trouble when dogs are involved. And Laurel and Hardy, what was all that about! And the caged lovebirds! Horrible! Blaise and Colin knew that I positively hated anything caged. I should have let those lovebirds go. I could easily have opened the cage and set them free.

I was so agitated and worked up that the bite on my leg pulsated. Under cover of the tablecloth, I extended my right arm down my leg and clawed at the huge red bulbous lump that had now developed on my calf. I lifted the tablecloth and peered at my leg. To my horror, there wasn't just one bite, but four! They were dotted all over my lower leg and were the size of marbles.

"Now look here!" I shouted to everyone at the table.

"The third villa might be your idea of paradise, but I nearly got eaten alive there. All those fruit trees and that vast expanse of garden mean trouble, insects whose bark is not worse than their bite. Look at my legs! Just look at my poor legs. I've been eaten alive!"

Everyone looked at me.

"Just because you don't like it mum," said Blaise, breaking the silence.

I shot her a fiery glance and she lowered her eyes, aware that she had made me cross.

Sally very diplomatically led us on to the fourth property.

For once, we all agreed.

"Great grounds, lousy house," we all chanted.

And with that, the patron arrived with three plates of salad, followed quickly by two more and a soup. Sally was going to have the salad as her main course. We said silent prayers and tucked in. We were ravenous.

Lunch was excellent and we all chatted away happily to each other. Tempers were calmed, insect bites were soothed, thirsts were quenched and relaxation ruled the mood. It was a very leisurely lunch, but there again, what reason was there to rush it? The temperature outside was almost 33 degrees while inside was a cool 21 degrees. There was absolutely no point whatsoever in venturing out until it cooled down. Anyway, as Alfredo explained, we had made good time in the morning and we only had two more properties to see in the afternoon, one having been withdrawn from sale.

I looked at Blaise's little face. She was turning browner by the hour and I wondered how much longer she would be able to go on without becoming very bored and weary of it all. I was surprised that we had kept her interested for so long. I guessed the dogs could take the credit for that. At least they kept her reasonably amused and interested.

It was almost four o'clock by the time we left the restaurant. The pork in peppercorn sauce had tasted delicious. We were cool and ready to press on for what would be the last two viewings. Once again, we all piled into Alfredo's air-conditioned car and headed out of Villamarchante. I didn't have a clue where we were going. Eventually we stopped outside the fifth property.

The fifth villa had the most wonderful views. The gates were unlocked and opened and Alfredo drove in and parked up. We looked around the grounds with awe. It had the most wonderful view of the surrounding countryside. I noticed one or two bits of DIY paraphernalia lying around as I walked the perimeter of the house. Colin and I had agreed over lunch that we simply could not buy a villa with vast plot of land. We just hadn't got the resources to finance its upkeep and anything

31

requiring major work would mean lost rental income whilst work was under way. Spain was not the easiest place in the world to get labour and jobs were not undertaken or completed with any sense of urgency. Not that I minded that because that was part of the attraction of Spain. It has its own pace and rush jobs are non existent. Its slow and easy pace of life draws people like a magnet. For this reason it would make it particularly hard to make things happen fast and get things done, since we were based in England.

Sally led us along a white concrete path to the back of the house. We climbed 8 steps to a full-length veranda, which overlooked a large plot of orange and lemon groves.

"Those belong to the house," Sally informed us.

"Oh how wonderful," I exclaimed, enraptured by the thought of picking my own oranges and lemons.

"Angela, we have just agreed that we can't maintain anything with large grounds, you yourself made the point," Colin groaned.

His words fell on deaf ears, as I sent Blaise running down the grove to where Sally thought the boundary was.

"It's here mum," I heard Blaise shout from somewhere down the grove.

"Where are you Blaise, I can't see you?" I shouted from the veranda.

"Here I am mum," she shouted back, but I still couldn't see her.

"It's a big grove isn't it Sally?" I remarked jovially.

Sally, ever diplomatic, agreed and left me to my thoughts. I caught a glimpse of Blaise some way off.

"Blimey Colin, it's a plantation. We would have our own orange plantation," I gasped.

Blaise and I were caught up in our own little dream world. I pictured us riding donkeys to market, wicker baskets strapped over the donkeys backs, oranges and lemons piled high. I imagined Colin striding down the hill behind us, stick in hand, encouraging the donkeys to keep going, a straw hat on his head and a length of grass between his teeth. I was carried away in my very own wonderland.

"It's too big Angela. Far too big! What on earth are we going to do with an orange and lemon grove?" Colin asked, confounded by my interest.

"A couple of trees, well yes, that's fine, but a whole orange plantation. I don't think so! Angela, are you listening to me or what?" Colin asked impatiently.

My dream was shattered and I sighed deeply.

"Come on back now Blaise. Blaise? Blaise? Can you hear me?" I yelled across the grove.

"OK mum, I'm coming," she replied, trotting back into view.

We decided not to view the house. Colin was right. I had got totally carried away. Now I could see how easily Colin and Blaise got carried away with the Laurel and Hardy house. Everyone had their own idea of what their little piece of heaven on earth was and I had just seen mine.

"One day Colin," I whispered, "I will have my very own oranges to pick. One day."

We packed up into Alfredo's car and set off to view the last property.

Once again, I had no idea in which direction we were headed. I felt listless and even the usual bright and chirpy Blaise had quietened considerably. The insect bites on my right leg began to itch again and I sat on my hands to stop myself scratching them. It was almost five o'clock. Arriving at the last villa, Alfredo rang the buzzer several times. The owners of this house were supposed to be at home. They too had a large dog. We peered in through the gates. I didn't particularly like the location of this house. It was in what appeared to be a cul-de-sac along a dirt track road. The fence was made of silver chicken wire. The hedges looked sparse and the area didn't quite have the look we were after. It looked rather plain and bare.

Alfredo tried for several minutes to raise life from the premises. The only life seemed to come from the dog that barked away on the end of its chain. Just as we were about to turn tail, a rather weary looking chap emerged from the side of the house. He explained to Alfredo that we had woken him from his siesta. He told Alfredo that the house wasn't in any state to view but he said that we were welcome to look around the outside if we wanted to. I hesitated; after all, having had enough mad dogs at my heels in two days to last me two years, I didn't feel particularly happy about venturing too near what looked like a very hot and ill-tempered dog. Blaise was really feeling the heat too. I looked over at her. She looked a little swollen around the face.

"Mum, I don't feel well," she whimpered. "I want to go home."

"We won't be long now darling," I assured her.

We entered through the gates and Blaise followed us listlessly. We stared at the plot with blank expressions on our faces. We looked one to the other. We were hot and tired. I noticed that our legs had taken on an orange hue. Perhaps the sun had caught us. We stood listless on the concrete drive and made a full 360-degree turn.

"What's there to look at?" I said quietly.

Over on the left there appeared to be some sort of vegetable patch, with its wigwam canes bound carefully together. There was a plunge pool in front of us with stagnant water in it. But other than that, the canvas was bare.

Sally explained that this house was the most expensive. I couldn't for the life of me fathom out why. I glanced over at her with a puzzled expression.

"It's because it's a two-storey house," said Sally.

"Well, two-storey or three-storey, I like this one the least. What about you Colin?" I asked.

"There's not much to look at is there?" he said calmly.

"I think we have seen enough for one day. Let's call it quits," I concluded.

We thanked Alfredo and Sally and explained that we had viewed enough houses for one day.

It was just after six o'clock and we had missed our time slot in the pool. We were permitted to swim between the hours of ten o'clock and noon in the morning and between four and six o'clock in the afternoon. I looked at Blaise huddled in the back seat with us. She looked listless. I was worried and told Colin.

"I think she has heat exhaustion," I said quietly, a worried expression on my face.

"We'll ask Helen if we can dip her in the pool to cool her down. We must get plenty of fluids into her and cool her," Colin responded.

Alfredo started the engine and we headed back to VSI's office.

We arrived at VSI at quarter past six. The last house must have been in a suburb of Villamarchante. We took our cool box from Alfredo's boot and filed into his office. We thanked everyone for their hospitality and especially for the lovely lunch. We had fully expected to pay for

Alfredo and Sally, however Sally explained that Alfredo was our host and, as such, he was glad to pay for our lunch. This was very different from our experience in France.

Alfredo and Sally were keen to know what our first impressions were. Out of all that we saw, I liked the second house; Colin and Blaise preferred the third. One thing was certain though, the Turia Valley was definitely the most pleasant area we had ever visited. It would suit us just fine. And as for the properties, it was definitely between the second and third villa. However, wanting to be honest, we explained to Sally and Alfredo that we had two viewings booked the following day with another agent. Sally asked if we would like to view any of the properties once more. Colin and I looked at each other and said we would think about it and let Sally know the following day. After a good evenings rest and reflection, we would be better able to let them know more and make some sort of a decision before we left for England. We shook hands and performed the usual three kisses routine before leaving VSI's office.

We arrived back at Helen's covered in tangerine coloured dust. On closer inspection of my leg, it transpired that I had indeed been badly bitten probably by mosquitoes or fruit flies. The intense heat had finally exhausted us. We were utterly captivated by what we had seen during the day and although we didn't know exactly which house we liked best, we thought that the Turia Valley was definitely a place in which we could happily live.

We trooped across the little faded zebra crossing, through the archway to the car park, where our Fiat Punto was parked. We gave Blaise all the drinks that were left in the cool box, climbed in the car and headed back to Helen's in Lliria.

Moxy and Ben barked a welcome at the gate as we approached. Moxy was still wearing his red polka dot bandana and Ben, true to character, retreated to wait quietly in the shade.

"Ben must really feel this heat," I remarked to Colin. Ben had wiry, jet-black hair that easily absorbed the heat.

"No wonder he never runs around getting hot and bothered," replied Colin. "It must take terrific effort just to stay on his legs in this heat."

"Yes, poor Ben," I sighed.

The heat must have got to me more than I thought. Me! Sympathizing with the plight of a dog. I chuckled as I followed Blaise and Colin into our room. I placed the empty cool box near the fridge while Colin went to ask Helen if we could take a quick dip in the pool. He said he was sure she wouldn't mind and Colin being the excellent judge of character that he is, was absolutely right. Helen didn't mind at all.

Blaise was jubilant and forgetting all about her nausea, she peeled off her clothes and ran from the room towards the pool, still putting her bikini top on as she went. Colin and I thought a ten-minute dip would refresh us too and we followed her to the pool. We slipped quietly into the water to the sound of crickets clapping their hind legs. Another hot, balmy, orange scented breeze fluttered the Palm trees. I inhaled deeply and filled my lungs with the sweet aroma. I let my thoughts drift and imagined day upon day of such sweet night air.

Chapter 3
Just My Imagination

"What time is it?" I asked while yawning and stretching atop my bed.

I noticed the pile of quilts in exactly the same place on the floor again.

"It's nine o'clock mum," Blaise replied.

Blaise was already sporting her bikini ready for a dip in the pool.

Fortunately for us, our appointment with Craig wasn't until noon, enabling us to take a morning dip in the pool. Craig had two properties to show us and we had arranged to meet him at his office in Lliria.

The properties we viewed yesterday had been on my mind all through the night. I had to keep pinching myself to make sure that I hadn't dreamt it all. It was simply unbelievable what you could get for your money in the Valencia municipality.

Sally had assured us before our visit that our budget would definitely buy us a four-bedroom villa with a pool. To be honest, I had doubted it. It seemed so unrealistic; especially as a three-bedroom semi detached house in Kent cost a cool £250,000!

I padded along to the bathroom, threw some water on my face and returned to my bed. I peered through the little iron-gated window to the patio and pool area. Moxy's dusty nose appeared at the grill. He eyed me hopefully and I heard his claws scratch the concrete as he made his way to the internal gate. Colin opened his eyes.

"What time is it?" he enquired, sitting up in bed.

"Just after nine darling," I answered, laughing at his hair which was stuck up on end like a cockatoo's.

Colin and Blaise followed my routine in turn, each of them padding to the bathroom, splashing water of their faces and returning to sit on their beds. I took the contents of the fridge to the patio table outside.

"Hmmm," said Blaise. "Have we any Brie left mum?"

Blaise had a love of the soft French cheese, as did I.

"Yes, we have plenty of it treasure," I reassured her.

The table was laden with croissants, fruits, cheese and ham and a pitcher of cold orange juice. It felt much hotter than the previous day and I was more than a little glad that we didn't have to view any properties until lunch. We could at least spend the morning at leisure.

The properties of the previous day were still milling around in my head and our conversation at the patio table consisted of Blaise and Colin extolling the virtues of the third property. However Colin did agree with me that if the circumstances were such that we were moving to Spain permanently, the third house would have been top of the list. But our objective was to buy a house that we could rent out long or short-term so that the house costs would be covered. I estimated that if we could get ten weeks rental a year, the entire running costs of the house would be covered and any profit could be used to improve it. It was not about making huge profit, but maintaining the house and keeping it in order. If at some time in the future, we wanted to live in Spain permanently, the house wasn't going to fall down around us. We needed a house that would accommodate us, with a room for guests, preferably well-maintained and easy to care for. A garden would be nice but it had to be an easily manageable garden.

My thoughts drifted back to the second property. The villa was a perfect size with four double bedrooms, a modern kitchen and bathroom, grounds that were mostly laid to patio with plenty of storage for Colin's tools and Blaise's toys. There were touches of luxury that really made the second villa appealing. It had a dishwasher and the bathroom mirror had blue check ceramic tile border and a solid wood frame. The huge colourful peach and white striped Dutch awning that framed the front patio and the cheery looking blue and orange upholstered swing bench with matching canopy, nestling in the corner of the patio next to the pool, gave the house a real holiday feel. It was very picturesque. Blaise had particularly loved the garden swing seat. The gardens looked very easy to care for. They were mainly border gardens with huge exotic red and yellow iris. It was a very private villa with the pool and patio areas well hidden behind a mature box hedge of cypress. The orange tree, heavy with lime green unripe oranges, had scented the air.

"It's got air conditioning in **every** room," I suddenly blurted out.

"What has?" asked Blaise.

"And the pool house is fully tiled, it's a second bathroom in effect," I stated plainly, as I continued voicing my thoughts aloud.

"Yes, I like the second property best Colin. In fact, the more I think about it and the more I like it. It will be really easy to clean because everything is fully tiled. All it will need outside is a really good sweep and someone to water the borders once a week," I said between mouthfuls of croissant.

"I like the swing chair," said Blaise with a radiant smile.

Realizing that I would have to find some feature that appealed to Colin and that would grab his attention, I added "And, it's got a sunken pool with a pump!"

Colin's eyes met mine.

"Let's just see what today brings shall we? We might find something better. Best to keep an open mind Angela and then once we have seen everything, we can think it over," Colin cautioned.

I knew he was right of course. Colin was always right. On numerous occasions Colin had proved to have much better judgment than I had. I found it frustrating at first, in the early days of our relationship and then over a period of time, I came to realize that it had saved us time and money over and over again. I often quietly thought to myself that I should listen more to his council. But on this occasion there was this little voice telling me that the second house was the one for us.

We finished up breakfast and headed back into our room carrying the dirty plates and glasses. Helen offered to wash them for us since we were without cooking or self-catering facilities. Blaise had already gone to the pool.

"Don't sing that stupid song," Colin bellowed from the bathroom. "Blaise, do you hear me?"

"Yes dad," Blaise shouted through the little iron-gated window, while Moxy stood at her side wagging his tail.

I pulled my bikini on, located my holiday paperback 'must read' and grabbed my towel.

"We could move the pool to the bottom of the garden and sink it Ange," Colin shouted from the bathroom.

Colin was obviously thinking as much about the third property as I was about the second property. The memory of the third house was painful and not just because I got eaten alive by fruit flies. Being a lady of ample proportions, I had gasped when I saw that the narrow gap between the pool and the side wall of the house would only just fit Twiggy through it, let alone a mature woman with a fuller figure. Blaise got through the gap quite easily, while Colin had to make more of a concentrated effort to squeeze through. Not to be outdone, I decided to follow suit, only to find that the upper part of my body was well and truly wedged against the pool wall. With considerable effort and a lot of pushing and pulling from Colin and Blaise, I squeezed, inch by inch, through the narrow gap. It was so embarrassing and Blaise had laughed until she almost cried.

"Mum, it's just like when Winnie the Pooh got stuck in his door after eating too much honey," she had chuckled.

"Perhaps we need to lose a bit of weight," winked Colin, using the term 'we' so as I wouldn't think he was having a dig at me.

Thank goodness Sally hadn't seen me. And thank goodness I was wearing a black T-shirt too or you would have seen the evidence of a squashed bosom blatantly displayed across my front.

Reflecting on Colin's remark about moving the pool, I sighed deeply for maximum effect and calmly replied, "Yes. You could move it darling, but you would have to kill all those fruit trees to do so, not to mention getting a digger to totally tear up that beautiful garden."

There! I had played my trump card. Colin, knowing that I would be distraught if he killed the trees, simply wouldn't have the heart to do it. Yes, the third house would be discounted in favour of the second.

"I'm off to the pool darling, are you coming in for a dip?" I asked nonchalantly.

"Shortly," Colin replied. "I just want to check something on the video."

I laughed at the mention of the video camera; it brought back happy holiday memories.

The video camera was only a couple of months old. Colin purchased it during our April holiday in Gran Canaria. It never ceases to amaze me that when women go on holiday, they buy souvenirs such as shell bracelets, fans, leather belts, purses, handbags, and sandals. Occasionally they may buy a lace tablecloth from the local market to take back as a present, or they may buy a brightly coloured tie-dyed sarong that can be packed each time they go on holiday. 'I got that on holiday in such and such a place,' they would say. Men, on the other hand, go on holiday and buy things like MP3 players, video recorders, BB guns, laser pens and cameras. The monetary value of a woman's purchases is probably about £50. The monetary value of a man's purchases is more likely to be about £250.

Colin's video camera typically fell into the 'man' category, although to be truthful, he did negotiate a very good deal. He also got a carry case and a mini tripod thrown in for free. But the negotiations for the product were an education. Colin knew how to offer the most ridiculous price and was a master at playing one shop off against another. He was always prepared to travel from town to town to get the best deal. He was expert at bartering, having had plenty of practice during two holidays in Tunisia. He had a real flair for it and was not at all embarrassed at offering a ridiculously low price. However, in some countries, applying the same principle isn't always taken in good humour, as Colin found out. One particular shopkeeper in a shopping mall in Maspalomas, Gran Canaria, came very close to throwing Colin out of his shop.

Ryan had saved up his pocket and holiday money and wanted to buy an MP3 player. Colin wanted to browse the electrical shops in the mall and help Ryan choose one at a good price. Entering a small electrical unit in the mall, Ryan and Colin proceeded to look at the goods for sale. There were two or three other men in the small unit and one of them was looking at a video recorder, the same model as Colin had bought a few days earlier in Playa del Ingles. Blaise and I were browsing the shops a couple of units away when we heard raised voices.

"You are mad, mad, you shouldn't be allowed out!" ranted the Asian shopkeeper as he marched out from behind his counter, drawing the attention of everyone within 100' of his shop.

I had laughed till my sides ached. Well, he was only voicing what I had been saying for the last ten years after all, but the situation was really quite comical. I don't think Colin had ever been asked to leave a shop before. He sort of smirked as he sauntered very slowly through the mall towards me. A small crowd had gathered and they stared intently at me as I walked up the mall to meet him. Ryan followed a good two paces behind him. As I continued to walk towards them, Colin entered another shop to browse and I peered in to the first shop to see what had happened. The shopkeeper was very agitated and strode hastily towards me.

"Take him back to the asylum, he is mad!" the shopkeeper shouted to me.

Of course I pretended Colin had absolutely nothing to do with me and continued to stare blankly through his shop window. The shopkeeper puffed heartily on his cigarette and looked down the mall, his head turning this way and that. I wondered what on earth Colin had done to upset him so much. Had Colin said his prices were daylight robbery or some other censuring remark? I turned tail and walked towards where Colin and Ryan were browsing souvenirs. Most of the goods were trinkets, like bracelets and ankle straps, things that Colin had no interest in whatsoever.

"What happened mum?" said Blaise excitedly. "Did Dad have a fight?"

Blaise was looking a little too excited at the prospect, her face all aglow and eyes glassy, her eyebrows raised in expectation.

"No he most certainly did not!" I exclaimed fiercely.

"Where's Dad?" she asked.

"He's in that shop over there," I said, pointing to the souvenir shop.

Colin and Ryan appeared in the trinket shop doorway. Ryan laughed heartily. The first shopkeeper appeared from his retail unit yet again.

"Mad, mad, you are mad, go back to your asylum," he called out in a very loud voice that carried down the mall.

I must admit that by this time, I felt a fit of the giggles coming on. Ironic really that the man who'd accused Colin of being mad was behaving as if **he** was the one who had just been let out of an asylum. Colin must have really upset him.

"Colin, what on earth did you do?" I asked earnestly.

"Nothing," he replied very calmly. "I just told the chap who was making enquiries about a video recorder that I got one of better quality, much cheaper in Playa del Ingles. I told him how much I had paid for it and the shopkeeper just went loco on me. He said I wanted to rob him of his livelihood, that I was a liar and that I couldn't get it for that price at all. So I offered to take him to the shop in Playa del Ingles so he could see for himself."

"Well, I bet that made him feel good," I said exasperated by the whole thing.

By now, I noticed that there were several people lingering around where we stood. I faced a dilemma. I wanted to browse the shops at the top end of the mall and that meant we had to pass the crazed shopkeeper once more. I groaned. Colin, not bothered by anything or anyone, proceeded to walk towards the top of the mall. We all followed and sure enough, just as we passed the electrical unit on our left, the raving lunatic of a shopkeeper appeared again, shouting at Colin, cursing him and calling him mad!

"Go on, get back in your shop!" shouted Colin, as cool as cucumber.

By now, I was definitely seeing the funny side of it, as there were about a dozen people who appeared to be following us, procession style, through the mall. Perhaps they thought Colin was a trading standards officer. Whatever they thought, Colin had definitely brought amusement to a Maspalomas Shopping Mall in his quest to find the best deal for an electrical gadget. I was happy in the thought that at least Colin had paid £100 less in Playa del Ingles than in the shop of the madman of the Maspalomas Shopping Mall. And of course, thanks to Colin's superb bartering skills, the Playa del Ingles shop had thrown in the carrying case and mini tripod for free.

Chuckling at the thought of the Gran Canaria Mall experience, I made my way toward the internal gate. I was almost at the gate when a woman appeared from the doorway of the next room. She had long blonde hair and had come outside to smoke a cigarette. It transpired that she had been looking around the area for the last three days. Her husband was planning to come over and teach English to the Spanish. She said they preferred it slightly further south, around the areas of Gandia and Oliva. She suggested that we go and explore further south if we had the time. I said we had viewed a lot of houses and that we were delighted with what we could buy for our money in the local area. I mentioned some of the properties we had seen but thanked her all the same for the suggestion and said we would definitely think about exploring a little further afield, after all, Colin did say we had to keep our options open. I wished her a pleasant day and said goodbye.

I slipped through the gate quietly, but ready to hurdle any obstacles on the path in order to get to the pool without being savaged by the dogs. I couldn't see the dogs anywhere. I sauntered up to the pool, threw my towel down on the sun lounger, placed my coca cola on the little plastic side table and headed for the pool steps. Blaise was still drowning wasps with the paper cup.

"Play with me mummy," she shouted, as I slid into the cooling water.

"OK, what shall we play?" I asked.

"Synchronized swimming," she replied, launching herself like a mermaid into the turquoise depths.

She surfaced, giving me instructions on where to hold her, what direction to pull her, how to swirl her around and so on. She asked if her toes pointed correctly and if it looked very elegant. Even though I could hardly move her for fear of hurting my back, it was great fun.

"Whatever happens to your imagination when you grow up?" I shouted over to Colin, who was heading towards the pool steps, a beach towel flung over his shoulder. "Where does it go? Do you think we lock it away in a filing cabinet in our brain and never let it out again?" I asked in a philosophical sort of way.

"You are a crazy woman," he blurted out, diving head first into the pool.

He surfaced, his hair splayed flat against his forehead. It made a fine looking fringe.

"What on earth are you talking about now?" he asked.

"Imagination Colin. That's what I am talking about. Imagination! Look at Blaise," I commanded, pointing to her in the water. "She pretends that she is an Olympic standard synchronized swimmer and she's having loads of fun. That's because she has got a great imagination," I finished.

Colin looked at me with a puzzled expression.

"You still have imagination Ange," he said reassuringly. "I certainly do. For example, I can imagine that third house with the pool moved, the trees re-located and the garden beautifully laid out, with shady spots for you to sit and relax on your swing seat."

Colin had mentioned the swing seat just as Blaise was swimming over to us, well within earshot. I let out a long slow groan and walked slowly towards the deep end. The water covered my mouth at just over half the pool length. I heard Blaise and Colin's laughter as the cool water of the pool covered my head and I blew loud bubbles for maximum effect.

Now that Colin was around to amuse and entertain Blaise, it was my chance to relax on the sun lounger and read some of my holiday novel. To be honest, I found it hard to concentrate on it, as too many thoughts were going round and round in my head. However, I persevered as I was determined to relax and blot out images of Laurel and Hardy and my angry, swollen, itchy, throbbing, scarlet coloured insect bites. I arranged my towel neatly over the spongy cover, pushed my spectacles further up my nose and collapsed on the lounger. A huge Palm tree provided excellent shade. I looked up, blinking at the suns rays that shone through the cascading Palm leaves. I studied my book again. I had read the same paragraph twice already. My concentration was in shreds. I tried again on the following page, but it was no use. My concentration was lost. Feeling very thirsty all of a sudden, I reached for my drink. Unfortunately, the table was just out of arms reach and I didn't want to move off the bed incase I roused the dogs. Wherever they were hiding, it was best if they were not disturbed.

I caught sight of Ben lying flat out in the shade, his back against the whitewashed side wall of Helen's house. But I couldn't see Moxy. Perhaps he had found a shady spot at the back of the house. Colin and Blaise were cursing the wasps that congregated and plagued the shallow end of the pool. Colin karate chopped them in mid air while Blaise collected them in her plastic cup and drowned them in their unconscious state. I put my nose back into my novel.

After a few minutes had passed, I slowly started to drift off. It felt lovely being able to take a warm and cosy nap underneath the canopy of the Palm tree. Suddenly I felt something just above my right knee. I opened one eye carefully, terrified of what I would find. Peering through a half opened eye, I froze. It was Moxy! He sat lopsided against the sun lounger, his head resting dopily upon my leg. Oh no! It was too late. Blaise was looking over!

"Mum, Moxy wants to make friends," she screamed excitedly, as she climbed up the pool steps and ran towards me.

Moxy stood and wagged his tail in a friendly greeting.

"Mum, he wants to be friends, don't you Moxy woxy," she said, talking to him like he was a little baby.

"Now don't excite him Blaise, he's being nice and quiet, let's leave him like that," I pleaded. "Pull the table a little closer please Blaise, so I can reach my drink."

Blaise obediently moved the side table closer to my sun lounger and started picking up Moxy's toys that were strewn around the patio. She threw them enticingly near to him. Sure enough, Moxy took the bait and grabbed the end of a rope pull. Blaise pulled him around on it, laughing wildly, but after a few minutes, decided she was too hot to play any more and wandered back to the pool to cool down. She dropped the rope pull on the pool side and joined Colin in the water. Moxy trotted behind her and waited at the top of the pool steps. I wondered if he would follow her into the pool. He looked very hot and was panting heavily. I closed my eyes in thought.

Did Moxy really want to be friends with me? I really didn't like strange dogs but I decided to try and be a little kinder to him. Perhaps I could offer him a tit bit, or something else that would make him associate me with something nice. I placed my coca cola back on the side table and sat up. Quick as a flash, Moxy took it as a signal that I was up for play. He trotted towards me, the dirty, limp, red rope pull hanging from his mouth. I quickly lay back and pretended I hadn't seen him. He began to make strange noises, like a sea lion. He dropped his rope pull at my side and just as I reached for my drink, I felt his teeth close around my arm, just above my wrist. In utter panic I withdrew my hand in an instant and jumped off the lounger. Colin on seeing my panic stricken face looked over in my direction.

"He nearly bit me," I screamed, heading towards the safety of the water.

"He didn't you baby, he wants to play with you and it's just his way of asking you to play. Is the skin broken?" Colin enquired.

"No but I definitely felt his teeth," I replied anxiously.

Moxy headed towards me and before I could escape, took my wrist in his mouth once more. I was terrified and froze, firmly rooted to the spot. Strange sounds escaped subconsciously through my clenched teeth!

"See mum, he's not hurting you, he's holding your hand," Blaise said trying her best to reassure me.

All I could recall were the old familiar words *'If a dog knows you are scared, he'll have you! Dogs can smell fear.'*

I couldn't remember who had said them or when, but the words had stuck with me for many years. I figured it was best to try and bluff my way out of the situation before I suffered loss of limb, so I playfully pulled my hand from Moxy's mouth and pushed his head away. He wagged his tail and came back for more. I repeated the process several times, calling him a 'daft old dog.'

"Look, mum's playing with Moxy," Blaise called out to Colin in excitement and surprise.

"Look dad, look! Mum's actually playing with Moxy."

Blaise's face was exuberant at the sight of us playing together. I was so happy to see her excitement that I forgot to be afraid. Before long I was pulling Moxy's bandana, feeding him bits of ham, wrestling with the rope pull and generally having a good old time with a dog the size of a small Shetland pony. I imagined that I lived In Spain and Moxy was my dog. Moxy saved me from drowning in the pool; Moxy saved me from a vicious wild boar, Moxy at my bedside when I was poorly, Moxy, my brave and faithful dog, Moxy… my hero! I laughed aloud at myself and Colin and Blaise laughed along with me. Eventually, it got too hot for Moxy and he dropped the rope pull and retired to the shade of the Palm tree, panting heavily.

"Well that was an exciting morning wasn't it mum?" Blaise remarked.

We showered and changed into long trousers and T shirts and locked the apartment. It was time to meet Craig in Lliria.

We made our way to town in the little white Fiat Punto, the map of Lliria town centre firmly clutched in my hand.

"Can you remember where it is Colin?" I asked anxiously.

"Yep, it's on the main road through the town," Colin replied calmly.

We parked the car in a small clearing that we were told was a car park. We walked down the street and joined the main road. Arriving at the estate agents, we announced ourselves for our meeting with Craig.

"Señor Craig," repeated the man his voice deep and gruff as he sat behind his desk.

I repeated Craig's name.

"C R A I G," I said, pronouncing each letter, very slowly.

The man seated at his desk arose, walked through a pair of double glass doors, peered up a staircase and repeated the name again.

"I don't think he understands English," I whispered to Colin.

The man looked over at the girl who sat at the other desk and they both shrugged their shoulders in unison.

"Es Señor Holden, Señor Craig Holden aqui?" I asked.

"No es Señor Holden aqui?" he replied.

"A que hora es Señor Holden aqui?" I asked trying to find out what time Craig was due to arrive. "Señor Holden trabaja aqui, si?" I asked, in what I thought sounded like passable Spanish.

"No!" the man and the girl said in unison.

"What's he saying Ange?" asked Colin, concerned.

"He said Craig doesn't work here," I replied.

"Well ask him if he knows where he does work," said Colin, losing patience.

"Es Señor Holden cerca de aqui?" I said slowly, not sure if I had said the right Spanish words for 'near here.'

The man just shrugged his shoulders.

"Come on Ange, it's no good staying here, we are not going to get anywhere with this chap," said Colin.

We all turned tail and filed out of the estate agents office.

For the next hour, we walked the entire town of Lliria, searching for Craig in any estate agents offices that we found. But nobody seemed to know of him.

"Oh dear, it's not looking good is it?" I said with a tremble in my voice.

It was one o'clock and we were all hot and tetchy.

"Where's the map Helen gave to you?" Colin asked.

I rummaged in my bag and found it. I handed it quickly to Colin. He studied it.

"Well according to the map, it should be right there," I said, pointing to the corner of the road on the opposite side to us.

We glanced over to the corner, puzzled by the markings on the map. It was a Chinese Restaurant.

"Hang on a minute," said Colin, "there's more than one cross on this map. In fact, there's another three crosses on it," he exclaimed.

"Let's walk to where the next cross on the map is," I suggested.

We set off and after a few minutes arrived at the point on the map. It was a small bistro on the sidewalk. We continued walking to the next cross. Not surprisingly, it was another restaurant, an Italian Pizzeria.

"These crosses are markers for restaurants and places to eat out you madwoman," said Colin, exasperated.

"Well I'll phone Helen, she can tell us where it is," I suggested, hoping to rescue the situation.

We were now over forty minutes late for our appointment. Colin decided that it was just as quick to drive back to Sunny Ridge, but I felt awful having broken the appointment and insisted on telephoning Helen anyway. I rang Helen and explained what had happened.

"Oh that's no trouble at all," she crooned in her soft Irish accent. "I'll phone Craig and let him know. He can meet you back here, that will save any more trouble for you."

We arrived ten minutes later and Helen entered through the internal gate, Ben and Moxy in tow. Moxy was delighted to see me but Ben stayed near Helen. I didn't trust Ben, a hint of my old phobia creeping up on me perhaps. I shouted to Moxy and he merrily trotted over to me. I pulled at his bandana and gently stroked his head. He dropped his head to the floor and licked at the crumbs from the croissants we had eaten at breakfast. At the sight of Moxy scavenging, Ben joined him and in a minute flat, the two dogs had cleared up all the crumbs on the floor and were enthusiastically setting about clearing up those on the patio table. I watched as Ben and Moxy licked the crumbs from the tabletop.

"These are seriously big dogs," I whispered to Colin, who winked at me.

Craig arrived about half an hour later. We shook hands and talked about niceties such as what we thought of the town, where we had been, what we thought of the Pollos Asados and Heron City, all that sort of stuff that one says to break the ice. We hadn't really ventured far because we were so exhausted from the previous day's viewings, but we were all looking forward to going to Heron City, the huge entertainment and eating complex, not too far away.

Craig said he had two houses for us to view, so hopping back into our car we followed him out of the urbanization towards Pedralba. We pulled into a side road that Colin said he thought we had driven along yesterday.

"This road looks very familiar Ange," Colin said, pulling up behind Craig's car and securing the handbrake.

We peered through a pair of large iron gates. It was the fourth house that we had viewed with VSI. I remembered it as soon as I saw it. It had the same overgrown garden, Palm trees at the front and the Pine forest at the rear. We made our apologies to Craig and told him that we had already viewed this house and discounted it. I felt terrible but he said he didn't mind and that it was quite common for two agents to have the same house on their books.

Craig had another villa to show us situated opposite his own home, Sunny Ridge. The area was very well maintained even though you had to drive through an industrial estate to reach it. This too was quite common in the area. Residential areas were often built next to industrial areas. However, industrial areas in this region were very small scale compared to those in England.

The house was conveniently situated for nipping into Lliria for your shopping and of course Lliria had a mainline metro link to the heart of Valencia. I particularly liked the idea of free parking at the metro. We headed back in the direction of Sunny Ridge.

We pulled up more or less opposite Craig and Helen's place. The house was reasonably good sized, reasonably well maintained and had a small plunge pool to the side. The gardens were laid to lawn at the front and were quite big. Colin and I glanced at each other and smiled, both thinking the same thing. Neither of us were gardeners nor green fingered so to speak. The last thing I wanted to do in Spain was mow the lawn. The grass would be dead within weeks. Who would water it for us while we were away? We would most probably have to employ someone to water the garden and lawns every day. Someone, somewhere, would simply delight in having such a big front lawn, but unfortunately, not us.

We thanked Craig for his time and said we would think about it carefully before making any decision. Before Craig left, he gave us some very good advice. He told us to get a solicitor. After all, one wouldn't buy a house in England without one. We shook hands, thanked him once again and watched as he returned to his car and set off back to work. We all breathed a sigh of relief. It was at this point that I realized that I had already made my decision. I decided to keep my thoughts to myself until such time as Colin wanted to discuss it.

We spent the afternoon in the pool, frolicking around, cooling down, mulling things over, enjoying the sun, enjoying the surroundings and imagining what a life in the sun would be like. And for once, none of us spoke our minds, content to just relax and unwind.

Chapter 4
Storm Chaser

After a shower in piping hot water, I dressed for our night on the town at Heron City. Helen had given us a small information leaflet about it and we were all eager to let our hair down and have some fun. Any serious decision-making could wait. This was our penultimate night in the Turia Valley. We had sufficient time to look at the surrounding area, its delights and fancies. We were free to indulge ourselves, visit places of interest and surround ourselves with the sights, sounds and smells of Valencia. Blaise and Colin had also made an extra effort to look good and I felt deliriously happy to be going out for the evening.

According to the map, Heron City was just off the CV35, (the main road we had driven in on.) It would probably take about twenty minutes to get there. I looked at the brightly coloured leaflet in my hand. The cover photo looked wonderful, the huge Heron City sign standing like a beacon, probably visible for miles around. The coloured fountains and fluorescent lights of Heron City's entrance looked very enticing. Colin grabbed his video camera; I packed a small compact digital camera and Blaise clutched her fully loaded purse! Dressed in our summer finery, we clambered into the little white Fiat Punto. We looked like typical tourists, which in itself was strange in this part of the country.

We set off down the highway and arrived at Heron City some fifteen minutes later. It was clearly signed and Colin pulled off the highway, down a long road that wound its way around the back of the complex and led directly into an enormous car park. As I got out of the car, I noticed that it was covered in tangerine coloured dust. It was filthy and badly needed a wash. It was hard to travel anywhere in the region without driving along an orange dust track at some time. Our car had taken on the tangerine hue that had coated our legs on our first day of house hunting.

"Be careful getting in and out of the car," I shouted to Blaise and Colin. "It's full of dust; it will make your clothes filthy if you accidentally brush against it."

"OK," Colin and Blaise chimed as they got out.

Heron City was situated next to a huge retail outlet store called Porcelanosa. I was overjoyed when I saw the huge Porcelanosa sign and thought it clever that someone would put a huge ceramics store next to an entertainment complex. We walked towards Porcelanosa and looked through the huge glass windows, only to find that it was a bathroom showroom and didn't sell the kind of porcelain I was expecting at all. I had imagined rows of brightly glazed pots, the sort that you could see on patios all over Spain. There would be Lladro and Nao pieces, lamp bases and various 'objets d'art!' Still, on a positive note, at least we would know where to buy a new bathroom suite should we ever need one in the future. We crossed the road opposite Porcelanosa towards the entrance to Heron City, whose bright fluorescent pink logo was hoisted some 50' or more high in the air. It was fantastic. You could see the sign for miles. It was a huge circle, lit with bright red and purple rings with the words

'Heron City' brightly lit within the circles. The mast upon which it was set looked like a small electrical pylon. Perhaps it was, after all, that amount of fluorescence would need a mini grid to power it. The sign was most impressive and no doubt attracted people for miles around.

Inside Heron City was a huge complex that consisted of shops, eating-houses and leisure facilities. There was a Frankie and Benny's restaurant, a toy store, a sweet shop, a bowling alley, several pizza houses, several burger houses, traditional Spanish tapas bars, a couple of sandwich bars, a couple of souvenir shops that sold everything from scented candles to linen baskets and various other bars and shops. There were large cinema billboards showing movie previews, play areas for toddlers and photo booths that took tourist type photos. Yes, everything you could want was here and everything was open until ten o'clock.

We strolled around leisurely, taking in the smells and sights and Colin and I took lots of photos of the coloured fountains. Blaise climbed up on to the perimeter wall around the fountains, pretending she was a ballerina, dancing her way along the narrow wall, her imagination fired. The pools of water cascaded down small ledges that gave a miniature waterfall effect. Each pool was lit with a different fluorescent colour and the colours rotated between the pools. First pink, then green and finally purple. The middle of each pool had a large hole in it where the water fell down and where the coloured screens for the lighting were housed. I suddenly became very scared. I had visions of Blaise falling off the wall into the pool and down the hole, the hole in each pool being sufficiently large enough for her to fall through.

"Off the wall now Blaise!" I commanded.

"I'm dancing mum," she answered happily.

"Blaise get off the wall **now!**" I repeated in my sternest voice and with enough tone to imply that she had better do as I said and quickly.

Blaise jumped down from the wall, a pained expression on her face. I explained my reason for concern to her and she accepted it, agreeing that it was quite dangerous, although she continued to scowl at me. I was most surprised that there were no warning signs and I considered putting the idea forward in the suggestion box. However, there didn't appear to be a suggestion box anywhere on the complex. Perhaps they just assumed parents would keep their children in order and that accidents wouldn't happen!

With Blaise safely back on terra firma, we headed in the direction of the shops and restaurants.

Heron City was undoubtedly colourful, bright and cheerful. Just being there made you feel happy. Colin shepherded us along to get something to eat, choosing a traditional Spanish bar. He indicated for us to take a seat at the nearby table. Blaise ordered Spaghetti Bolognese and thoroughly enjoyed it. She wore most of it on her face and T-shirt. Colin and I ate a simple dish of rice and chicken, washed down with fizzy orange. Even though it was late evening, it was still hot and we were parched with thirst. We finished our meal and continued our stroll through the arcade. Blaise noticed a photo booth and ducked inside it. The booth produced different styles of photos. You could have your photo printed on a wanted poster, or you could pick a style that made your look like a cartoon character. Blaise was fascinated by it.

"Please mum, can I have my photo taken, **please?**" she pleaded.

"Not now Blaise," I replied. "We still have a lot to look at and it's getting late. You can have your photo taken the next time we come here," I assured her.

Blaise pulled a disappointed face before following us through the arcade. I could hear her muttering to herself as we strode along.

"Do you promise I can have my photo taken next time?" she asked and added, "You've got to promise."

"We'll see," I replied, in the way that mums always do.

"What does she want this time?" Colin asked, in the way fathers always do.

"She just wants her photo taking," I answered. "She can have it taken the next time we come."

We completed our tour of the arcade, ending at the coloured fountains where we had entered. We crossed the road to the car park, located our car and climbed in. Night had closed in quickly and it was dark. The bright neon lights of the Heron City logo shone iridescent against the black sky. We watched the neon lights fade in the distance as we drove back to Sunny Ridge.

We hadn't travelled far when Colin and I noticed something in the distance on our right. Bright flashes lit the sky.

"There must be fireworks somewhere," I said looking out of the car window, scanning the sky for light.

We continued along the road, watching excitedly as the sky lit up at regular intervals. Colin glanced toward my passenger window. A wall of silver flashed brightly.

"That's not fireworks Angela," Colin remarked.

"What do you think it is then? Laser beams?" I suggested.

"No, I think it's lightening," Colin stated. "There's a storm coming."

I looked out in the distance to the silver glow in the sky. The sky lit up every few seconds or so.

"You may be right Colin," I said as I continued to stare at the flashes of silver.

We arrived home just before ten o'clock. The sky flashed silver in the distance. We had just got out of the car when we saw a huge bolt of lightening fall in a jagged line from sky to earth. It hit once, twice and then a third time. It was awesome! Colin got out his video recorder.

"I've got to see if I can catch this on video Ange, its spectacular," he said excitedly.

We both looked at the bolts of lightening as they forked like silver daggers to the ground. Colin was right. They were spectacular.

I took the apartment key from Colin and unlocked the door. Blaise and I entered the room. Blaise went straight to the bathroom while I switched on the small lamp atop the bedside cabinet between Blaise's bed and mine. I suggested she get ready for bed while I poured each of us a glass of cold milk. I put the drinks on the bedside table.

"Don't forget to brush your teeth when you've finished your milk, I'm just going back outside to see Dad. I won't be long; we're going to watch the storm."

"OK mum," she yawned, as I slipped through the gate to where Colin stood at the side of the car.

Colin had set the video recorder to tape and pointed it in the direction of the storm. It was some way off in the distance and looked like a laser light show or firework display. The only clue that it was neither lasers nor fireworks was in the colour. Silver only. No greens, reds, purples, oranges or yellows.

Colin walked up the dirt track road past Sunny Ridge; his feet crunching on the gravel track, alerting the dogs to his presence. They barked furiously at the gates.

"Where are you going?" I asked in a muffled voice.

"I'm going up here to see if I can get a better view, are you coming?"

"No, I'll stay here with Blaise. Be careful Colin," I said anxiously, adding, "Don't do anything daft, it could be dangerous."

"I'll be OK," he called back over his shoulder, as I watched him walk up the track until his outline disappeared over the ridge.

I went back inside our apartment, quietly closed the door and got ready for bed. Feeling very tired, I reflected on the day's events. We had really enjoyed the much slower pace of life. Blaise was especially happy that I was being kind to Moxy and that I wasn't scared of him any more. I too, felt glad about it and was quite proud of myself. It's not easy overcoming an inbred fear and I had been making a conscious effort to take a deep breath and slow down my breathing when the dogs were around. It had been quite an adventure walking around all the houses for sale. Blaise told me she'd had great fun running through the orange and lemon groves. I told Blaise how much I really liked the second house we had viewed. She said she already knew and could understand why I liked it.

"Mum, if we were going to live here in Spain, it would be different. We would probably buy the third house, but we are not going to live here for some time, so I understand."

I was taken aback. To hear such words of wisdom drop from the lips of a ten year old made me warm inside and immensely proud of her. Perhaps I had grossly underestimated her. She had just celebrated her tenth birthday the week previous, but Blaise already spoke with such wisdom for her age.

"I'm going to sleep now mum," Blaise said, tucking up with her soft 'night night' tucked neatly under her chin.

I laughed softly to myself. Blaise might say wise things from time to time but as long as she went to bed with her 'night night,' she would always be my little girl. I wondered how much longer she would keep hold of it.

I remembered my cousin John having a 'night night' and my auntie Cath used to sneak in his room and take it when he wasn't looking, in order to wash it. I chuckled at the memory. I tossed and turned in my bed, strange memories flooded my thoughts. I remembered my own mother trying like mad to get me to throw away my dummy. I had dummies in every colour, white, pink, blue, cream and my favourite, lemon. I was about eight years old, or so I have been told, before I stopped taking a suck on my dummy and finally gave it up for good. My mother had often told me that I used to rush in from school, take my dummy out of the dresser drawer, take half a dozen sucks on it and then throw it back in the drawer again, before going back outside to play.

I threw my dummy into the fire several times. I can remember people telling me it was dirty. It couldn't have been that dirty otherwise mum wouldn't have let me suck on it. I remember one particular occasion very well. I must have been no more than four years old at the time. I tossed my lemon 'dodi' into the open flames of the fire in our living room, thinking I was a big girl at last. All was fine until the evening, when I desperately wanted it back. I came home from nursery and cried with despair when I realized that it wasn't in the top drawer and remembered I had thrown it in the fire.

I remembered my mum saying, "It's gone, you threw it away, it went in the fire. You're a big girl now."

I often wondered if there was peer pressure on my mother to wean me off my dummy. I don't think for a minute she would have made me throw it away if she had known how much it comforted me. Of course, even at that very tender young age, I always had a reply.

"Jayne's got some more, they are hung up on the wall. I've seen them!" I had shouted in desperation.

I had cried mightily and finally my mother had given in and sent my sister Norma to Jayne's shop to buy another one for me.

Dummies are fantastic gadgets. I used a dummy to help me give up smoking. I bought myself a lovely pink one to help me over the bad times. Giving up smoking was difficult enough, but not knowing what to do with your hands and mouth when you were not talking or gesticulating was weird. My pink dummy was wonderful, even if I did accidentally answer the door one day with it stuck in my mouth. Luckily it was our reliable milkman Stewart Clayton who saw me. Stewart had been my milkman for years. He looked very surprised and I was very embarrassed, but I explained that it was to help me give up smoking.

"Well, if it helps you give it up Angela, it's worth doing," he had said.

My thoughts returned to my cousin John. I wondered if he was of a similar age when he finally gave up his bit of nylon cloth. Perhaps he hadn't thrown it away at all but had it safely tucked away in a drawer as a comforting reminder of his childhood. Would Blaise keep her soft flannel in her drawer? Would she tell her children about it and keep it forever? I have stored lots of Blaise's things that she has treasured over the years, like her favourite reading book, 'The Princess and the Pea,' her first soft toy, an orange dinosaur called 'Ding Ding,' her favourite Peter Rabbit bib, her musical cot toy and a musical sleep inducer. The latter was her favourite, a white plastic cloud that you placed on a bedside table. You wound it up and it played nursery tunes while projecting images of lambs and teddy bears on the ceiling. Of course, all the baby memorabilia was safely stored in the top of my wardrobe together with other bits and pieces of treasure, memories of Blaise from birth through childhood. And I would probably keep collecting bits and pieces until she reached adulthood.

Lots of 'motherly' questions filled my thoughts and I dozed off feeling totally at peace with the world. Blaise could keep her *night night* forever if it made her happy. It's strange to think that a soft white face flannel could give such comfort. Why would I want to take it away from her? So what if she was ten years old, she could keep it forever if she wanted to. I looked over to where Blaise lay. She was resting peacefully. I sighed contentedly. How wonderful, the blessings of motherhood.

A low buzzing noise woke me from slumber. I looked over at Blaise who was snoring softly. There was a feint glow about the room. I looked over in the direction of Colin's bed, the source of the glow. He was viewing his recorded masterpiece on the small pull out video display.

"What time is it?" I asked rubbing my eyes.

"It's just past midnight; I videoed the storm. It was terrific, I'm just viewing it now," he whispered.

"Have you been out in that storm all this time?" I enquired through a yawn.

"Yeah, I walked up the track quite some way, to the top of the hill, but figured it would be safer in the car. I came back, got the car and drove up the hill. The view is fantastic. I saw the lightening fork its way to the ground. Want to come and look at this with me?" he asked.

I swung my legs over the side of the bed and sat up. I was still half asleep. Our plans for the following day were a little vague and we hadn't planned an early start.

"Why not," I replied padding over to Colin's bed.

I arranged myself in a comfortable position and looked at the video screen. Colin was right! The storm was truly fantastic. The entire sky had lit up with a fluorescent purplish white glow, followed by a thick dagger shaped bolt of lightening that fell in a jagged line to the ground. At one point, there were three lightening bolts touching the ground at the same time, each connected by a horizontal line at the top. I don't know how far apart they were but the scene reminded me of a silver Christmas streamer. I wondered what would have happened if one of those bolts had made contact with a person. I had heard somewhere that 99% of all people struck by lightening survive and I wondered if it turned their hair silver, like it was portrayed in the movies.

I found it strange that I couldn't hear any rain or thunder. My experience of storms in England was a reliable and repetitive series of events. First, there would be heavy rain; second a bolt of lightening followed some seconds after by a great big clap of thunder. I had never seen an entirely electrical storm and I was mesmerized and fascinated by it. I could easily understand why some people chased storms. The element of danger can be very exciting and the thrill of outrunning it or escaping unscathed must be something like the feeling you get when you take your first white knuckle ride at a theme park.

"You didn't get too close to it did you?" I asked quietly, thinking about how dangerous it might have been.

"Nah, it was miles away Ange. I bet I could have driven another thirty miles before I got near it," Colin answered, still looking at the screen.

"Oh that's OK then," I replied, as a giant yawn involuntarily stretched my mouth wide open, "I'm going back to sleep now," I attempted to say, but with my mouth contorted and twisted, it sounded like utter nonsense.

"Goodnight darling, see you in the morning," I whispered as my head hit the pillow.

"I won't be too long after you myself Ange. Goodnight," Colin said tenderly as he pressed various buttons on the video recorder.

Chapter 5
The Dilemma

We woke to yet another gloriously scorching hot day. It was our last day in the Turia Valley. There would be decisions made and actions taken. The weight of the impending responsibility lay heavily upon me. Colin and Blaise roused from sleep and we took a dip in the pool before heading to Villamarchante to look around and explore the town.

Moxy heard us shuffling around through the little iron-gated window and came padding round to the internal gate. I started my morning relay of food transportation from the fridge to the patio table, instinctively pulling a few more dead blooms off the geraniums on my way to and fro.

"The shower's not working! The water's not emptying," Colin shouted from the bathroom.

I made my way to the bathroom. Blaise was sitting on the edge of her bed squealing.

"What's wrong Blaise?" I asked with concern.

"I need the toilet mum," she said through clenched teeth. "I have a tummy ache."

This was a common situation. It seemed that whenever Colin wanted the bathroom Blaise was in it and whenever Blaise wanted the bathroom, Colin was in it.

Fortunately, when we left our first rented house 'Beaverdell' and moved to our second rented house, 'Little Acorns,' our troubles were over, as 'Little Acorns' had three toilets. My refereeing days were over! However, here in our little apartment in the Turia valley, it seemed the same old situation was back to haunt me again.

"Oh I'm sure Dad won't be long," I said cheerfully, as Blaise rocked back and forth holding her tummy.

"How long will you be Colin?" I shouted through the bathroom door.

"Not long, no point having a shower because it will flood the bathroom if the water won't drain away. I'll have to tell Helen about it," Colin replied testily.

"See Blaise, dad won't be long," I assured her calmly.

Colin appeared in the bathroom doorway, his towel tucked firmly around his middle. He smelt fresh as a daisy. Blaise ducked past him in a shot.

"Good job the weather is hot or I'd be freezing to death now," Colin stated, rubbing his hair briskly with a hand towel.

"Perhaps we've blocked it with all the dust we've showered off," I joked. "Everything seems to get covered in orange dust doesn't it?"

"Hmmm," he replied gruffly, still rubbing his hair.

I transferred the final round of drinks to the patio table.

"Breakfast is outside when you are both ready," I shouted, taking a seat at the plastic table.

"I'm just going to tell Helen about the shower," called Colin, heading off in the direction of the internal gate. "She'll need to get it fixed."

I watched as Colin patted Moxy fondly around the head and the pair of them walked towards the main house. I continued serving breakfast and pouring drinks, happy for the peace and warmth of the morning. Colin returned within minutes. He sat down and tucked into the delicious goodies laid out on the table.

Blaise smiled and chirped a friendly "Morning dad."

She had already put her bikini on ready for the pool.

"So, what are we doing today?" she asked, between mouthfuls of Brie and croissant.

"Please don't talk with your mouth full Blaise," I checked, thinking 'drat that mother business again,' as I said it.

I was probably conditioned from my own mother.

"Sorry mum. What we doing today then?" she repeated.

"We are going to swim and then we will have a look around Villamarchante. It looks like a pretty little square. We can have a late lunch there if you like," I added.

"Are there any shops there?" Blaise enquired.

"Yes I think so. I'm not sure what sort of shops, but there must be some Blaise. After all, it is quite a large village. I saw the hardware store when we were waiting for the estate agent to open," I continued.

"Oh, **that's** Villamarchante," said Blaise, recognition registering on her face.

"Are we going to say hello to Sally?"

"I'm not sure sweetheart, perhaps," I replied.

Colin hadn't said a word yet. He blinked at the sun and we heard a cheery Irish accent shout from the internal gate. It was Helen followed closely by Moxy and Ben. Colin stood up from the table and ushered her into the apartment.

Blaise and I tried frantically to stop Ben and Moxy eating everything atop the patio table. But the smell of ham and Brie was too tantalizing for them. Being very large dogs, their heads were slightly higher than the tabletop. Not only could they smell the food, they could see it too. Helen, hearing our efforts to shoo the dogs away, called them over to her. They reluctantly obeyed and headed towards the internal gate. I overheard Helen and Colin's conversation. Apparently, Helen had experienced the same problem with the shower in our apartment before. On the previous occasion, the plumber had fixed a leak on the main pipe that ran under the concrete from the guest's front gate to the bathroom. Helen said she would call the plumber out again and ask him if he could fix it today. She said it would probably be OK to shower later that evening. Colin informed her that we would be out for most of the day and that we would probably be back at about five o'clock for a quick dip in the pool. If we could take a dip later on in the evening, about seven o'clock, then we wouldn't come back until then. Helen said she had no problem with us taking a dip in the pool a little later. After all, it would give the plumber more time to repair the problem. She wished us a nice day and returned to the main house, Moxy and Ben following behind her. Colin returned to the patio table to eat the few bits that Blaise and I had left him.

"Where's all the ham gone?" he asked, scanning the table for food.

"Those blasted dogs!" I remarked, winking at Blaise in an attempt to keep her quiet.

A quick look of disbelief covered Colin's face. Blaise and I kept our faces straight, not daring to look at each other incase we burst out laughing.

"I bet you two have eaten it," Colin said, laughing. He picked up the remnants of the pack of Brie.

"Us!" Blaise and I chanted in unison, staring wide eyed and feigning shock that he could even think such a thing.

Colin winked at us and we all laughed loudly, our secret discovered.

Villamarchante was some ten to twelve minutes drive south of Lliria. It had two 'Ferreteria' (hardware stores selling anything from patio tables to drills) two supermarkets, a town hall, an estate agent, an ice-cream parlour, several restaurants and bars, a clothes and shoe shop and shops that I couldn't fathom out what was on sale. There was a lovely little town square, which seemed to be the hub of village society. It was in this square that we had bought drinks on the morning we met with the estate agent, VSI. There was also a police station and what looked like an empty, run down German bank. It looked like it had been closed for quite some time, its windows filthy and its interior filled with rubble and cobwebs. One of the small bars in the square had a picture of Che Guevara, the Cuban guerrilla, drawn on it's frontage.

"We should come to the square for breakfast tomorrow," I suggested to Colin. "That will save us having to buy anything else from the supermarket. We can eat up what we have left in the fridge this evening and then the fridge will be clear for morning. All we really need to leave in the fridge are drinks."

"Yeah, that makes good sense," Colin agreed.

We crossed the worn out zebra crossing that led from the car park to the village square. It was not what you would call a proper zebra crossing. It was painted black and white, but like most places in Spain; cars ruled the roads and pedestrians gave way to them. We explained this to Blaise, stressing that she must never step out on a zebra crossing and expect the

Orange Blossom Beginnings

cars or wagons to stop, as they most definitely wouldn't! We asked Blaise to think carefully about which direction the cars would come from.

"Remember Blaise, they drive on the right here," I cautioned.

"I know that mum, I'm not daft!" she retorted crossly.

I saw Colin shoot her a sharp glance that meant she should apologize to her mum instantly.

"Sorry mum," she said softly.

"It's OK Blaise; I'm only worried for your safety, that's all. I know you're not daft."

Blaise took my hand and squeezed it as we crossed the road.

We walked past the town hall entrance and saw the chairs and tables laid out neatly in the square. The square was not really a square at all. It was a rectangle. If you imagined a rectangular shaped clock, at seven o'clock is the town hall, the first building on the left as you stand on the pavement at six o'clock. Next to the town hall, a doorway formed the entrance to several apartments. The estate agent, VSI was next at nine o'clock, followed by another entrance and finally, the Salon de Jamon at eleven o'clock. At twelve o'clock was the Ferreteria, with town houses either side of it. At between one and two o'clock was the clothes and shoe shop and the entrance to yet more apartments. Between two to three o'clock was Che Guevara's bar. Another small bar stood next to that, then between three and four o'clock was the ice cream parlour and finally at five o'clock, stood the empty building that was once a German bank. At the back of us at six o'clock, were disabled parking bays for the town hall. It seemed strange that Villamarchante did not have one single working bank or cash point machine!

Dotted around the back streets off the square were the narrow, cobbled streets of terraced houses. At intervals along the way, set high up in the brick walls, were rectangular recesses of about a foot high. Statues of the Virgin Mary or Jesus Christ were placed in them and small bundles of dried flowers decorated the floors of the recesses. I wondered how they managed to place the flowers up there. Perhaps people threw them in, basketball style, although I couldn't really imagine anyone actually doing that. After all, it wouldn't be very reverent to throw a bunch of flowers at Jesus or the Blessed Virgin Mary! More likely that a very tall stepladder was used. It did make the narrow cobbled streets very interesting though and you never knew what religious scene awaited you around the next corner. Occasionally, a tiled, portrait style image of Jesus Christ greeted you, ornately put together high up on the street wall.

Beautiful carved heavy wooden doors marked the entrances to private houses. The woodwork was varnished in dark oak and mahogany. Some doors had very ornate carvings upon them; vines, leaves, oranges and all manner of things that no doubt in time, we would come to know as indicative of the region.

We made our way slowly through the streets, wending our way back to the square. We took pavement seats at Che Guevara's bar and watched as the square filled up. Colin ordered cold drinks for us while Blaise and I sat happily passing the time of day.

"There's not many English here are there?" I remarked.

"No there isn't," Colin replied, his eyes lighting up. "Great isn't it?"

"That girl at the other restaurant can speak a bit of English because I heard her talk," said Blaise and added, "And the lady in the property shop can speak really good English can't she?"

"That's because she **is** English," Colin and I said in unison, laughing.

"Oh, that's why then," Blaise replied.

Colin and I talked about what we had seen, what we liked about the region, what we thought holiday guests would find of interest, which village or area we would prefer to buy a property in, what we thought of the scenery and what we thought of the people. We both agreed that we really loved the triangular area around the towns and villages of Lliria, Villamarchante and Pedralba. It was so lush. Neither one of us had known what to expect in the Valencia municipality nor had we any idea how fertile the Turia Valley was.

Having travelled to the Costa Brava many times, we had a special fondness in our heart for Estartit. Flanked by the Medas Islands and declared a marine reserve, this would have been our first choice of area; after all, Blaise had been conceived there. But having returned to Estartit several years running and following inspection of every estate agent we could find there, the verdict was that we simply could not afford to buy there, as much as we would have liked to. From necessity, our net had been cast wider.

Sipping our drinks in the busy little square, we recalled our visit to the Costa Calida, just south of Cartagena in the Murcia region of Spain.

A close friend of mine had a house in Mazarron and I had enjoyed a girly holiday at her villa for three years running before Colin and the children had accompanied me on a two-week holiday one late October. The weather had been fantastic. We had jumped rollers in the ocean, holding each other's hands so the huge waves didn't knock us over. We'd played bat and ball on the fine sandy beach almost every day, until seven o'clock most evenings and we'd met a really friendly couple, Ken and Carol that still remain as friends today.

I had shown Colin the urbanization where my friend's house was. It was a Sunday that we would never forget. Someone on the urbanization had organized a car boot sale and while the proceeds were for a charitable cause, Colin had been dismayed. It was typically British and Colin didn't want typically British in Spain.

As we sat in the square at Villamarchante and sipped our drinks, we recalled that holiday. I had cut the bottom of my foot on coral on the second day we were there. I had poured iodine down a 2" gash along the length of my heel, morning and evening. I had worn a bandage dressing with a thick bed sock over it for the remainder of the two-week holiday and limped my way around for the remaining twelve days.

Colin remembered how red the soil was in Mazarron. There were lovely sunrises and sunsets too. But some of the land had been baked dry and looked like barren scrubland. Although the soil was beautifully coloured, it was too desert-like for Colin.

Blaise remembered feeding the fish in the sea. We had chosen a small and very picturesque beach as our favourite. It was called Ermita Beach and it was a small, crescent shaped beach, backed by small cafes. A small rocky outcrop reached 40' out into the sea from the shoreline. It was good for snorkelling and home to a variety of fish. Ryan and Blaise waded waist deep into the sea every day to feed the fish. There were some quite large fish too that bumped into your legs in their frenzy to eat the bread. This had frightened Blaise at first, but after a few days she had become used to it.

Blaise and Ryan had befriended a small boy of about three years old whose name was Graham. He had turned out to be a real handful, but they had enjoyed playing with him even though he was a little spoilt at times. After all, what child wasn't spoiled at some time or other? The saying 'spare the rod and spoil the child' comes to mind and I thought it might have been true in Graham's case. However, I have never liked that saying and think some people use it as an excuse to take discipline to the extreme. Colin, Blaise and I agreed that we had enjoyed our holiday in Mazarron but we didn't want to live in that particular area of Spain.

"Too many English," said Colin.

It was fact; the small urbanization where my friend had bought her house some years ago, had turned into a massive estate of white painted houses. A recent account given by one of the couples we befriended there told of high crime rates and prostitution. The estate had been described as 'an English ghetto.' By all accounts, the Spaniards dumped their dogs on the estate because the English were a soft touch and took in all the strays. One of my friends recently told me that there's also an animal rescue shelter there now. I wondered how much of what we heard about it was true. Some of the people I knew who lived on the urbanization seemed perfectly happy, whilst others we knew were definitely unhappy. I guess it's all a matter of personal preference at the end of the day and the truth is probably somewhere half way. All the same, I couldn't blame Colin for not wanting to buy there. I have very fond memories of Mazarron and would highly recommend it as a holiday destination. It's quite wonderful, with good beaches, good restaurants and a pleasant promenade. However, in my own personal opinion, the greenery of the Valencia region has the edge.

We continued chatting about the houses we had seen, what we thought of the area, how beautiful and lush the landscape was, how pretty the orange groves were and how friendly everyone had been. Colin and I discussed the possibility of hiring out the villa, perhaps on a long-term basis for those wanting a base in readiness for the Americas Cup in 2007. We agreed it would be a good time to buy in the Valencia municipality.

"There will be lots of companies setting up business in preparation for The Americas Cup," Colin stated.

"And if we don't get a long term let, we can rent it out as a rural holiday destination. Blaise, what do you think of the idea?" I asked.

"It's a good idea mum but I think we will have to learn Spanish or we might order something to eat that we don't like!"

Colin and I laughed. We could tell from Blaise's remark that she was thinking about food and was probably quite hungry. Several groups of people arrived and sat down at the next table to us. They were English. I laughed and Colin raised his eyes skyward.

We introduced ourselves to the party on the next table. There were two couples and both had bought houses in the area. One couple had bought a huge farmhouse further down the coast and their friends had bought a house in Villamarchante.

The group of people all looked dusty, hungry, thirsty and worn out. They told us that they had been working hard, renovating a property. They asked us why we were visiting. Colin told them we were considering buying a house in the area and they were delighted for us. Colin went on to explain that we didn't really want to buy where there were lots of English. Unsure of how they would react to this, I held my breath. But I needn't have worried. They all agreed that the Turia Valley was probably one of the best places in Spain for us to buy if we didn't want to be surrounded by lots of English people. They told us that the only English people we were likely to meet were those who had fallen in love with the area, those who liked the prices of property and the cheap cost of living and had moved there to live.

'It's not really a holiday destination is it?" Colin asked adding, "However, that might change with The Americas Cup."

The group nodded in agreement.

"So far, there are about nine or ten couples in or around the region who come from England, there's a German woman who's married to an Englishman and there's one Dutch man," one of the group informed us.

During the next hour or so, more couples arrived. We were invited to push our table together with theirs and make up one big happy British contingent. One thing that we all had in common was a love of the region. Whether it was North or South Valencia, it was all great.

"This is real Spain," one chap said with what was now slightly slurred speech. "Home of paella, oranges and the 'Bull Fight.' It's got culture, history, great gastric treasures, folklore and traditions. There are still communities here."

"The Spanish encourage the English to join in. If you make an effort, however small, the people here love you for it and will go out of their way to help you," another chap told us.

At this point in the conversation, the bar owner himself appeared carrying trays of freshly baked pizza. He placed them down on the tables in front of the group.

"Enjoy my friends," he said in a fine English accent.

By this time, our jolly English and Welsh contingent were all a little merrier, having consumed several beers. We had been in the square for at least two hours and yet more wine and more beers arrived. They told us that a week or so ago, they had arrived for lunch and didn't leave until the next day. They had enjoyed themselves so much that when they had got up to leave, they realized they were too 'merry' and had to stay for the night.

"You can do that here," one chap remarked through a mouthful of pizza.

"You can simply please yourself!" said another chap to my left.

I could see Blaise's eyes following every slice of pizza they picked up.

"Would you like a pizza Blaise?" Colin asked.

"Oh yes please," she answered enthusiastically.

"What about you Ange?" Colin enquired.

"Yes please. Blaise will probably want a plain cheese and tomato and I'd like a cheese, tomato and mushroom," I answered, licking my lips.

Colin made his way inside the bar to place our order. About twenty minutes passed and realizing he'd been gone for quite a while, I wondered if he was having difficulty ordering. Still, the owner spoke very good English and so I discounted it as the reason or the delay. I wondered what the problem was and decided to go and investigate.

The interior of the bar was narrow and dark. Cigarette smoke curled its way around the slot machines. It was extremely busy, a mass of bodies propped up the bar and every table was occupied. I spotted Colin stood at the bar and made my way over to him.

"Busy isn't it?" shouted Colin over the noise of the nearby slot machine. "I've been trying to catch his eye for ages, but he's busy taking trays of food all over the place."

I waved my hand and tried to catch the attention of the girl behind the bar. The owner, observant as ever, saw us in our effort to catch someone's attention. He whistled loudly and pointed to us, signalling for the waitress to take our order. Finally she approached us with her order pad and pen at the ready. Colin placed our order in a fine Spanish accent. More Fanta lemon and cola was promptly placed on the bar and we carried them out to our table. Our freshly cooked pizzas arrived soon after, aromatic with fresh oregano and sage seasoning, with hot cheese bubbling away on the top. We tucked into the pizzas as if we hadn't eaten for a week and the hours passed in jovial conversation with our new found friends. Realizing the time they reluctantly emptied their glasses and made ready to leave. They needed to resume working on their renovation projects. Colin and I wished them all well for the future and waved goodbye. It was almost seven o'clock and we had been at the bar for four hours. We finished our pizza and pushed the empty plates towards the middle of the table. We emptied our glasses and looked for the waitress.

"La cuenta por favor," Colin asked, as the waitress approached to clear our table.

The waitress obliged and slid the bill ticket under the clip of a small silver tray. She placed it on our table with a casual 'vale,' (pronounced bali,) the Spanish equivalent of 'OK.' The cost of nine drinks and three pizzas was incredibly cheap at just under €22. Colin picked up the tray, placed €25 under the clip and ushered us from the table. The square had filled up with extended families, out for the evening. We walked down the side of the square, Colin leading the way, Blaise and I following behind. Colin stopped and turned to face us. His face lit up, and he grinned from ear to ear, his dimples clearly showing.

"Want an ice cream?" he asked.

"Oh yes please!" Blaise and I exclaimed with delight.

Colin herded us into the ice cream parlour and we stared at the tubs of colourful ice cream. It was a wonderful sight; there were cornets and tubs for one, two, three or four scoops. You could choose a single flavour or have a mixture. The possibilities were endless. We stood transfixed, our noses pressed against the plastic casing of the ice cream cabinet. After much 'oohing' and 'aahing,' we each chose a tub filled with three different mouth-watering flavours.

"Hmmm. This is divine," I exclaimed, savouring a spade full of chocolate ice cream.

"Mum! Taste this," Blaise commanded, moving her ice cream spade towards my mouth.

I took a taste of the green concoction.

"Hmm, chocolate mint, delicious Blaise."

"Taste this flavour," Colin commanded. "It's just like the real thing. It's Melon."

I slurped first from Colin's spade then from Blaise's and finally from my own. No wonder my middle age spread had spread everywhere else!

We made our way from the square and trekked across the faded, foot worn, zebra crossing, through the stone archway and across Villamarchante's dusty, pot-holed car park. We slurped melted ice cream enthusiastically from our colourful ice cream tubs, tired but happy, the perfect end to a perfect day.

Chapter 6
Mulling It Over

I awoke early. There was a bit of packing to be done before our return to the airport and I was restless, my mind constantly mulling over this and that. I stripped the sheets from the bed, folded them neatly and stacked them one on top of the other on the bed. I took the pillowcase off and did likewise. All the time my mind went over and over the properties we had seen. I crossed the room in a semi-daze and tripped head first over our partially packed suitcases. Cursing loudly, I made my way to the bathroom.

Standing in the shower, I felt the powerful spray of the hot water jets; the pressurized droplets making my skin tingle as they bounced off my body. My mind wandered as the angry jets of water beat against my face. I remembered a hasty purchase I had made some years ago. I had bought the most enormous, green, ugly, fabric suitcase from a stall on Ashton-under-Lyne's outdoor market. I had fallen for the salesman's patter.

"It's the last one I've got in stock love; it's been substantially reduced too."

It did have a good set of wheels on it and a very sturdy handle for pulling it along. It would easily transport sufficient clothing for up to four people. The other bonus was that it only needed one person to pull it along and having given due thought to the weight of four people's clothes, the only person strong enough to pull it without self-injury was my dearly beloved husband, Colin. Although Colin was more than strong enough to take charge of the enormous case, its sheer size meant that it really was the most bulky, inflexible piece of luggage I had ever bought. It didn't fit easily into any make of saloon car boot and the depth of the case meant that it was difficult to house in any reasonable sized hatchback. I think part of me hoped that one day it would get so badly treated by the baggage handlers that it would appear on the carousel looking battered, bruised and broken. Of course we would simply have to throw it away. However, the case had turned out to be as tough as old boots and was packed full of storage items in our loft in Kent. Would we ever use it again for travel purposes? Hmm... perhaps.

"What on earth had the ugly green giant suitcase got to do with buying a property in Spain?" I said to myself.

Colin's words had been playing over and over in my head all night, like a needle stuck on an old 45-rpm record.

"We won't make any decisions now Angela, we'll talk it over when we get home and make our final choice then," he'd said.

And he was right again of course; I was an emotional wreck and couldn't hold a single thought for more than a moment without it flying off is some direction or other.

I towelled myself dry and returned to the room to find Blaise and Colin awake. Colin was in the middle of stripping his bed and Blaise sat on her bed staring into space, in that sort of half awake, half-asleep state. Colin asked her to strip her bed but she continued to sit motionless, blinking like an owl. She reminded me of the pretty barn owl we had seen one evening on our way to Villamarchante. I would definitely have to bring my binoculars the next time we returned.

I looked over and saw Colin emptying the fridge.

"You're very quiet," he said.

"Yes, I didn't sleep well, I'm probably just tired," I replied.

It was the truth but a sense of panic rose within me.

"Why am I panicking?" I said aloud.

The second property was going over and over in my mind. I saw myself sweeping the patio, sitting on the bright blue and orange swing seat, picking the oranges from the tree and walking barefoot on the floor tiles. I imagined all the family sat under the shade of the Dutch awning, munching croissants and drinking freshly squeezed orange juice. I saw myself placing kitchen utensils in the drawers and pondering where I would place an artificial plant inside the house. In short, I had made up my mind. I wanted the second house. Everything about it suited our purpose. Having seen several properties, I simply knew it was the best of the lot. I wanted to go home and think it all through logically. Any snap decisions made now could result in heartache down the line. I needed to review everything carefully and take my time.

Once again, a sudden overwhelming fear crept over me. What if someone beat us to it? Why there might be aeroplanes full of potential house buyers heading straight to Valencia at this very moment and all of them would declare the second house to be their chosen villa and our chance to buy it would be gone. Colin could sense my unease, as could Blaise. They both looked furtively at me.

"You alright mum?" Blaise asked, concerned.

"Yes of course my treasure," I reassured her. "I'm just thinking about going home. I mustn't forget anything. We need to make sure we pack everything we came with," I said in the most casual tone I could muster.

I put on my 'going home clothes' and started taking everything Colin had emptied from the fridge to the patio table. I don't know if I fooled them, but at least I was out of the room. I dead headed the geraniums and looked towards the internal gate. I wondered where Moxy was. He usually appeared within minutes of hearing the plates chink on the patio. He appeared just as I reached the apartment door.

"Hello Moxy, who's a good boy then," I crooned.

Moxy wagged his tail happily. He was still wearing his red polka dot bandana.

"Mum, can we get a picture of the dogs before we go?" asked Blaise.

"I don't see why not Blaise," I replied. "It will be a good memento for us won't it?"

We sat down at the patio table, asked for a blessing on our food and tucked in. Breakfast didn't look at all appetizing. We had a bit of left over Brie, jam and juice. Maybe I had lost my appetite at the thought of going home, as I wasn't hungry. As it turned out, none of us were! Perhaps we all realized that the decisions we would soon make and the steps we would take over the next few days would have a significant effect upon our lives forever. We were one step nearer to realizing our dream.

I felt an inner glow spread throughout my being. I thought about how blessed Colin and I were. We had a lovely daughter, a wonderful son, no debts, money to buy a home and enough drive and ambition to succeed in building whatever future we wanted for ourselves. It hadn't always been so. Colin and I had endured hardship throughout most of our life together. Blaise was a blessing that I, for one, had not expected to enjoy. We had endured trials and tribulations enough to last a lifetime and yet we were close to realizing our dream. I smiled in the sunshine.

"You look happy now mum," Blaise said.

"I am Blaise," I chirped. "I'm very excited too. Your Dad and I are certain that this is where we want to buy a house. It's so lush here. Do you know they call this region the garden of Spain? Just imagine Blaise, we live in the garden of England and we'll buy a house in the garden of Spain. All Dad and I have to do is make a final decision and then that's it. Can you really believe it?" I asked, feeling very jolly.

"Are we going to buy number three house?" Blaise enquired.

I was dreading answering her and was relieved when Colin repeated exactly what Blaise had said to me. Had my darling daughter talked Colin round or had Colin talked my darling daughter round? Either way, it looked like the second house was the favourite. The second house had a name too. It was called 'Bona Gent.' The owner told us it meant 'Good People.' I liked the name; after all, we **were** good people.

"We'll have another look at the video recordings when we get home," Colin said between mouthfuls. "And we'll call into the estate agents before we leave for the airport. We can say goodbye and thank you to Alfredo and Sally and register our interest in the second property. It's got good rental potential and it will be easy to maintain. It could be rented out more or less immediately."

"That's a good idea Col," I said with a million butterflies churning in my stomach. "It's by far the best property for investment and rental potential, but you know, if you and Blaise want the third property, that's OK with me, even if it isn't practical. It's important that you are happy with what we decide to buy Col. It's no good going along with property two if you really want property three because you will always blame me and say I got my own way. And I know I nearly always get my own way, but this is too important to us for me to take that stance," I spluttered, the words tumbling out before I could stop or check myself.

An air of silence fell upon us. I lowered my eyes to my plate. I didn't want to buy the third house. In fact, the thought of it made me shudder. But I knew in my heart that if Colin and Blaise really wanted it, I would agree just to make them happy. After all, Colin was a very handy person. He could move swimming pools, move trees, fix plumbing, build walls, roof houses, paint and decorate. In short I knew he was more than capable of making our Spanish home a palace. But I could see every holiday we took there being a burden on him, knowing my own character and my 'want it done now' personality. I could see us being driven mad with the sheer size and scale of the work that would need doing. Our holidays wouldn't be holidays; they would be hard work all the time. Maybe we would even resent having bought it in the first place. I simply didn't know. I was preparing to ask Blaise to go inside so we could talk privately when Colin broke the silence.

"No, you've got a point. If we lived here permanently, I'd like a house like the third one. I loved it, but it needs major work doing on it. If we bought it we would lose rental potential. When we came here, we had a certain framework to work to. We had a list of what was desirable and what was essential. The plot needs to be a good size but the gardens need to be easily manageable. We want four good sized bedrooms and a pool. The second property is ideal as a rental property and that's really what we want here, an investment property, not a home. When we retire here we'll have a good home, modern and easy to manage. If we want to buy a different house once we move here to live, then that's different. The second property has a lot going for it. The pool is better than any we've seen and those railings and lockable gates mean it can be secured too. That makes it safe for families with young children. It's fully air-conditioned and temperature controlled. That's a bonus. Remember when we went to Turkey in 2000. They said it was an air conditioned apartment but only the main bedroom had an air conditioning unit in it."

"I remember that Dad," Blaise said loudly. "You and mum ended up sleeping on the sofas in the lounge and letting me and Ryan sleep in your bedroom, because it was too hot for us in the lounge."

I laughed at the memory. It had been awful accommodation, a top floor apartment and naturally, as the air got hotter and rose, it roasted us. Colin and I sacrificed our own comfort and swapped rooms with the children.

"The fact that the air conditioning has the dual function of warm air heating in winter is priceless Ange. It's also got modern appliances by Valencia standards. Not many self-catering accommodations have a dishwasher. The house has a lot of indoor living space too. They tend to have the space outdoors here, probably because they spend more time outdoors than in. But, if we want to rent it out over winter too, then it's got to have central heating. It's pretty much got everything we want," Colin concluded.

I feasted on every word. All my anxiety disintegrated and I was overjoyed. I grinned from ear to ear.

Happily for us, our packing was finished off with everyone in the best of moods. Our holiday snaps were taken with Moxy and Ben and our farewells said to Craig and Helen. We loaded our belongings into the little dusty Fiat Punto and set off, Villamarchante bound, to let Alfredo and Sally know our thoughts and mind set.

We arrived at Villamarchante at about half past eleven. Colin parked the car in the pot-holed car park and we made our way through the arch, across the faded zebra crossing and into the village square. The Salon de Jamon's tables and chairs were laid our ready, but most of the other café bars were only just setting up their patios ready for the day's guests. We pushed open the door to VSI to find Sally and Alfredo busily working away. They rose to greet us and we indulged in the usual greeting of three kisses on alternate cheeks. I had been counting how many kisses the locals gave each other. In Villamarchante it was three kisses. We sat down opposite Alfredo and Sally, eager to tell them our thoughts.

Colin and I briefly gave an account of how pleased we were with what we had seen on our visit. The countryside was very beautiful and the wealth of greenery the area seemed to enjoy was in stark contrast to what we had seen elsewhere in Spain. We recalled the seemingly endless groves of orange trees and the scattering of olive, almond and lemon groves, the picturesque columns of vines that stretched neatly across the open terrain near Cheste. Pretty white villas with terracotta roofs, draped deep purple bougainvilleas over their garden fences. The old tiny terraced houses, their verandas crammed with bright red geraniums in terracotta and blue pots and finally the mountains covered with Pine trees that scented the air. The late afternoon breeze carried the scent of Orange Blossom and Pine and scattered it over the valley. The landscape of the Turia Valley had surpassed everything we had ever hoped for.

We assured Alfredo and Sally that we were not wasting their time and that we were seriously interested in buying a property in the region. Colin went on to confirm our desire to be in a region that was predominantly Spanish. We didn't want to end up on an urbanization filled with English people. One or two English neighbours were acceptable but not an estate full of them.

When asked about the houses we had viewed, Colin's opinion was that they had got better and better as the day had progressed. Colin explained that after careful consideration, we wanted to register our interest in the second house. Sally said Alfredo had only just measured the house in order to advertise it. We explained our reasoning for discounting the other houses and each of us in turn voiced our delight at certain features of the second house, 'Bona Gent.'

Sally agreed that 'Bona Gent' had excellent rental potential, if that was what we were thinking of. It was modern, well maintained, of a good size and whilst a little over our budget, not excessively so. We told Sally we would make a decision within the next couple of days and that I would contact her by email. I felt like I was keeping a secret and was bursting to tell her that I, for one, definitely wanted to buy it. However, I held my tongue.

We assured Sally and Alfredo that we would not dally over it and thanked them sincerely for all the help and assistance they had given us. We promised to recommend VSI to anyone we knew who was looking to buy a house in Spain. After more hand shaking and kissing, we left the shop and strode with purpose to our car. We climbed in, settled down and made our way to Valencia airport.

The journey to the airport was made in eerie silence, each of us lost in our own thoughts. Blaise peered out of the window. Colin's eyes were transfixed on the road. I looked at the landscape, as if seeing the area again for the very first time. The traffic was light; the roads were good. Typically Spanish drivers tailgated each other, driving right up to each other's bumpers in an effort to force one another back into the slow lane. Motorways and main roads were free of police cameras. Driving in Spain was enjoyable and relatively easy, with most roads traffic jam free. Life in the Turia Valley was calm, people took the time to talk to each other and pass the time of day. 'People watching' was a well-loved pass time and small communities sat outside on the basket chairs of the pavement cafes, eating and drinking together. Young babies were passed around from waitress to waitress, so that parents could eat and drink in peace. Life in the Turia Valley was pleasing to the eye, pleasant on the ear and food for the soul. What more could we ask for?

We arrived at the airport late and Colin was worried that we wouldn't get seated together.

"Come on Ange, hurry it up a bit," Colin said, breaking the silence and ushering us through the airport departures door.

I handed the car keys in at the car hire desk and followed Colin through to the departures door. We hurried to the check in desk and much to our surprise found there were no queues. I handed over our tickets and passports. We were tagged, bagged and ready in about five minutes flat.

"This is the most fantastic airport," I said thoughtfully, adding "No hoards of holiday makers, no queuing. Isn't it great Colin?"

"It is," he agreed, herding Blaise and I towards the departure lounge, which was situated through a door to the right of the check-in desks.

"It may be a small airport, but it's perfectly functional," I commented dryly.

"I hope it stays like this," Colin remarked, before calling, "Hey come on, that's our flight they're announcing."

We stood up and made our way to the gate. It took all of a few minutes to go through to departures and within twenty minutes of arriving at the airport, we had boarded the aircraft. The plane taxied down the runway, turned and gathered speed, as the markers flew by our window. I smiled as the plane lifted into the air and reached into the net pocket of the seat in front of me. I took out my book, pushed my spectacles further up my nose and dived into the text. Two hours and one in-flight meal later, we descended into Gatwick Airport and watched as the pouring rain made zigzag patterns on the aircraft window.

Chapter 7
Judgment Day

It was cold and wet when we touched down. We followed the arrivals sign and the trail of people heading for baggage reclaim. Since the flight from Valencia was aboard a small aircraft, there were not many people waiting at the carousel and luggage appeared quickly on the conveyor belt. We cleared customs, phoned BCP and waited in the bus shelter for the BCP courtesy bus to arrive. We didn't have to wait long before we saw the familiar bus pull into the courtesy coach lane. We were first in the queue and boarded quickly. We took our seats near the front and watched the other passengers load their luggage and board. We watched as the rain pelted the windscreen of the coach. With a long hiss, the coach doors closed and the driver pulled out of the bus lane.

Our car keys were waiting for us in BCP's reception, together with a note of the location of our car. Fortunately, it was only a few rows away from the reception and in just over an hour from collecting our luggage; we arrived back at our house, Little Acorns.

We went through the motions of unpacking. Colin packed his tools ready for work and got everything Blaise needed for school ready for her. Funnily enough, none of us referred to our trip. It was amazing how easily we had fallen back into our normal everyday routine.

We rushed here and there, got this ready, got that ready, checked if we had done this or that. The evening passed quickly. Colin and I sat down exhausted, while Blaise climbed the stairs wearily to her bed.

Colin carefully put the video recorder down next to the TV and pulled the connection wires from their pouch in the video carrier. For a moment I thought he was going to wire it up but then he strode over to the sofa and sat down.

"When do you want to take a look at the video footage of the houses?" I asked, trying not to sound impatient.

"We'll take a look tomorrow, let's just relax for now," Colin replied.

"Good idea. Do you want a Horlicks or a hot chocolate?" I asked.

"Yes please, that would be nice," Colin answered.

I disappeared into the kitchen to make the drinks. I took Blaise a small glass of milk and put the kettle on to boil. I kissed her tenderly on her cheek; I knelt down at her bedside and said prayers for the evening. I gave her a tight tuck and returned back downstairs to finish off making the drinks.

The kettle had boiled and I stirred the water methodically into the Horlicks powder. I placed the tip of my battery operated froth maker into the liquid, pressed the button and whizzed the milky concoction into frenzy. The milky drinks frothed instantly, just like the ones we had drunk in the Salon de Jamon. I carried the two large piping hot mugs of Horlicks to the lounge, placed them on the coffee table and settled myself on the large sofa.

Colin lay full length on the small sofa. He looked weird with his calves and legs dangling over the side of the armrest. Ever since my slipped disc, I had been told not to sit upright if I could help it. It was fine to stand, potter about or lie flat. So, having already spent three hours in a sitting position, my back felt rather the worse for wear. There is no way you can hide back pain, it tells on your face and so I couldn't hide my discomfort from Colin. Consequently, he had told me to take the large sofa and I didn't hesitate to take up his offer. We watched TV for a while and an hour or so later, I packed my swimming bag for my physiotherapy session at the pool and made my way up the stairs. I hoped the exercises I had done in Spain had done me some good. The combination of warmth, light exercise and water therapy had eased my symptoms and the mental diversion had stopped me from thinking about the pain so much.

Colin followed me up the stairs, ready to catch me if my back suddenly pulled or went into spasm. We climbed into bed, re-living our first impression of the Turia Valley. We chatted about Valencia airport and how easy it was to get through customs. We remarked how it only took a couple of hours to get there and the pleasure of driving on traffic free roads. We recounted the names of nearby stores and services, discussing what we thought may be places of interest for visitors. We finally agreed that being in close proximity to Valencia City itself was a great benefit, ideal for short-break rentals and The Americas Cup. Happy with our choice of area and with our wonderful memories, we both settled down to sleep. Colin dropped off so quickly that he let out a loud snort and woke himself up again.

"Did I go off?" he asked sleepily and without waiting for me to answer added, "Sorry."

He turned over and let out another loud snore before I had time to answer him. I smiled and snuggled closer to him, placing my cold feet on his warm calves. I laughed softly to myself, thinking 'England and cold feet!'

We awoke early in order to get Blaise ready and off to school. Colin had been taking her to school ever since my disc slipped. It was impossible for me to drive. The doctor had advised me to refrain from driving until further notice, so Colin dutifully ferried Blaise to and from school and the childminder.

All day I felt elated. I was so excited, I was positively bursting with joy. I waited for Colin to return from work with Blaise in tow. I desperately wanted to see the video. I had picked up the leads several times but had thrown them down again in true techno phobic manner. I heard the key in the front door and quickly dished out the dinner. We sat down at the dining table, said prayers and ate our meal quickly, eager to finish and watch the video footage of our trip. Colin and Blaise took the dirty plates and stacked them in the dishwasher. I sat on the sofa waiting for them, my rolled tea towel placed in the small of my back as a lumber support.

"Come on Colin, hurry up!" I shouted towards the kitchen.

"Come on Blaise, we're going to watch the video recording of the houses," I announced.

Blaise didn't look particularly excited about it.

"Don't you want to watch it?" I questioned.

"Yeah, sure mum," she answered.

I could tell from the tone of her voice that she really didn't want to watch the video footage. It was a very half-hearted reply, more to please me than her.

"Just stay for a short while Blaise and then you can go, after all, it's important that you have some input," I encouraged.

"What for?" she asked sulkily and continued, "You and dad have already made your mind up, that's what we told Sally. Do I really need to watch it?"

"Well I suppose not, not if you don't want to," I replied, accepting her decision.

"You sure mum?" Blaise enquired.

"Yes, off you go my treasure," I replied, patting her arm reassuringly.

Colin and I sat glued to the TV as we watched the video footage of the last few days. We watched the old couple and their little white dog in the first house, both of us remarking how fantastic his tomatoes were and how lovely their vines looked. We agreed that the garden needed too much maintenance. The price was within budget at €146,900 but we discounted it.

The second house appeared on the screen. We both agreed that it had a good set of lockable double gates. They were made of ornamental wrought iron and lined with a privacy cover. Over the gates was a pretty terracotta tiled roof canopy with a lantern style courtesy light. The entrance looked very appealing. There was good access from the main road too. Directions to the villa would be easy to follow. There was a mature cypress hedge set in between a terracotta wall and a dark wood fence. It provided excellent screening for the garden, making it very private. Driving in through the iron gates, the front of the house was laid to patterned flagstones, making the patio and paving easy to keep clean; they would only need a sweep and perhaps a jet wash in springtime.

Everything inside the house was quite modern and of course it had the benefit of temperature controlled air conditioning in every room.

The windows were double-glazed and the house had been electrically re-wired. The villa floors were tiled throughout making it cool under foot and easy to clean.

There were four outside buildings consisting of two sheds, a pool house and a paellero, which doubled as a utility room. The villa was pretty much perfect. The price was €159,000 and at the top end of our budget but still affordable.

The third house appeared on screen. It was definitely quirky and very Spanish and looked every bit a traditional Spanish Villa. We watched the huge gardens appear on screen and I thought about all the major work it would need. My right leg started to tingle at the memory of the insect bites and I looked at the scars on my legs. We quickly discounted it and thankfully Colin didn't zoom in on the Laurel and Hardy statues.

The fourth house, I would have liked to have bought as a renovation project. If we could have extended the house, it would have been perfect, but not a house you could have rented out for quite some considerable time. The house needed grand design work and was quickly discounted.

The fifth house and its orange and lemon groves looked fantastic. This was the sort of house I would love to live in, if just for the view alone. But we definitely couldn't manage the work that an orange and lemon grove would demand. With my memory of donkey rides to market and a small heartache, it too, was discounted.

Colin hadn't bothered to video the sixth house. We agreed the most expensive house we viewed was the least appealing.

Colin sat on the floor, rewinding the video back and forth. We looked again at the second house then the third house. Eventually, some two hours later, we judged 'Bona Gent' to be the best investment property. We asked each other over and over again, were we sure about it? But there was no contest really. It was just perfect.

Colin and I needed to act fast. If someone else saw it and wanted to buy it, we would both be devastated. Well, perhaps not Colin, it takes a lot to phase him, but I certainly would have shed a bucketful of tears. I couldn't contain my joy, I wanted to let Sally know our decision and at some ridiculously late hour, I sent an email to her, offering the full asking price for the second property, 'Bona Gent.'

An email arrived from Sally the very next morning. The whole of the weekend was spent with email zooming back and forth down the wire. I couldn't sit at the PC long enough to be any real use and poor Colin was in and out of the computer room all of that weekend.

I kept rewinding the videotape and hugging myself. Yes, it was really happening to us, we were going to buy a house in Spain. Fortunately, Colin brought us back down to earth with a bump. It seemed that Spain had as much bureaucracy as England in that once you have agreed to buy a house, you must complete the purchase within forty-five days. Our lounge transformed into a scene from Dads Army!

"Don't panic, don't panic!" I repeated over and over again.

"Angela for goodness sake, calm down, you'll start hyperventilating and pass out!" shouted Colin from the study. "Take a deep breath, it will all be OK."

"Colin, what are we going to do?" I ranted, "What if someone buys it before us? Ask Sally what we should do now?" I panted.

Colin wrote to Sally without delay and we were advised of the procedure for the handing over of the deposit and then setting the completion date. We had to return to Spain post haste with the deposit. Sally told us that we must pay the deposit direct to the vendor and not to the solicitor. Once this has taken place, if the vendor pulled out on us, they must, by law, pay us twice the deposit back. If **we** pulled out for whatever reason, we would lose our deposit.

Colin told Sally we would organize our flights quickly and would contact her with the date of our return. I can honestly say that I have never booked flights and a hire car as quick in my life. Kneeling on a stool at the PC in our study, I booked our return flight and car for two-weeks hence. It was the earliest date that was convenient for Colin. We would fly out on the Sunday evening and return on the Tuesday morning. I couldn't wait to email Sally and let her know. I pressed the 'send' button and felt deliriously happy. Sally sent an email back within minutes. The meeting with the owners was set up for the Monday and there would be an opportunity for us to take another look at the property if we wanted to. Colin would be able to take more video footage of the villa and grounds. Sally confirmed all was in order on VSI's part and so the meeting with the vendor was arranged for noon on the Monday at

VSI's offices. Sally was very reassuring and told us not to worry about anything. The villa would not be marketed to anyone else.

"Whoopee!" I cried, ecstatically.

Meanwhile Colin stood in the doorway behind me smiling. I hobbled over to him and gave him a hug. Well a kind of hug. Hugging is difficult when you think that your back is going to unhinge at any given moment.

"What are we going to do with Blaise?" Colin asked bluntly.

"Well, we will simply have to find her somewhere to stay, perhaps with friends. I know. I will ask Jackie if she will have her for the weekend. That way she will have Sammie for company too. And Blaise thinks of Jackie as her second mum. Since we arrived here, she has taken really good care of Blaise and helped us wherever possible. Yes, I'll ask Jackie, if she can help us. I know she will," I went on.

"Do you think she will mind?" Colin asked.

"Who will mind, Blaise or Jackie?" I queried.

"Jackie of course," Colin replied.

"I don't think so, if she does, she'll tell me. And if she's got something else on, I will ask Sue Mansfield. Blaise likes going to Sue's too. Sue always gives her a big stuffed cat to play with and Blaise loves Sue's cat, what's its name?" I muttered.

"OK. Well I will leave that to you then," Colin said, switching on the TV and settling down.

"Widget!" I said loudly.

"What?" Colin asked, looking over at me somewhat confused.

"Widget!" I repeated and added, "That's the name of Sue Mansfield's big black cat."

"Wonderful," Colin laughed.

The weekend passed in a blur. I met Jackie and asked if Blaise could stay with her. Jackie said it wouldn't be a problem and the entire week passed at breakneck speed. I had to organize a lift to get to the bank and a lift to the post office to order euros. The one thing I found strange living in Kent is that you have to order currency. I suppose you can't live the village life and expect town benefits. I also had to organize transport to the physiotherapist, to the Doctors and to see the hospital consultant. I had come to understand why people who were not very mobile felt like they were a burden. I too, felt a nuisance begging lifts from everyone.

I arrived at the hospital and was shown in to see my consultant. This was my last appointment with him. After a few minutes update on my condition, I was told that I needed to exercise like my life depended upon it. The consultant said that swimming and exercise in water would be the best form of exercise for me and between us we worked out a regime that we thought would help.

Although the disc had worked its way back into position, my right sacroiliac joint was excruciatingly painful. The osteopath said it was the result of a twisted pelvis, probably caused by sitting with my legs tucked underneath me in my youth and all the time spent driving in the car in an unnatural position. At all costs, I was, whenever sitting, to keep my pelvis square. Of course, I wasn't able to swim on my front yet, but I could float on my back and continue with the exercises I had previously been given by the physiotherapist. I was also told to try jogging in water, about chest deep, so that my body weight was supported. No more than five minutes to start and I was to try over the coming weeks to double it to ten minutes.

Each day, I made the trip to my local leisure centre pool to exercise. Sometimes, my friend Becky would join me. I must have looked very strange holding on to the side trying to jog. But I kept at it. After the first four days, my back started to give me a lot of pain again. I was worried incase the disc had slipped out and so I telephoned my consultant. If I couldn't sign the preliminary paperwork for the Spanish house, we would inevitably lose the sale. But after another examination, he advised me to double my efforts on exercise. He said that I was going to feel a whole lot worse before I felt a whole lot better and that I needed to continue and build up the exercise a little more. He seemed pleased with my progress in four days but said it was a long job and that I needed to keep at it. The disc was just fine. It was most likely the sacroiliac joint trying to straighten that was causing the pain. So feeling quite relieved, I was ferried home to collect my swim bag and be dropped off at the swimming pool once more.

The water therapy continued and in the two-weeks prior to returning to Spain, I pushed myself as hard as I could, just as the consultant had suggested. I could swim two lengths of backstroke, float for another two lengths and jog for ten minutes. I still couldn't do breast stroke, as my position in the water really hurt my back and made my neck stiff. In addition, I wasn't easily able to lower my feet to stand from swimming on my front, whereas it was a lot easier to stand after swimming on my back. Still, I felt I had made real progress. Fortunately, the healthy exercise regime and my determination to get better proved to be a good distraction during those two-weeks, that and the trip to Sloane Square in London with Colin.

"Why do we have to get the Spanish Consulate to certify the passports?" Colin questioned, galloping down the stairs.

"I don't know, but Sally said we have to bring copies that are certified by them and only them. Something to do with the bank, probably a bank requirement," I answered, while picking my way around the house making sure we had everything we needed.

Flying by the seat of our pants as usual, Colin drove Blaise and I like a Formula 3 rally driver all the way to Borough Green railway station. I had my tube map and a London map that clearly showed where the Spanish Consulate was located. We were taking the train to London Victoria. The plan was to drop Blaise off at Borough Green School, catch the train at Borough Green station, hop on the tube once in London and we would be at the Spanish Consulate by about ten o'clock. That would leave us some time for a little sight seeing in London before returning home to collect Blaise from school just after three o'clock.

Colin parked near the entrance to the ticket office, so I could get out and buy the tickets, while he parked the car. The station was very busy. It seemed that everybody was getting the train to London. Finally I was in front of the ticket clerk. I called him 'Mr. Charisma,' as he had often sold me my ticket on visits to my employer's London office. He was always cheerful and jolly. The station attendant worked out the cheapest fare for Colin and I just as Colin arrived.

"This train will be packed full and we won't get a seat," he said crossly.

"Don't worry Colin, we can sit in the first class carriage," I stated, and added nonchalantly, "I always do if it the train is full. If you pay for a ticket, you are entitled to a seat. Anyway, wait till you see the first class carriages. True, you have more seat and legroom, but they are filled with graffiti and left over breakfast. School children dump loads of food in the carriage before they get off. You'll see what I mean when we get on."

Just as Colin predicted, the train was full and just as I predicted, the first class carriages were awful. They were filled with rubbish and crumbs. I couldn't imagine what these children ate for breakfast in the morning, but the evidence seemed to suggest crisps, MacDonald's and Mars bars. We settled down and watched the fields of Roe deer zoom by us.

We arrived in London and caught the tube to Sloane Square. Map in hand, we were soon walking up the stairs of the Spanish Consulate. Once inside, we reported to reception and were told to go to the first floor and wait. Colin climbed the stairs with me following behind. There was a young girl waiting on the landing. There didn't appear to be anywhere to sit, which was just as well, having sat for almost an hour on the train. I was more than happy to stand so I could stretch my back out. Colin and I waited for about twenty minutes. Finally a door opened and a dark haired woman appeared. The woman disappeared through a nearby door, reappeared some two minutes later and re-entered the first room. This was repeated a couple of times. At last, a folder was handed to the young girl on the landing who smiled, thanked the woman and made her way down the stairs. A young man of about twenty, quickly replaced the young girl. He joined us in the queue on the landing. Rather naively I thought we would be seen more or less immediately, but then we were in the Spanish Consulate and the Spanish cannot be rushed. Aware that the Consulate closed at one o'clock, we had arrived at twenty past ten, which we considered was in plenty of time. The minutes ticked by. I looked at my wristwatch, impatient for attention. It was ten passed eleven. I wondered what was keeping them. Colin looked agitated. He hated hanging around waiting, especially when no one could explain the delay.

"This is ridiculous," he said, pacing back and forth along the small landing.

The young man looked at us troubled. Perhaps he was worried in case Colin kicked up a fuss and delayed matters further.

"What on earth is she doing in there?" Colin asked angrily.

"I don't know Colin, but I don't think it will be long now," I answered, trying to sound positive.

"Perhaps she has gone for her lunch and will be back just in time to close the office at one o'clock," Colin said indignantly.

"Colin, don't be daft, she can see we are waiting, she wouldn't have gone for lunch, would she?" I asked, a worried look crossing my brow.

The door opened.

"Señor, Señorita, come this way please," said the dark haired woman, smiling.

I flashed a look of 'I told you so' to Colin before following her into the office. We told her that we needed copies of our passports certifying for our bank in Spain. The dark haired lady took our passports from us, opened them at the photograph page and looked at us both. Gazing from Colin to me and back to Colin, she promptly took the passports to the photocopier, placed them down on the glass plate, zapped the green button and left the room taking the copies and the originals with her. Some two or three minutes later, she reappeared with the originals and the copies, duly stamped and signed. We paid the fee and I placed the passports and the certified copies safely in a folder I had brought with me. I placed the folder in my bag and we shook hands.

"Thank you, goodbye," Colin and I said in unison.

"Good luck!" she replied with a warm smile and opened the door for us to leave.

All the anxiety of the long wait had gone and Colin and I walked arm in arm down the Consulate steps, as jolly as could be and mightily relieved that we had our essential documents for the Spanish bank.

"Let's celebrate by having a mini shopping spree on Sloane Street," I suggested.

Colin happily agreed and we set off arm in arm down the street.

There were so many wonderful shops to look in and Colin and I had never shopped in London before. One shop particularly attracted our attention. It sold men's clothing and both Colin and I really liked the window display. The shop was called 'Fat Face.' Once inside, there was so much to choose from. There were a huge variety of colours, styles and textures and it was hard to find things we didn't like. Colin chose two T-shirts and two pairs of shorts. They were very trendy looking and Colin said they felt really comfortable. The shop assistants were polite and helpful and we nominated 'Fat Face' as our favourite men's clothing shop. With shopping bags in hand, we detoured into 'The Pier' and I had a great time looking around at all the fabulous things. There were colourful beaded lamps, mosaic tables and brightly coloured linen. I bought several items of kitchenware to take to Spain. We continued cheerfully arm in arm down Sloane Street, Colin loaded up with shopping bags.

"Let's have lunch," Colin suggested merrily.

"OK. That would be really nice Colin," I answered, happy for the one to one time with Colin.

We chose a small bistro style café and sat people watching until the waiter arrived. Colin ordered a light lunch for us, salad, pasta and cold drinks. The food was simple but delicious. After finishing up the inclusive ice cream dessert, we strolled down the street, browsing the shops on the way to the tube station for our journey back to Victoria. Colin and I agreed that the shops in Sloane Street were marvellous and promised ourselves a return trip at least once before the end of the year.

Colin and I took seats in first class back to Borough Green, happy and looking forward to returning to Spain to buy 'Bona Gent.' After all, the Spanish Consulate had stamped our copy passports now. Everything would be just fine. We were busily admiring our shopping when the guard appeared to inspect our tickets. I handed the tickets over with a smile. The guard scowled.

"These tickets aren't for first class," he mumbled in a monotone voice.

"But the train is full and I have a back injury. The guard at Victoria told me that I could always sit in first class if I couldn't get seated in ordinary class," I added.

"But this train's not full. There's room in economy," he replied and added, "You really shouldn't be sat here."

"But my back is injured," I pleaded, not wanting to be squashed into some uncomfortable seat in second class.

"I can only tell you that you really should move, you could be fined," the guard continued.

"But just look at this carriage, its dirty and full of graffiti," I went on, determined to put the point across. "You can't really say this is first class can you?"

"It's your choice," he finished grumpily, moving on to inspect tickets in the next carriage.

"Come on Ange, let's move," said Colin grabbing my shopping bags.

Feeling sorry for myself, I sulked and followed Colin into the second-class section. Although not full, it was still crowded and we were not able to sit together. Still, at least we had a seat. Colin held our shopping bags and we spent the rest of the journey to Borough Green huddled next to strangers.

"Where's his compassion?" I said to Colin, as we descended the train.

"He's a jobs worth," Colin replied.

"What's that?" I enquired.

"You know, it's more than his job's worth to be kind or considerate to anyone. He won't bend the rules. The saying originated from Esther Rantzen's show 'That's Life.' They used to give these 'Jobs Worth' awards to those people who wouldn't budge from the rules, even if it meant being horrid to someone. They would say it was more than their job was worth to bend a little, hence the name of the award 'Job's Worth.'"

"I agree with you," I said angrily. "Maybe we should nominate him for that award."

"Well, that programme isn't on TV anymore, but there are lots of people like him around Ange," Colin concluded.

I had to agree with him, however, I determined that it would not spoil our good mood and so with a big smile, I slipped my hand into Colin's and we strode to the school to collect Blaise.

Shortly before our planned return to Spain, I realized that I had everything booked except our accommodation. I was so cross with myself. How could I have forgotten something as essential as somewhere to stay? I tried Helen and Craig, but they were fully booked. Fortunately, Sally at VSI knew someone who would probably let us rent a property for a short-term stay. She gave us their telephone number and I made contact. The couple were taking care of the property for relatives who still lived in England. The owners were gradually renovating the property. The whole of the ground floor was finished and it had three good-sized bedrooms, a kitchen and a lounge. We agreed a fair rental price and I breathed a sigh of relief. We were to telephone their mobile on our arrival in Valencia and they would meet us in Villamarchante's square near VSI's office.

The day before we were due to leave, I checked to make sure I was prepared with everything I would need packed ready. I helped Blaise pack her weekend bag. Blaise didn't want us to leave her but she understood it was necessary and that it would only be for a few days. She promised to be good and helpful to Jackie. We reminded her to be her usual well-mannered self. Colin and I packed a handful of things and then the enormity of what we were doing hit me full force. Were we really doing the right thing? Had we made enough enquiries? Had we visited enough places? Was it the best place to put our money? Once the deposit was paid, we couldn't change our mind without losing the deposit. Did we want to change our mind? Did we check everything, like outstanding debts or bills on the property? What if the vendors had changed their mind? I drove Colin mad with a hundred and one questions, repeated over and over again. Poor Colin, he was re-assuring and confident and told me that everything would be fine.

I tried to think of all the positive aspects of buying the villa. It was situated in an area of outstanding natural beauty. No housing estates would be built nearby. The urbanization was situated between two country parks. We had fresh mountain air, scented with Jasmine, Orange Blossom and Pine. We would have our own orange and fig tree, our own swimming pool and enough rooms to invite our family and friends over. We would taste the real Spain, not some English urbanization that just happened to be in Spain. We would learn the language and have Spanish friends. And when we were old, we would have our bolthole, somewhere we could spend our days peacefully out of the rat race. We could climb the mountains or walk in the country parks. We could spend evenings outside sipping iced chocolate from pavement cafes. We could watch the local youths run with the bulls and we could take part in the worlds biggest tomato fight, La Tomatina, in the village of Buñol, a short drive away. We could enjoy the culture of a city break in Valencia and we could go to the beach any time we wanted. We would have our own piece of paradise and heaven on earth. What on earth was I so worried about? Excited, nervous and feeling more blessed than ever, I climbed the stairs to bed. Tomorrow was just a short sleep away and then we would be on our way to fulfil our dream.

Chapter 8
Making the Deal and Dealing the Dosh!

"Oh Colin, it's really grim outside!" I shouted over my shoulder. "It's pouring down with rain and it's that fine drizzle that soaks you through," I lamented.

It reminded me of the weather back in Manchester. A grey sky blanketed the daylight. I often used to say to Blaise that somewhere behind that grey veil there was a powder blue sky. I think I used to say it more for my own benefit that hers. Colin told me several times that he thought I suffered from seasonal affective disorder or SAD for short. I do seem to recall that the winters were very long and the summers, well, non-existent some years. The North seemed to have a long spring and an even longer winter. You couldn't really tell that there were four seasons in the year. The worst months were February and March but one year it even snowed in April. I smiled to myself. I remembered our first winter in Kent. It seemed to me to be a very long autumn. I had telephoned the lady who used to rent the house before us and who had lived in Kent for most of her life.

"Has winter arrived yet?" I asked.

"Well, this is it really, it doesn't normally get any colder than it is now," she'd replied.

I remembered laughing when I relayed the story to Colin. Daffodils and other spring flowers bloomed in February in Kent and in October there were some very warm days. Colin and I went to view a house in the village of West Malling one late October. We ended up swapping our long sleeved tops for T-shirts before we even got out of the front door. 2003 had been our first year in Kent and it had been an exceptionally warm year, the hottest summer temperature ever, being recorded in Gravesend.

"Come on Colin, wakey wakey, rise and shine!" I sang, happy to be up and about and glad that we would shortly be on our way to bright, warm sunshine. We had arranged to drop Blaise off at Jackie's on our way to Gatwick Airport. I didn't want to be late; I was eager to be off and all my doubts of the previous evening had disappeared.

"Blaise!" I shouted from the landing. "Wakey wakey, up and at 'em!"

Blaise appeared with fuzzy hair and weary limbs.

"Morning mummy," she muffled through a giant yawn.

We dressed, grabbed our bags and sat down to eat breakfast. It seemed strange not to be rushing around, as Sunday was usually spent getting ready for church. I cooked breakfast at breakneck speed, cooking extra bacon so that Colin and I could take sandwiches with us to the airport. Colin asked for our food to be blessed, that things would go well in Spain; Blaise would enjoy her weekend at Jackie's and for us all to travel in safety. I was so excited; I couldn't sit still for two minutes. I ate my breakfast with gusto and determined not to be late for the airport. I whipped the plates from under Colin and Blaise's noses the minute their cutlery hit the plate. I piled the dirty pots ready for Colin to load into the dishwasher, made sure instructions for feeding our old cat were easy to find and legible, made sure that everything was ready to be loaded into the car, checked our currency, passports, flight tickets and car hire confirmation and herded Colin and Blaise towards the car. I tucked my rolled towel under my arm ready to place in the small of my back and locked the front door.

Colin drove through the quiet country lanes to Jackie's house. We saw Blaise safely into Jackie's, said our goodbyes and hopped back into the car to continue our journey. Jackie and Dave wished us all the best and told us not to worry about Blaise.

"See you all Tuesday then," I shouted through my car window, as Colin pulled out of their drive.

"See you soon Mum, see you Dad, have a good time," Blaise shouted back to us.

"Bye!" shouted Dave, Jackie, Sammie and Jamie in unison, waving frantically at us as we disappeared around the bend in the lane.

The rain continued to drizzle down without any sign of let up, as we made our way to the motorway.

"At least the M25 won't be busy at this time," I said, as we joined the M26 motorway Gatwick bound.

"We're going to be at Gatwick very early Ange," Colin stated calmly. "Do you fancy pulling off at the services for a drink?"

"That would be lovely thanks," I replied.

Colin pulled into Clacket Lane services and the heavens opened, sending rain the size of garden peas bouncing off the floor. Colin tried to park as near to the services entrance as he could, but we still had to run to the entrance through the pouring rain. I took the plastic carrier bag that doubled as a rubbish bag from the car, ran to the nearest bin, emptied the contents out and put the carrier bag over my head. I walked as quickly as I could towards the services entrance.

"Now I know why those old plastic granny bonnets are so popular," I said exasperated, shaking the rain drops from the carrier bag. "They are very practical."

Colin ordered hot chocolate at Costa Coffee and treated us to a small cake. Having just had a big breakfast, I didn't really feel hungry, so I nibbled on the cake and wrapped it in my serviette for later. It was so good to sit down with Colin without having to worry about where Blaise was. Although Blaise usually headed to the toilet for a good old sing song, she had occasionally been drawn to the flickering bright lights of the games area. This always worried me because so many men, young and old, seemed to congregate there. But today, we were 'foot loose' and 'child free' and the sheer freedom from responsibility was wonderful.

It seemed strange to be going away without Blaise. We had only ever left her once before, a couple of years previous, when Colin and I had a weekend break in Monmouthshire for Colin's birthday. Blaise had been eight years old and she'd stayed with my sister Norma. Blaise had never been left behind before and she really didn't understand why we had gone away without her. She wrote a letter in her sadness. My sister Norma found the letter some days after we had returned. The letter had been stuffed inside the pillowcase. Norma had read it out to me. It had made her tearful and I cried too, once she had read it to me. I remember I gave Blaise lots of attention and fuss when we got home, just to reassure her that we still loved her and that we wouldn't be making a habit of leaving her behind. Now, some two years older, Blaise fully understood that it was necessary for Colin and me to return to Spain to buy the Spanish house. Colin had missed Blaise terribly on the Monmouthshire break and I knew that this trip would be no exception.

"Come on Ange, we had better make tracks," said Colin, handing me the Glamour and Hello magazines he had bought.

"Thanks Col, these are two of my favourites," I responded, as we dashed back to the car in the heavy rain.

We parked the car at BCP yet again, took the courtesy coach and arrived at Gatwick an hour before departure. It was perfect timing. The flight was on time and Colin and I were seated together. The aircraft lifted off and once more, we were on our way to Valencia.

I stuck my nose in the 'Hello' magazine while Colin listened to music on his MP3. Fortunately, Colin knew better than to pester me during the flight. I needed peace, tranquillity and two hours worth of my favourite reading material to ensure I arrived in a good humour. A couple of hours later, we touched down after a very pleasant and uneventful flight.

We arrived at Valencia Airport to gloriously warm sunshine. We made our way through the small airport and in no more than ten minutes after touch down we had collected our luggage and made our way to the car hire desk. Marvellous! The smell of strong coffee wafted towards me from the small café close by. Hmmm... it smelt lovely! The car hire company I had booked with was new and I hadn't heard of them before my Internet search. They were not a name I recognized and I hoped that they were a reputable firm. The firm must have had some degree of standing to be based in the airport building. I crossed my fingers that it would be OK. Actually, the truth is that I didn't really have a choice because all the other car hire firms were already fully booked. The lady on the desk looked very pleasant though and she smiled at us.

"Good day, can I help you?" she enquired.

"Yes thank you," I answered, handing my printed email confirmation to her.

"Have you used us before?" she enquired.

"No," Colin and I both replied.

She busied herself, tapping information into her computer. She reached over to a nearby drawer and took out a bunch of keys.

"OK, here are your keys, your car is in bay number 36," she said with a smile, indicating parking bay 36 with a cross on the airport map. She continued, "You must go out of the doors, turn right, cross the road and then take the second right parking lane and you will find your car."

We thanked her and quickly made our way out of the airport building. We followed her verbal instructions and found our allocated car. It was a silver estate. Colin and I stared in disbelief. There were only two of us and we were only staying for two nights. We didn't even have two bags.

"But I only paid for a Corsa or similar," I stated, slightly bewildered at our good fortune.

"Perhaps they have upgraded us so that we use them again next time," Colin explained. "They do that to hook you in, so you book with them again."

We seated ourselves in the huge car and set off to find David and Ann in Villamarchante.

"You've got their telephone number haven't you?" Colin questioned nervously.

"Yes darling, we've got to ring them when we are nearly there because the villa is only five or ten minutes away from Villamarchante square," I replied confidently.

Colin and I set off up the ramp from the airport, heading for the A7 to Alicante and Barcelona. We picked up the CV35 to Ademuz and arrived in Villamarchante twenty-five minutes later. I rang David and announced our arrival in the square. He said he'd be with us in ten minutes. Colin parked the car in the familiar car park and we strode over the faded zebra crossing to the square. We sat down outside the Salon de Jamon and met the same young waitress as we had two-weeks before. Colin ordered our drinks in what was a very good Spanish accent and much to our surprise; the friendly waitress answered us in very good

English. She told us that she was trying to learn a little English because there were now quite a few English living in the area and they came to eat and drink at the café. Her accent was excellent and we complimented her on it. She told us that she studied English at school but that she had never got the chance to speak in English before. She gracefully accepted our compliment and disappeared to get our drinks.

It was a very hot day and there were many people sat in the square with their families. Sunday is still very much a religious and holy day in Spain and the Spanish people seem to be very good at keeping the Sabbath day holy. Most people were happy for the chance to relax and spend time with their families. Extended families joined each other in the day of rest, rejoicing in each other's company, catching up on news and strolling around the town. Little children played together within their family groups. Babies were cooed over and handed round to relatives for cuddles. Grandmothers and grandfathers, their grandchildren clutching their hands, were pulled around the square. Dishes of olives, pistachio nuts, slices of fresh bread, squid and other assorted seafood dishes were laid out on the tables. Garlic, olive oil and tomato were mixed together to make a delicious dip, much favoured by the Spanish.

Colin and I sat amazed at everything that was going on in the square on this hot and sunny Sunday afternoon. Older generations sat in clusters, having dragged their tables together to form a long trestle. Newly weds and new parents talked to each excitedly over the tapas laid out on the tables, swapping babies and wedding pictures back and forth. Neighbours, friends and relatives greeted each other in a never-ending stream of hugs and kisses. They were genuinely pleased to see each other, their love for each other plain to see. Young or old, all were welcomed. We were so caught up in the goings on in the square that we didn't see a brown faced, white haired man come bounding toward us, his hand outstretched.

"Colin and Angela?" he enquired.

"Yeah that's us," Colin answered. "You must be David," Colin added, with a faint note of uncertainty in his voice.

"That's me," David replied, with a huge grin and an extended hand. We shook hands in turn.

"Where are you parked?" David asked.

"We've parked over there in the car park," Colin said indicating with a nod of his head to the car park through the arch.

"That's good, me too," said David. "You can follow me to the villa, it's not far away," he said cheerfully. "I am in the middle of a BBQ, so I will show you around and then depart and leave you to it if you don't mind," he said politely.

We thanked him for coming out to meet us and followed him to the car park and through the back road out of Villamarchante towards the villa.

David was right. The villa was only a five-minute drive from Villamarchante square, tucked away on a small urbanization just past the local cemetery and a small industrial estate. David unlocked the double gates and we drove through on to the concrete driveway. David indicated that we should park under the carport, which was heavily draped in vines that dangled large green grapes provocatively through the metal grids. Although there was only one vine root, it had wound and weaved its way across the entire metal frame and had fruited profusely, providing excellent shade for the car. David told us to help ourselves to as many of the grapes as we wanted. He told us that his wife's sister owned the villa and that they were renovating it with a view to moving over to Spain to live permanently.

The villa was really quite lovely. The plot was quite large with a good garden and patio area and a very inviting filtered plunge pool. You could walk around the entire circumference of the villa. It had plenty of parking space and sunbathing areas. David nodded to us to follow him as we made our way inside the house.

The lounge was very tastefully decorated with sofas in bright gold chenille with matching drapes. A very ornately carved dining table with matching chairs and a matching sideboard stood to the left. The wood was highly polished and you could see the reflection of your face in the tabletop. To the right was an open brick fireplace with a huge artificial plant in the hearth. Over on the far left corner of the room was a heavy metal door that led out to a shaded terrazzo tiled patio. The view from the patio was wonderful and overlooked mountains and Pine forests. The scenery was simply stunning.

The kitchen and bathroom were modern and well fitted. The bathroom's pale dark green marbled tiles looked like they had just been laid. They looked brand new. There were three spacious bedrooms, but furniture was very sparse. The main item was the bed and a freestanding corner fan but as we were only going to be there for a couple of days, we didn't really need wardrobe units and drawers. We were quite happy to dress from our overnight bags.

The view from the outside patio was magnificent. There were two white plastic sun loungers and a white plastic table and chairs set.

"The villa is lovely. I am sure we will be very comfortable here," I said, handing David €50 for the breakages deposit.

We shook hands, agreed a time to check out and then were left to enjoy the peace and tranquillity. It gave us the chance to reflect upon events, a time to enjoy the wonderful scenery and dream a little. I marvelled that by this time the following day, we would be taking our first steps to become owners of a place in Spain.

Colin and I pulled our bathing suits out of the overnight bag, changed quickly and headed to the pool. I carefully descended the ladders into the water and Colin dived in at the far end of the pool The water was cool and refreshing, in stark contract to the hot afternoon air. Colin and I were both sticky with the heat of the day. It was wonderful to slide into the turquoise coloured pool and forget about everything. It was peaceful, wonderfully tranquil and a perfect spot for chilling out. I looked over and watched Colin swim length after length, up and down the pool. I simply floated on my back with the sun glaring down on me. There was no shallow end in the swimming pool. The depth was a level 4'6" and so I had a choice of floating on my back or swimming. Unsure of how my back would behave if I tried to do breaststroke, I floated on my back for a while, blinking at the sun. Once Colin had eventually swum the energy out of his system, I fully intended to try and swim a few lengths myself. I lay motionless in the pool. Colin splashed up and down the pool and eventually stopped at the poolside, wiped the water out of his eyes, slicked back his hair with his hands and got out.

"I'll go and fetch us a cold drink," he shouted, disappearing through the metal door.

I decided to try and swim backstroke, very slowly. My arms still had an incredible amount of strength in them and backstroke had been my racing stroke at school swimming galas. Having done about ten lengths of the small pool and feeling pleased with myself, I clutched the metal rung of the pool ladder and slowly climbed out. I joined Colin on the patio sun loungers to dry off. Although it was half past seven in the evening, the air temperature was still very hot. We lazed on the patio, listening to the 'Sounds of the 80s' CD. We laughed and sang along, sipped cold fizzy orange, ate bacon sandwiches, and watched the sun set on the horizon. We were remarkably calm considering tomorrow was going to be a big day for us. Making my way down the corridor to the bedroom, I climbed under the crisp cotton sheets of the double bed, called goodnight to Colin and fell fast asleep.

Colin awoke before me and was up, showered and dressed before I opened my eyes. I don't recall what we ate that morning, what clothes we wore, whether we took a swim or if I watered the garden. The plan was to meet Sally, Alfredo and the vendors at VSI's offices at noon. The vendors, Don Ramos and Dona Martinez, would be there to take delivery of the deposit. VSI had already told us that they had a key to the villa, so we could visit the property again to take more video footage if we wanted to. The process would be that Colin and I would meet with the vendors, Alfredo would go through everything step by step and Sally would translate for us. Sally had already assured us that everything would be clearly explained and that VSI would ensure that the property was debt free. An initial contract had been drawn up. The vendors would sign it and we would sign it. We would give proof of our identity by providing certified copies of our passports from the Spanish Consulate in London, hand over the €4700 deposit and agree our completion date. It all seemed very simple and straightforward. Colin and I had decided that since we wanted to be in the Spanish 'system,' we would take a small mortgage on the house. Alfredo arranged this for us with a reputable bank, the CAM bank, at their main branch in Valencia. Similar documentation was also needed for the CAM bank so we had various other documents with us. These comprised of proof of employment, wage slips, proof of address and all the usual things that a lender in England would require. Alfredo would then arrange to open our bank account and apply for the mortgage on our behalf. To be honest, I was expecting an interview with a bank official, or Mayor, but everyone had told us it would all turn out to be a very simple and easy process. Once more with hope in our hearts that all would go well, we set off for Villamarchante.

We arrived in plenty of time, parked the car in our usual spot, exited the car park though the stone arch and crossed the faded zebra crossing into the square. We walked the few paces to VSI's office and were warmly welcomed by Alfredo and Sally. We sat around the large table to the side of the reception area and engaged in the usual round of 'how are you' and 'what a beautiful day' type chitchat. Sally offered us a cold drink, which we gratefully accepted. We were excited and watched for Don Ramos and Dona Martinez to arrive, our eyes fixed on the doorway. We had just finished with pleasantries when the door opened and Don Ramos and Dona Martinez entered. They were quite an old couple, probably aged somewhere in their mid to late 60s. Alfredo rose to greet them and ushered them to the table. They sat down opposite us and shook our hands. Alfredo sat at the head of the table and Sally sat at the opposite end, facing Alfredo. Once the formal introductions were over, we made polite conversation to break the ice and even though we couldn't speak fluent Spanish and the vendors couldn't speak a word of English, we got along just fine.

Don Ramos showed us a photograph of him and Dona Martinez when they were in their forties. Their children and their grandchildren surrounded them in what looked like the lounge at 'Bona Gent.' Picking out bits of Spanish I understood here and there, Don Ramos told us he was 79 years old. Colin and I were astounded at the news. He was selling the property because he found it difficult to drive now he was old. He and Dona Martinez lived in the centre of Valencia and 'Bona Gent' was their holiday home. They had brought their children to 'Bona Gent' nearly every weekend and they had stayed there for the whole of the main summer holidays. When their children had grown up and got married, they had stayed at 'Bona Gent' with their grandchildren too. Don Ramos explained that his son and granddaughter were currently staying at 'Bona Gent.' Don Ramos was now totally dependent upon his children driving him to the villa and he felt he was becoming a burden and a nuisance. He said he simply couldn't keep up with the maintenance work required to keep the house in order. He had put every modern convenience in the house, double-glazing, new electrics and a filtered swimming pool, which was very rare in the Valencia region.

Don Ramos said he had shared many happy moments in the house. It was as if all his happy memories were of times spent at 'Bona Gent' and I felt a tear prick my eye. Their lives had been summed up in one short conversation with total strangers from England. I looked at the photograph that Don Ramos had placed on the table. It was such a happy family scene, with everyone laughing. Don Ramos had been a handsome man and Dona Martinez a good-looking woman. I handed the photograph back to Don Ramos.

"No, no," he said, pushing the photograph back towards me.

"He wants you to keep it," Sally intervened.

"He has many photographs just like it; he had many family gatherings at the villa. It's good that you keep it," Sally added.

"Thank you so much," I replied smiling at him.

Don Ramos nodded and gave me a huge grin. There was a moment's silence.

"We lived near Manchester," I said, smiling at Don Ramos.

Sally interpreted for me and I watched his face light up.

"Manchester United, David Beckham," Don Ramos said with a big smile.

Colin and I both grinned like Alice in Wonderland's Cheshire Cat.

"Yes, David Beckham, Manchester United," Colin said and shook Don Ramos' hand enthusiastically.

I am sure Colin would have hugged him too if we had been standing.

Coughing to clear his throat and gain everyone's attention, Alfredo tactfully brought us around to the subject of the house, the legal stuff and of course the money. The vendors confirmed that there were no debts on the property or land. Sally had ensured that Alfredo had included this in the initial document and pointed it out to us on the paperwork. The agreement to buy was between us and Don Ramos and Dona Martinez. The agreement was turned on its side and the vendors signed along the top. The paper was pushed towards us.

"You must sign next to the vendors' signatures," instructed Sally.

Colin pulled the document towards us and we signed in turn alongside the vendors' signatures. Alfredo retrieved the document and flicked to the back page. He read it aloud and motioned for the vendors to sign on the last page of the contract. We watched transfixed as Don Ramos and Dona Martinez signed. Alfredo motioned for us to sign too. Colin and I smiled at each other and signed. A moment's silence fell. Colin and I looked at each other and then at Don Ramos and Dona Martinez, the silence becoming slightly awkward. Sally coughed discreetly.

"It's time for you to give them the deposit now," she instructed.

Colin counted out the notes and handed the money over to Don Ramos. We all shook hands and Don Ramos and Dona Martinez grinned from ear to ear.

"OK. We need to agree a completion day now," added Sally, sobering the mood.

It was the 12 July and we knew completion must occur within 45 days. Through Sally's interpretation, Don Ramos asked if we would mind completing sometime in the last week of August. He wanted to have one last summer at the villa with his children and grandchildren. He told Sally that he had paid the council tax for the year. Even though they would not be in the villa for the full year, under Spanish law, it falls upon the seller to pay this in full. Colin and I were grateful and offered our sincere thanks. We were delighted to know that €150 was the total annual cost! Our monthly council tax bill in Kent exceeded £150 per month and I wondered how Spain could function at a fraction of the English cost. It was obvious that you could live very well on a budget in Spain. No wonder the British flocked like seagulls to live there. I wondered what sort of house £102,000 would buy in the South East. Possibly a garage, but certainly not a house. A three-bedroom semi would not give you much change from £250,000. No wonder Spain was a very popular retirement destination.

We shook hands once again. Sally told us that the vendors were happy for us to go and visit the house again. Don Ramos's son in law was at 'Bona Gent' with his daughter, but Don Ramos assured us he wouldn't mind us calling by. In the meantime, Alfredo checked all the paperwork and suggested the 26 August for our completion date, to which we all agreed. Everyone seemed very pleased and happy.

"That's it, all done," I beamed at Colin.

Don Ramos and Dona Martinez left the building with €4700 tucked in a plastic supermarket shopping bag. Sally gave us the name of a couple of companies who were very good at securing a good exchange rate for transferring the balance of the money over from England. She assured us that she would keep close contact with us via email and bade us farewell until the 26 August. The wheels were now in full motion. We had signed the first formal contract. Our Spanish bank details, mortgage details and other necessary information would be sent to us. We bade farewell to everyone and walked out into the bright July sunshine.

"Well we've done it. We've finally done it," I said breathing a sigh of relief.

Colin smiled, his dimples clearly visible. It was a real smile, as Colin's dimples only appeared when he gave a true smile.

"Fancy an ice cream?" Colin asked loudly.

"That's a great idea Col," I replied.

We strolled hand in hand across the square to the heladeria, in a state of mild shock. I was trying to remember how I felt when I bought my first house in England. It certainly hadn't been anything like buying a house in Spain.

"Colin, could you imagine handing money over the table like that in England?" I mused.

"You'd be mugged before you got to your car," answered Colin.

We both chortled at how ludicrous it all seemed.

"Fancy, meeting over an estate agents table and handing over the dosh," I said snapping my fingers and adding, "just like that!"

We scooped the delicious ice cream with our little plastic spades and walked back to the car.

"Well what now?" I questioned.

"Let's go and get some good photographs of the villa and some video footage to take back with us," Colin suggested cheerfully.

We climbed in the car and set off for 'Bona Gent.'

"Can you remember where it is?" I asked, marvelling at Colin's good sense of direction.

"Yes, of course," Colin replied adding, "Can't you?"

"No I can't, all the roads out of town look the same to me," I replied, hoping Colin really could remember where the villa was, as I didn't fancy getting lost in the intense afternoon heat. The engine started and Colin drove out of the car park. I sat silently staring out of the window as we passed grove after grove of oranges. Colin seemed to know where he was going and so I closed my eyes for a catnap.

I awoke with a start as the car bumped over a pothole in the road. We arrived at the double gates of the villa, pressed the outside buzzer and waited for someone to appear. Don Ramos' son in law was sat outside under the porch, working on his laptop. His young daughter was playing in the garden with a little chestnut coloured dog. He walked towards the gate and greeted us warmly. He had been expecting us and said we could take as many photographs as we wanted. He cleared some of his paperwork away and left us to wander around. Colin was busy videoing and looking at the water pipe outlets for filling and emptying the swimming pool. Don Ramos had told us that if we ever emptied the pool to clean it or repair any tiles, it would fill up overnight as it had two feeder pipes. One was an automatic feeder and one was a manual feeder, a hose from a water outlet further along the side of the house. If we turned the water on at night, the pool would be full when we awoke in the morning. I looked around the house, making mental notes of things I would need to buy, crockery, cutlery, rugs, sheets, pillows, chopping boards and other bits and bobs.

Sally had told us that it was quite normal for vendors to leave all existing furniture in the house. If that were the case, the villa already had two sofas and a TV stand with aerial. There were also bunk beds, two single beds and a double bed. The villa was ready to occupy immediately. Sally had mentioned that she knew someone who was managing properties in the area. It was a friend of hers who had just started in the business. She would give us the name and telephone number of the lady if we were interested in renting out the villa. I looked up at the ornate nameplate at the front of the house.

"Bona Gent, Bona Gent, Bona Gent," I repeated several times over.

Don Ramos' son in law watched me as I repeated the words.

"It means 'Good People' I think," he said politely.

I smiled and thanked him. He went on to say that he could speak a little English. He was working from home during the holidays so that he could take care of his daughter while she was off school. He wished us luck with the house and said he hoped we would be very happy. The house was too much for his father in law to maintain now, as he couldn't drive so well in his old age. Would I still be driving when I was 79? Would I still be alive at 79? I shuddered and decided to think of something more positive. I asked Don Ramos' son in law if he had enjoyed staying at the villa. He said that he had and that all the family loved the place. But they all had their own lives now and were too busy to take it on themselves. I thought it was sad really, bad luck for them but exceedingly good luck for us.

Colin and I made one more turn of the gardens and sheds and then thanked the young man for his hospitality. We shook hands with him and said goodbye. Colin said he had taken some great video footage. Content with the day's events and feeling elated, we headed back to the rented villa in Villamarchante.

"Time for some rest and relaxation I think. We'll have a swim, laze about, take in that beautiful scenery and then have an afternoon siesta," Colin said with a wink.

"With an offer like that, how could I refuse," I giggled.

And that was just what we did. We took a refreshing swim, lazed on the sun loungers, listened to 'Sounds of the 70s' on the CD, enjoyed a cold drink and a few snacks and lay blissfully relaxed and happy. In the late afternoon, Colin and I fell into the crisp white linen of the comfortable double bed and slept like Angels.

We awoke at just after eight o'clock. We emptied the fridge and packed our stuff ready for leaving. We hadn't brought a lot with us on such a short visit, so packing up had been quick. We took some scraps of ham to the dog guarding the property opposite. Her name was Probenta according to the shiny metal tag on her collar. She was honey coloured with white patches. The plot she was guarding was huge but very bare. The villa wasn't anywhere near finished; in fact it didn't even look half built. Great mounds of orange coloured earth covered the plot. It would have made a great home for a Meerkat colony. I couldn't help but wonder who fed and watered her. Colin and I never saw anyone arriving at the plot the entire time we were there. Of course, they could have called by while we were out. I pushed the tasty ham and some bread through the wire fence and she wagged her tail enthusiastically. I felt quite safe with the large metal bars separating us. I am not sure how I would have felt if I had seen her loose on the road, though she seemed very friendly and appeared to love our company. But then, if I were on my own except for maybe a few minutes when neighbours fed me, I would probably crave company too.

"You can go insane on your own," I said aloud and added, "That's why years ago, solitary confinement was considered the worst prison punishment. I do hope Probenta doesn't go mad," I shouted over to Colin. "Look how happy she is to see us."

Colin also wondered where the owners were, since he hadn't seen anyone call to feed her or give her water. He stroked her neck through the fence and scratched behind her ears. She seemed to love it. Fortunately, the sun was at its coolest and I didn't feel guilty having called her from the shade to stand in the baking hot sun. The ham was gobbled up quickly and Colin and I returned to the car. Colin reversed the car out of the drive and we headed off to eat.

"Where do you fancy going then?" Colin asked.

"Let's go to Che Guevara's," I suggested. "We haven't been there for erm... oh, let me think... at least ten days," I laughed.

"OK, back to Villamarchante," Colin said cheerfully.

We set off for yet another adventure in Villamarchante square.

The evening was lively for a Monday. The children had finished school for the main summer holidays and everyone was in a holiday mood. Colin ordered steak and onion sandwiches, French Fries and four bottles of Coca Cola. The beef was scrumptiously tender. There were several English people in the square and Colin had great fun spotting them. He seemed to be able to tell who was English at first sight, apparently something to do with socks and sandals. It was really good fun finding out if he was correct. Sally had told us that several English people were considering buying houses in the area. House prices were low and English people who had already made the move were bringing their relatives over to see just how good the quality of life was and those relatives in turn were buying properties, renovating them and moving to Spain to live. It made great sense to me. Who wouldn't want to move to Valencia? It's was lush, tranquil, inexpensive and you could enjoy a very good lifestyle with a modest amount of income. Who wouldn't want to quit the rat race back in England and opt for an altogether slower pace of life? Communities were important here, people cared about each other and people had respect for each other. Crime rates were very low and I couldn't imagine a more perfect place to live. Slowly it began to sink in that one day, Colin and I would arrive and never leave. This would be our home and on that merry thought, I kissed Colin on the cheek tenderly.

"What was that for?" Colin said awkwardly.

"Oh, I don't know really," I tittered, "I just wanted to."

"How much is it going to cost me?" Colin chuckled.

"Well, that's nice I must say," I replied angrily, which seemed to make Colin laugh even more.

I yawned and stretched my arms up over my head.

"Shall we go Colin?" I asked, holding his hand affectionately, "I feel really tired. I know I shouldn't be, but I'm shattered."

"It's probably because the worry of buying the villa is over now. It's ours," he said joyously.

"Well almost ours, only another forty five days to go," I gently reminded him.

"I'll get the bill," Colin said, trying desperately to catch the eye of the waitress.

The patio was heaving with bodies and the waitress was nowhere to be seen. Colin made his way inside the bar to pay our bill. I waited for quite a while and was just about to go and look for him when he appeared.

"I've been chatting to the owner. He's quite old you know," said Colin, adding "a lot older than you think."

It seemed to me that everyone and everywhere in the Turia Valley had a history and a story to tell. I heard Colin mouthing the words, but I was already lost in a semi-trance state and practically fell asleep while walking back to the car. Once inside the car I dozed off instantly and had to be woken up to open the villa gates.

I entered the villa, fell on the bed and from what Colin told me the next day, zonked out and snored heartily all night long.

I had slept soundly and woke feeling wonderful. Colin said he'd slept reasonably well; despite the neighbourhood dogs howling every time someone drove past in a car. It was a bit like listening to the dawn chorus from the Disney film, 101 Dalmatians. As soon as one dog started to bark, it was like a Mexican wave throughout all of the immediate area and way beyond. It was Monday morning. During the summer months, manual workers started work very early in the morning and finished late in the evening. The afternoons were too hot and most people had at least a two hour siesta or longer. And so it was that at seven o'clock sharp, the Villamarchante dawn chorus woke us up.

I decided to water the garden for the owners. The roses had shrivelled and died and everything that looked like it might have flowered seemed to have done likewise. I grabbed the hosepipe and began watering the flowerbeds and trees. Colin arose and headed to the pool to exercise before breakfast. He was determined, once we had our own house and pool, that he would swim at least fifty lengths every morning before breakfast. I finished watering the garden and joined him in the pool. He had almost finished his fifty lengths. I floated and made a half-hearted attempt at backstroke. I finally gave up and floated around the pool again.

Colin brought out our breakfast and we lazed around on the sun deck, munching green grapes picked from the vine covering the carport. The view from the patio was breathtaking and breakfast over, we sunbathed for a while. An hour later, the temperature had risen considerably and we headed for the shade of the patio.

"It's a shame about the electric isn't it," I mused, as a loud buzzing noise began.

"Well that's what happens when you have a ceramic factory next door to your villa," said Colin cockily.

"This buzzing must be really irritating at times," I said shouting to make myself heard above the noise. "I didn't notice it yesterday, did you?"

Colin stood up and looked over the wire fence towards the small ceramics factory.

"We weren't here yesterday, remember?" Colin said, walking towards the fence.

The noise stopped suddenly and all was quiet.

"Oh they must have turned it off Colin, thank goodness for that," I said relieved.

"Perhaps it's time for their siesta," Colin added.

"Perhaps," I replied, as Colin turned and walked back to the sun lounger.

No sooner had Colin sat down, than the loud buzzing noise began again. This time, it seemed to get louder and louder.

"Oh well, perhaps it was just a power cut," I began and added, "They seem to have them a lot here. You only have to put the kettle on and turn on the hairdryer and POOF, It trips out just like that," I said clicking my fingers.

"Well, we're leaving today, so it won't really affect us will it. At least our house won't have this problem, the nearest factory is over three miles away," Colin said smugly.

"Thank goodness," I replied and added, "I suppose we had better get the villa sorted out ready for leaving."

"Most of our things are packed, only our toiletries are left out," Colin replied.

We entered the villa, showered in turn and changed our clothes ready for our journey home. Our wet swimwear was placed in a plastic bag, then rolled in our beach towels and placed in the overnight bag. David said he was coming to check us out of the house at around noon. Colin and I cleaned the house from top to bottom, wanting to leave it in a better state than we had found it. We would probably need to hire it again quite soon if we had to complete on 'Bona Gent' by the 26 August. The rented villa was going to make a lovely home. It would be a marvellous residence once the owners had completed the refurbishment. The entire first floor still needed fitting out, but it would be magnificent when finished.

Colin and I said goodbye to Probenta the dog. We handed her some tasty morsels and scraps of food and opened the gates ready for David's arrival. The house was gleaming, the garden watered and Colin and I stood on the patio staring at the Pine-clad hills, breathing in the scented air.

"That's David's car," I said and turned to see David parking his car in the driveway.

He checked us out and was delighted to see how clean the villa was. He was grateful to us for watering the garden too. We intimated that we may need to stay again and asked if he knew when the owners were coming over. He told us that they were coming over for two-weeks in the summer holidays but he thought it would be at the beginning of August. He told us that if the villa was empty, he was sure that we could rent it again for a short stay. We shook his hand, wished each other well and said we would contact him through Sally at VSI if we needed to rent the villa again. We climbed into the huge estate car and headed off to the airport and our flight home.

Checking in at Valencia airport was wonderfully easy just like the previous time. There were no queues, no waiting and no delays. We checked in and within half an hour, were heading for the departure gate to board the aircraft. We made our way down the aircraft aisle, found our seats and sat down. I took my glasses from their case and put them on. I found the book-marked page of my magazine and settled down to read. I wondered which would come first, food, sleep or Gatwick airport. Sleep came first. Colin left me to sleep peacefully until it was time to land. He said he had thoroughly enjoyed eating my food but had saved me the carton of water.

"We're here Angela, we're at Gatwick," Colin said, sounding muffled, as if a long way off.

"Wake up Angela; we've landed. We'll be getting off in a minute."

I blinked several times to try and focus. Colin had tucked my magazine securely in the pocket of the seat in front of me. I blinked again.

"Have we landed?" I asked bleary eyed, looking out of the window.

It was raining, pouring down in fact, heavy rain, the sort that drenched you through.

"Huh, raining again," I said disappointed, adding "we're back in England alright."

We left the aircraft via the departure tunnel and made our way in the direction of passport control and baggage reclaim. We waited for our case to appear through the rubber flap of the baggage carousel. I was still very sleepy and stared at the conveyor belt going round and round, relishing its hypnotic effect. Colin spotted the small case, grabbed it and shepherded me through the green 'nothing to declare' passage to await the coach to BCP long stay car park. It was cold and wet outside, utterly miserable weather.

"Look at this weather Col," I remarked.

"Just like when we left," Colin said, as if reading my mind.

We climbed aboard the coach and were ferried to long-term parking. Colin collected the keys and we walked to our car as quickly as we could. A shiver shook my entire body.

"Quick, put the heater on, I'm freezing," I said laughing, as I grabbed the travel blanket off the seat and snuggled underneath it.

"That's better," I said contentedly.

"We'll soon be home," said Colin, turning the ignition.

"Home," I said quizzically, looking at him bemused.

Colin never called the rented house home. Perhaps it was the rain that reminded him of our old house in Ashton, but my thoughts were somewhere else, somewhere 1700 miles away in a tiny village called Pedralba.

Chapter 9
Shopping, Money, More Money, More Shopping

The whole of the following four weeks were spent in a whirlwind. Friends came to look at the video clips of 'Bona Gent.' We showed them the photos we had taken. I was busy setting up an account to buy currency. In the throes of all this, I was trying to concentrate on getting my back to the stage where I could walk normally without the strange, slightly off centre gait I had developed. This entailed being shook like a rag doll by the osteopath. Happily, he achieved more in one session than in six sessions with the physiotherapist. I went to the swimming baths every day. I walked as far as I could and exercised like my life depended upon it.

The physiotherapist had sent me back to my doctor. She was frustrated because I hadn't taken 'relaxants' and without them, she said that it would be very difficult for her to help me. When I woke in the mornings, or if the physiotherapist touched my back, my muscles went into spasm. The pain was excruciating and so reluctantly I returned to see my doctor yet again. She asked me why I was reluctant to take the relaxants.

"I've seen what people who take Valium look like," I said glumly. "Some of them look half dead, like zombies and I really don't want to go there," I said, feeling depressed.

Fortunately, my doctor was a wonderful listener. She listened carefully to everything I had to say. I told her that I thought my reluctance stemmed from way back when my mother had died. My mum had died when I was twenty years old and at the time I thought I had coped very well. That was, until about six months after she died. For some reason, I seemed to take on all the symptoms that my mum had. I thought I was having a heart attack all the time. I couldn't sleep and as a consequence, I became very run down. Then, I started to cry and found that once I started, I couldn't stop. I was living on my own in a house in Manchester at the time. I felt very depressed and the doctor put me on some tablets called Diazepam. He said they would help me get to sleep and they certainly did. I ended up swallowing them whenever I could because at the time, it was the only way I could blot out the loss of my mother. Instead of letting me grieve and sending me to bereavement counselling, he prescribed the tablets. I became disorientated with everything and everyone around me. I became reliant upon drink and tablets and gradually, over a period of time, my appearance suffered. I lost my job, lost my friends and lost touch with my senses. By the time I realized I had a problem, I had sunk to the very depths of despair. I decided to quit them or risk something even worse. I gradually weaned myself off them and suffered all the usual withdrawals that you would expect from a tranquilliser addiction and it took me about a year before I could really function normally again. I couldn't bear the thought of going through all that again. After pouring out the entire story, my doctor said she supported my decision not to have them and said if the physiotherapist had to work that bit harder, then that was how it was to be.

Between my determination, water therapy and the skills of the osteopath, I began to get myself fit again. The hospital Consultant had told me that I needed a total change of lifestyle. He said if I went back to spending all my time in the car, I would end up in exactly the same position again. Thank goodness we had made the move to Kent.

The distraction of buying the Spanish house had really given me a boost but I found myself missing my work. I loved my job, even if it had affected my health. My employers had been very good to me and

I missed the challenges and camaraderie. But I was not fooling myself into thinking I could just pick up where I left off. It would be a few months before I could even think of returning and even then, I was told I should phase in my work over a period of time. I decided to double my efforts on exercise so I could return to work without fear of any further injury. I made an extra effort to exercise every day. Sometimes I walked, sometimes I swam. I even did a little gardening in an effort to keep moving. When I wasn't moving, I was lying flat. But with gradually increasing exercise, my back became stronger. And so my routine continued. I spent Saturday mornings pottering around car boot sales, shopping for bedding for the house in Spain, after all, I had eight beds to furnish. I found lots of inexpensive things, heaped my purchases in plastic bags, while Colin carried and loaded everything in the car and drive us home. He was great, driving me everywhere I needed to go and when he couldn't, enlisting the help of others to drive me. In his spare time at weekends, he took me to Chatham Dockyard, Ikea and other household furnishing shops, so I could buy more furnishings for the house while he was there to carry everything for me. He made sure there were rolled up towels to support my back in the car. He moved the position of the seat every half hour for me. In short, he was more supportive than I could ever have imagined.

One weekend, Colin decided to travel to Manchester to collect Ryan for the holidays. Blaise asked if her friend Chloe could come back with them and stay for a week. After telephoning Chloe's mum, arrangements were made for Colin to collect Chloe whilst he was in Manchester collecting Ryan. Blaise was delighted her best friend was coming to stay.

"Can I go to Manchester with Dad?" she asked giddily adding, "Why don't you come too mum? You can see Auntie Norma and Auntie Linda."

Of course, I would have loved to but I knew I couldn't sit in the car for four hours or more let alone do a return journey. I assured Colin and Blaise that I would be fine and waved them off, as they headed north to Manchester. I remember I slept quite a lot when they had gone. The house seemed so quiet. I didn't have Blaise to fuss over or Colin to motivate me into going out. Colin had set Blaise's walking machine up for me to exercise on. From Friday evening to Sunday teatime, I walked, read books and slept. I enjoyed the peace and made lists of things we still needed for 'Bona Gent.'

Ryan, Chloe, Blaise and Colin arrived home at five o'clock on Sunday evening. My peace was shattered but I was pleased to see them all the same. I could hear their excited voices from inside the house. The entire week was spent listening to the children's laughter while they pounded the trampoline, sang songs, made up dances and generally made themselves as loud and intrusive as they could. Colin took them to the seaside. Blaise introduced Chloe to her new friends in Kent. Life that week seemed to be centred on Larkfield Leisure Centre, Claire's Accessories, MacDonald's and Lush. I was delighted to see Blaise happy and smiling and pangs of guilt jabbed somewhere deep inside me. I tried not to dwell on them and managed to keep them at bay, savouring her happiness. I would worry about Chloe leaving when the time came.

Of course, the time for Chloe to go home arrived far too soon. Blaise's exercise walker was set up again. The children put all their stuff away, best friend bracelets and necklaces were exchanged and they climbed into the car Manchester bound again. Hands waved frantically at me through the windows of the car, as it pulled on to the road and disappeared from view. The house was still again.

Not wanting to sit or lie down, I decided to catalogue all the purchases I'd made for the villa. Colin had been stacking them in the spare room at waist height so that I could easily get to them without bending. Armed with my pen and pad, I started my list. The first thing I wrote down was bedding. I had colour coded the bedding for ease of linen changes. If it was blue or blue and white bedding, it was single bed linen. If it was lemon or lemon mix, it was double bed linen. I needed eight quilt covers for the single beds and four for the doubles. I worked on the basis of one set on, one set in the wash. And so, my list grew and grew. Thank goodness for Ikea's summer sale. I bought single quilt cover sets for £4.

I bought rugs for the winter, bath towels, hand towels, tea towels, dish clothes, place mats, chopping boards, scouring pads and any other items I thought would be useful. There were tablecloths, solar lights, linen baskets and a hair styling set. There were face cloths, shower scrunches and toothbrushes. I hadn't realized how much I had bought.

I wondered where on earth it was all going to fit. The list ran to two A4 sheets. Of course the problem of packing it all would be left to Colin.

In addition to the household items that needed packing I had asked Colin, Ryan and Blaise to find old summer clothes that could be left at the villa. This included everyone's favourite beach towel, as even though they had begun to look a little threadbare, they would be ideal to leave at 'Bona Gent.' I remembered I had bought some waterproof matting to put down in the pool house and pool area. It was in a tight roll leaning against the bedroom wall. Colin would definitely have his work cut out packing it all; although he seemed confident that it would all fit in our cases and that we would still be within our weight allowance. I hoped with all my heart he was right, but if the worst came to the worst, I would simply have to pay the excess baggage charge.

The afternoon sped by and I was happy cataloguing everything we had bought for the Spanish house. I was excited about going back for the final exchange of contracts. The date was set for the 26 August. It was hard to believe that in less than a month, we would have our Spanish dream home. I put the list of items carefully into our important documents wallet and had a long soak in a hot bubble bath. The wonderful scent of Neutrogena Rainbath permeated the whole of the upstairs. It was my favourite and smelt like fresh rain, or so I imagined. I didn't really know what fresh rain smelt like, but I imagined it smelt like the scent coming from my steaming bath. I tried to recall the smell of the dew on the grass and trees on a misty autumn morning. If I tried very hard, I could sort of agree that it was like the smell of the bubble bath.

I reluctantly got out of the bath, dried myself off, powdered myself with a luxurious after bath powder and put my cosiest pyjamas on. I took my Maeve Binchy book from my dressing table and looked at all the household stuff stacked the entire length and breadth of the bed. Colin would have to move everything back into the spare room when he returned. I crossed the landing to Blaise's room, lay on Blaise's bed, propped my neck up with a fluffy pillow and lay back to read. The sound of a car pulling into the drive and the shadow of car headlights on the wall alerted me. I heard the familiar slam of the car doors and the click of the front door key. I roused myself as quickly as I could and peered out of the bedroom window. My car was back in the drive. Then I heard

Colin and Blaise greeting our old cat 'Zoetje.' Had I forgotten to feed the cat? I looked at the clock. It was half past eight in the evening.

"Angela, you OK up there?" Colin shouted.

I walked to the top of the stairs.

"You were very quick," I exclaimed. "You must have driven terribly fast."

"The traffic was light, we made excellent time," he said smiling up at me. "What have you been doing then? Didn't you bother to get dressed?"

"You cheeky monkey," I retorted, making my way one foot at a time down the stairs. "If you must know, I've been sorting out all the stuff for Spain. I made a list and then had a bath. I only got out of the bath about an hour ago," I protested, adding "It must have taken me over six hours to sort everything."

"Hi mum!" Blaise chirped coming through the lounge door. She looked sad.

"Have you eaten anything?" Colin asked concerned.

"No, nothing. But I feel quite hungry now though."

"Do you fancy a kebab from West Malling?" Colin asked.

"Oh yes please!" Blaise and I shouted together.

"OK, what do you want? Donner or Chicken?"

"Chicken for me and Donner for Blaise," I shouted.

Colin was back out through the front door as quickly as he'd come through it.

"I'm off now Ange. I'll get the kebabs from West Malling," he shouted, pulling the front door shut behind him.

I hobbled upstairs to see Blaise. She said she felt sad now that Chloe had gone home but was happy she'd spent an entire week with her. It had renewed their close bond and they had vowed never to lose touch. Of course, she missed Ryan too but he was coming back in just over two weeks.

Blaise and I laid the table, ready for when Colin arrived with the kebabs. Blaise went to change into her nightclothes and I resumed my reading. I sat on the dining room chair with a rolled hand towel placed in the small of my back. Colin returned with the kebabs twenty minutes later. We all sat around the lounge coffee table eating the kebabs and reminiscing about the wonderful week with Chloe and Ryan.

Blaise and Colin were tired out after their long journey to the north and back. They tidied up the dirty cutlery and plates, put them in the dishwasher and said goodnight to me. I kissed Blaise and reminded her to say her prayers and clean her teeth. Colin looked like he was half asleep already. The drive must have really drained him. He kissed me on the cheek and followed Blaise up the stairs. I quickly checked our email and the exchange rate and then climbed the stairs for bed.

The next couple of weeks rushed by like a high-speed train. I was busy transferring currency to our Spanish bank account, keeping in touch with Sally and generally fussing about the amount of luggage we had to take with us. I had a great sense of foreboding about it. There was so much of it, Colin and I had already filled the massive, ugly, green suitcase, two large blue suitcases and there was still more to be packed. Ryan of course would be bringing his own suitcase with him, so already the count was up to four cases. The large green case alone was the size of two cases. I began to worry in earnest, but once again Colin assured me we would be OK.

"We still haven't got to our weight allowance," he assured me.

"But will we get it all in the car?" I shrieked from the spare room that was now packed from floor to ceiling with stuff for Spain.

"We should do. What car have you booked?" said Colin appearing in the bedroom doorway, his cordless shaver in hand.

"Oh my Lord!" I gasped hurrying with my limp like gait across the landing and down the stairs towards the study.

"Angela!" shouted Colin. "What's up?" he said, calling down the stairs after me.

"Oh no!" he exclaimed, tumbling down the stairs two at a time.

"You haven't forgotten to book the car have you? You have haven't you?" he groaned, answering himself immediately.

The look on my face said it all. I was red faced, uptight and hammering away at the PC. I could feel his presence behind me, making me even more nervous.

"Don't worry," I muttered, "I'll do it now. The good thing is that at least we know we need a big car," I said trying to look on the bright side of things. "At least we know what luggage we've got," I said, tapping at the keys.

The input screen was there before me, dates entered, airport collection and return point, flight number and arrival time if known. For some reason, I couldn't remember booking the flights either. A gnawing concern festered in my head. I took a deep breath.

"Please Lord, don't say I forgot to book the flights," I prayed under my breath. I quietly walked to the kitchen to look for our documents in the black leather travel wallet. I looked in the 'tickets' section. Nothing! I returned to the PC. I checked in my email for a confirmation of the BA flights. Nothing!

"Oh heck!" I said under my breath. I returned to the kitchen and quickly pulled every loose paper document I could from the drawer.

"It must be here, it must be here," I repeated, like a demented parrot.

"Are you OK mum?" asked Blaise, as she entered the kitchen.

"Can I help you look for whatever it is you are looking for?" she asked, desperate to help.

I stood back for a minute, counted to twenty and tried to stop my fingers from drumming the kitchen work surface nervously.

"Well, what a dope I am, what an idiot, why can't I remember things!" I went on, running my hands through my hair.

"Don't worry mum, you've had a lot to think about," she said lovingly and put her arm around my waist to cuddle me.

"What have you lost?" she asked concerned.

"Nothing!" I snapped. "You can't lose what you've never had!" I exclaimed angrily.

Blaise gave me a squeeze and nuzzled into my neck.

"I'm sorry Blaise, it's not your fault," I said, realizing I had almost bitten her head off. "I'm just really forgetful lately. I forgot to book the flights," I said, sticking my bottom lip out to make her laugh and for maximum sympathy.

"Oh mum, that's OK, just do it now, it'll be OK," she said reassuringly.

She was right of course. I could easily book them online, after all I was a British Airways Executive Club member and membership meant that you could pull certain strings. I grabbed my credit card and made for the study again.

"Have you told dad?" Blaise asked, concern spreading over her sweet face.

"No, no need to treasure," I said giving her a smile. "It will all be sorted shortly. Now don't worry, everything will be just fine," I reassured her.

Blaise went up to her room while Colin watched Orange County Choppers on the TV. I knew Colin would be glued to the TV once OCC started, he would be spell bound. I would creep past him and book the flights and car. Well, that was the plan anyway.

The only trouble with last minute plans is that they rarely go as planned! British Airways didn't have one seat left on the day we wanted to travel or two days either side of it for that matter. I began to sweat. I quickly thought of alternatives, Heathrow, Stanstead or Luton. Unfortunately, there were no flights to Valencia available anywhere. What were the choices? Well, we could fly to Alicante, Reus, Gerona or Barcelona. Either way, there would be one heck of a drive. However, if we didn't arrive in time for exchange, we would probably face a lynching by the townsfolk! With a heavy heart, a little fear and utter disgust at myself for forgetting something as crucial as flights to get us there, I booked the four of us on a flight to Barcelona on the 20 August. Well, at least we would be there in time, even if we were six days early. The next job was to book the car. We would be going within the week. The only car available was a Renault Megane through Europcar. It was the only car that would have the slightest chance of transporting four people with lots of baggage 300 miles. I quickly booked it and breathed a sigh of relief. Everything was sorted. I thought carefully about how to break the news regarding the flights to Colin. I was too full of nervous exhaustion to even consider telling him there and then, so I decided to sleep on it. Wearily, I turned off the PC and joined Colin in the living room.

"Is it sorted?" he asked casually.

"Yep, it sure is," I said happily. "I booked us a Renault Megane. It seems to have quite a lot of room and if we need to, we can always request a roof rack," I replied confidently.

"Are we staying at David and Ann's place again?" Colin asked.

At this point, I hobbled quickly from the room shrieking various obscenities!

"Oh mum, what will we do? We haven't got anywhere to stay," Blaise whinged, following me into the computer room.

"Now look," I replied taking a deep breath, "I have fixed everything up to now haven't I? I will fix this too."

I searched her face for some small sign of confidence.

"I am going to email Sally right this minute. She can contact Ann and David and see if their sister's place is available. You will really like it. Dad and I stayed there when we went to pay the deposit to the nice old Senor and Senora," I went on, not pausing to draw breath.

I hit the send button hard and headed back to the lounge. I would check the mail tomorrow and if Sally hadn't replied by mid-day, I would telephone her and explain our predicament. All sorts of ridiculous thoughts went through my head. Perhaps we could camp on the floor of VSI properties. Of course, my long-suffering husband had realized our predicament and kept his cool. He just looked at me and shook his head.

"You are really losing it. You are truly mad," he exclaimed with a deep sigh.

Fortunately, he didn't refer to it again and thankfully he wasn't aware of the flight catastrophe. That would be my next hurdle. With a certain amount of self-satisfaction, self-appreciation and a large dollop of humility, I said my prayers and lay carefully on the bed.

My head hurt and my conscience kept me awake for a long time. I should have told Colin we were flying to Barcelona. I shouldn't have lied to him. But, I wasn't lying was I? After all, I hadn't even told him yet, so I couldn't lie about something I hadn't mentioned. Ah yes, but by not mentioning it, would that mean that I had the intent to mislead or deceive? The questions played on my mind and wouldn't go away. I promised my Heavenly Father I would tell Colin in the morning, asked him to forgive me if he thought I was being dishonest and closed my eyes to sleep. But it didn't work. I would have to tell him. I would try and make it a positive experience. We could make it part of the holiday and I could suggest visiting a couple of places of interest on the way. There was Peniscola, a very pretty seaside town (according to the guidebook) and Morello (or something that sounded like that,) a medieval hilltop village. Yes, that would be great. It would be part of our holiday. We could enjoy some of the culture that was on offer and take in some of the sights and sounds of the Costa del Azahar on our way south. Yes, surely they would all love that. With this thought fixed in my mind, my anxiety lifted and I drifted off to sleep.

I arose early and pottered around in the kitchen. Colin and Blaise joined me and we ate our breakfast together. Colin had plenty of work to do, trying to get all his plumbing jobs done before we went to Spain. Blaise, bless her, helped me with jobs in the house. Colin had agreed that I should get some help at home until my back healed. I couldn't bend forward to load the dishwasher or washing machine. I couldn't push the Hoover. These were things that the consultant forbade me to do! He said it was a sure way to dislodge the disc again. I saw an advertisement in the newsagents in the local village. It read "I can do your ironing for £2.50 per hour." I had telephoned the number and spoke to a friendly lady called Margaret. I asked Margaret is she would come and clean for me too and she agreed. Margaret would clean upstairs and downstairs on alternate weeks.

Sometimes I was not sure who had the worse back problem. Margaret looked in more pain than I at times, but she was a most thorough cleaner. She was cheerful and nothing was too much trouble. She had a kind heart and loved animals. She had a collection of small animal trinkets, animal prints and drawings and photos of her pets. She befriended our sick cat 'Zoetje' and did everything that was asked of her. I enjoyed Margaret's visits because I had someone to talk to. I missed my friends and colleagues from work and Margaret was a good listener. She would listen to me telling her about my exercise regime, my work, the Spanish house and of course, Blaise. Today Margaret was going to get everything sorted as best she could before we went away to Spain. That meant I could have a quick friendly chat, take Blaise for a walk with me and then come home to a clean and tidy home.

I packed drinks and snacks for Blaise and I to take to Leybourne Lakes and waited for Colin to drop Margaret off. I heard Colin's key in the front door lock and then the sound of his van driving away. Margaret entered with a friendly 'Hello' and took her coat off. I confirmed that I wanted the downstairs rooms cleaned and explained that she wouldn't be able to move around upstairs for all the goods and the masses of cases that were stock piled for Spain. Margaret and I had our usual friendly chat. She told me that Blackie (one of her cats) was poorly and that she would probably have to take him to the vets again. Blackie was old and it was not surprising therefore that he often ailed. I wished Margaret luck with him, after all, my cat was very old and sick too. Poor Zoetje had just turned nineteen. Margaret was very kind to her and always spent time gently stroking her. Finally, Margaret rolled up her sleeves and put on her bright yellow Marigolds and Blaise and I set off for our walk.

The day was very pleasant; the sun was shining but not too hot and there was a slight breeze. Blaise had brought her camera along and our walk along the lake was a delight to the senses. Colin and I were both camera enthusiasts, so it came as no surprise that Blaise was also quite keen with a camera. The ducks and geese swam gracefully on the lake; the scuba divers were out practicing their open water techniques and lots of retired couples were out strolling and enjoying the scenery. It was a lovely place to take a stroll, good under foot with well laid paths. There were plenty of wooden benches along the way, for those in need of a rest or for those simply wanting to sit and enjoy the view.

Blaise and I each had a small backpack with drinks and snacks packed safely inside. We stopped near the scuba diving platform for a short break. There was a huge fallen log that we often sat on and sometimes a lady riding a disabled scooter, stopped to talk to us. Her dog, a black and white border collie, hitched a lift, sitting comfortably on the foot platform. Her husband walked along side. They were a very friendly couple and their dog had a ferocious bark that disguised its kind nature. When I first met them, I thought their dog was going to attack me, but it never did. They told me it was all bravado on the dog's part. But, having a fear of dogs, I was always prone to thinking that the worst would happen. Something about dogs being able to smell fear crossed my mind again, but once the couple had been talking to me for a few minutes, the dog jumped atop the scooter and sat quietly. And so, each time I had met the couple since that first day, we had become more familiar to each other. The dogs name was Sheba.

Blaise persuaded me to let her take some photos with Colin's new digital camera. I took the strap from around my neck and handed the camera to her. She took some wonderful photographs of the water lilies on the lake and we viewed them using the preview button. They were excellent, very good indeed and quite professional looking. We walked over to the log and I heard the faint familiar whir of the motorized scooter. The old couple with their dog, Sheba, would soon be here. I told Blaise she mustn't worry if Sheba barked and that she would soon stop. Sheba appeared on cue before the couple came into view. She bounded over to the log, sniffed it and ran back to the old couple.

"She didn't even bother with a short yap to let me know she was there," I called to the old couple, as they came into view. "She just carried on sniffing the nearby logs."

The old couple laughed and made their way over to join us at the log. We chatted for a short while and they told us what the area was like before the building of the new housing development. They said that it was much better now. There were proper paths that were easy for the scooter to travel along. They definitely thought the development had been good for the area. We chatted for about twenty minutes, about this and that and then Blaise and I wished the couple a pleasant day, waved goodbye and made our way back to the car.

Margaret had finished the cleaning when we arrived home and was enjoying a cup of tea and a sit down with our cat. Blaise went out to bounce on her trampoline and I rested on the arm of the sofa. Margaret and I chatted about the villa in Spain. She told me she had never been abroad and had never really travelled anywhere. She was the daughter of a farmer and there had always been too much to do on the farm to take a holiday. She had the odd niggle like her stiff back, but all in all, she said she couldn't complain. Money was scarce and I figured Margaret probably spent more on her animals than she did on herself. I realized how very lucky I was. I was going to get my back right. Margaret was right; you certainly couldn't buy good health.

I was excited about going back to Spain. There was something very comforting about knowing you had a bolthole, somewhere of your own where you could just relax and get a way from the rat race. I wondered if Margaret had ever been in a rat race in her entire life. I thought it highly unlikely. Lucky Margaret!

Chapter 10
Just a Few Bags

"Ryan, where's your case?" Colin shouted up the stairs.

"In the car Dad," Ryan quickly replied.

I had told Colin we were flying to Barcelona. He had not been pleased, but agreed that we could make a few stops on the way to Valencia and take in some of the places of interest.

"Ange, how long is the drive from Barcelona to Valencia?" asked Ryan, calling down the stairs.

He and Blaise were as thick as thieves since he had returned. I reckoned it was Blaise that wanted to know. Blaise had a certain way of manipulating Ryan so that he ended up asking what she wanted to know. That way, if we became exasperated by the questions, Ryan carried the can! And he always did. Still, he loved her that much that he always did what she asked. Blaise was lucky to have such a loving brother.

"About three hours Ryan, but we're going to stop at a seaside town on the way. It's called Peniscola," I replied enthusiastically.

Blaise appeared at her bedroom door, looking down the stairs at me.

"Why aren't we flying to Valencia?" she asked. "Three hours in the car, in the heat, we'll fry mum," she added in a high whine.

"That's why we are breaking the journey at Peniscola Blaise, it will be just fine."

Colin continued to load the car. It was five o'clock in the morning and trying to load everything into our car was an accomplishment in itself. I dreaded to think what it would be like loading it all into a small hire car. Ryan helped Colin to pack the boot. After a lot of shuffling and re-shuffling, everything fitted in and the entire stack of luggage was securely loaded. We climbed in the car and set off for Jackie and Dave's house.

Fortunately for us, Dave was going to drive us to airport in my car and keep it at his house where it would be secure, while we were away. Dave was ready and waiting for us upon our arrival. I shuffled in the back seat with the children. Fortunately, at such an early hour in the morning, the traffic was very light and we arrived thirty-five minutes later. Colin and Dave unloaded the car while Ryan and Blaise ran to get luggage trolleys. Colin and Dave stacked the cases on the trolleys and we checked they were secure before waving goodbye to Dave. We turned and pushed the heavy trolleys snail-like towards the departure doors.

"OK, let's find where we check in," I muttered, studying the departure screens.

"Easyjet flight 5131 to Barcelona. OK everyone, we have a ten minute delay," I announced.

Neither Colin nor I had ever flown on a budget airline before and we were not quite sure what to expect. We made our way to the check-in desk, Colin and Ryan using all their strength to push the heavily laden luggage trolleys. We found the check-in desk for our flight to

Barcelona and looked on horrified. There was the longest queue I had ever seen. It appeared everyone was going to Barcelona.

"We never have to queue like this for Valencia do we?" murmured Colin, firing a glance at me that said if I hadn't been daft enough to forget to book flights, accommodation and a car, we might not be in the queue at all. I decided to ignore it and look on the bright side.

"Well at least we got a flight, even if it is to Barcelona!" I retorted.

We eventually got to the check-in desk and heaved our suitcases onto the belt for tagging.

"How many bags are you checking in?" asked the assistant.

"Four and a cool box," Colin answered politely.

After the usual questions about if we had packed them ourselves, had anyone interfered with them etc., we took the cool box to the special luggage drop off point and headed towards the departure lounge. Ryan really enjoyed looking around the airport. He had only ever flown from Manchester Ringway; Gatwick was new to him. We browsed the shops and arrived at the departure gate ready for boarding. Our flight was scheduled to depart at just before nine o'clock and to our relief; there were no further delays.

The departure lounge was full and people spilled out into the corridor. Our tickets had been issued with a row number but not a specific seat allocation. We were called to board by row numbers and the seats filled up from the back to the front of the aircraft. It was really quite civilized. No waiting for people to load luggage, everyone just boarded, hoisted their luggage in the overhead lockers, sat down, belted up and were ready for take off in about ten minutes. It was impressive to experience. No one was annoyed at having been split up. Anyone who had a spare seat next to them found it quickly filled.

We were seated three on one side and one aisle seat on the other. Marvellous, we were together. Colin put our backpacks in the overhead lockers. Our food and drink could be conveniently taken out when we wanted it. I sat in the aisle seat with my spectacles poised and my book ready. I didn't feel too good. My bones had started to ache and within half an hour of take off, I was suffering with flu-like symptoms. My throat became sore and the aching in my bones worsened. I fished in my bag for some paracetamol. I had packed soluble painkillers for my back and pressed two tablets from the foil packet. I broke them up, put them in my water bottle and waited for them to dissolve. I drank the entire contents in one go and within about ten minutes, I felt a little better. I closed my eyes and slept like a baby.

I awoke at about quarter to eleven, having slept soundly. Colin remarked on how pale I looked.

"How are you feeling?" he asked concerned.

"Fine now thank you, I'll just keep taking the painkillers and see if I can get some more paracetamol on the way. The motorway services are bound to sell them."

The aeroplane lurched forward and dipped quickly, the fasten seat belts sign came on and a flight attendant told everyone to put their chairs in the upright position as we were experiencing some turbulence. Blaise laughed. Then everyone on the aeroplane seemed to be laughing. The flight was better than any ride at Alton Towers. For ten minutes, we all enjoyed a white-knuckle ride above the clouds. People tried desperately to cover the top of their plastic cups with their hands, so as not to spill the tiniest drop. It was hilarious. Some grabbed their drinks, while some continued to try and take a gulp. Of course this resulted in them being drenched and most of them arrived at Barcelona fifteen minutes later, thrilled with the flight but soaked to the skin.

After some very serious direction seeking with various people at Barcelona airport, we found the Europcar desk. There were three terminals at Barcelona. Our flight had arrived in terminal A however the car hire section was in terminal C. We had to walk out of terminal A, past B and into C.

On the way to the car hire desk, we saw an enormous sculpture of a Horse. The children stood and looked up at it in awe. It was a marvellous work of art and stood about 24' high. Blaise and Ryan danced around it, photographed it and climbed on its plinth, while Colin and I joined the queue at the Europcar desk.

"I hope Valencia never gets as popular as Barcelona," I whispered, not wanting anyone in the queue to hear me, hoping to keep the peace and quiet of Valencia a secret.

Once at the counter, I tried my best to upgrade to a bigger car. I looked at the luggage piled on the four trolleys and inwardly cringed.

"But we don't have any other cars left, we are fully booked, it is the Megane or nothing," the assistant said.

We reluctantly accepted the Megane and were given our paperwork, keys and directions to the car.

Thankfully we found the car with ease. We stood in the car hire compound and looked at the Megane and then at our luggage. It comprised: the giant green case, two large hard backed blue cases, one large purple and green diving bag, four large back packs, one cool box and one large handbag.

"It's not going to fit in is it? I sighed, the tears stinging my eyes.

"Let me pull the car forward a bit," Colin said, sliding into the driver's seat.

It was very hot and I was beginning to feel a little faint.

"What on earth are we going to do?" I sobbed.

There was no way we could upgrade to a bigger car. My bones ached; my stomach hurt and my head throbbed. I felt awful. Feeling very sorry for myself, I realized I had made a real mess of everything.

"I've messed everything up haven't I?" I sobbed, unable to stop the tears trickling down my face.

"It's all my fault, I should have remembered, I'm sorry everyone," I moaned.

"Don't worry mum," Blaise said giving me a hug. "Dad will fix it, he'll fit it in, he's very good at packing car boots mum."

I looked on wearily as Colin and Ryan pulled the cases this way and that, packing them in and then taking them out again. I couldn't bear to watch them any longer. Blaise handed them cold drinks. I put my hand to my forehead. I was burning up. Great, this was all I needed. At that instant my stomach cramped. I fished in my bag for another two painkillers, dropped the huge tablets in my bottle of Evian and waited for them to dissolve.

"Come on you two, get in," Colin instructed.

"Blaise, Ryan, you will have to put this case in between you and the cool box too. Can you manage that?" asked Colin, dragging one of the hard backed cases towards the back seat doors.

"Sure dad," they replied in unison.

Ryan and Blaise sat quietly without any word of complaint, their bodies separated by a huge blue suitcase and a cool box. But at least everything was in the car. The alternative was that one of us got the train to Valencia and met the others there. I was so relieved that we were still all travelling together. I lay my head back against the headrest and closed my eyes, desperate to rest until my navigation skills were needed. Fortunately, Colin found his way easily to the southbound A7 motorway and our journey was finally under way.

An hour later I started to feel queasy again. I had already taken the maximum amount of painkillers and my only option was to take anti-inflammatory tablets. I searched my bag for some Ibuprofen. I remembered my doctor saying it was OK to take them with paracetamol. I located them in the bottom corner of my handbag, quickly swallowed two with some more water and closed my eyes again. Colin stopped at the next motorway services and I limped into the shop. I bought a tuna sandwich, a large bag of ready salted crisps and more water to dissolve yet more tablets. Thankfully, the tablets seemed to keep the unpleasant symptoms at bay.

About a hundred and twenty kilometres further on, we saw the sign for Peniscola and exited the motorway. Ryan and Blaise needed a break and I was sure Colin needed one too. He had already driven to Manchester and back and was now driving a similar distance from Barcelona to Valencia. The kids were packed in the back seat like sardines with the heavy blue suitcase and cool box wedged in every available space. In reality, we all needed a break.

Colin parked up on the main promenade and we walked up and down the colourful sea front. Peniscola was a very pretty town, just as the guidebook had described it. The sea front was very picturesque, backed by a fortress. The sand was fine and pale cream coloured. It looked relatively clean, considering how many holidaymakers were on the beach. It reminded me of my childhood holidays. Buckets and spades hung from string lines on the shop fronts, there were airbeds in every shape and colour, lassoed by more string. Colourful sarongs, sun glasses, beach balls, leather goods, jewellery, shoes, beach bags, rubber rings and little ornaments made from shells, filled the wire baskets and shelves that lined the aisles of the shop and spilled out on to the pavement. It was fascinating looking at the crafts.

Blaise and Ryan saw some shoes that they really liked and I happily bought both pairs. Ryan needed a pair of sea shoes too. He had outgrown most of the clothes and footwear he had kept at our house and I had packed up his last pair for the charity shop. He saw a pair that looked quite durable, and tried them on. They were a good fit and reasonably priced. We added them to our basket. We also purchased a rubber ring to give my back extra support and Colin bought himself a seat shape airbed. It looked like a huge grey armchair with a cup holder inlaid into its right arm.

My newly acquired virus seemed to be under control. The walk and distractions of the seafront had done us all good, particularly Blaise and Ryan, who had been cramped in the back of the car for two hours. Somehow Colin had kept awake and alert and, delighted with his new pool toy, was eager to try it out.

"If I ever bought another house in Spain, I would consider buying one here," I said to Colin, as I squeezed his hand.

He agreed with me. Peniscola was a lovely seaside resort. It was a very strange sensation discussing buying yet another Spanish house and silly to be talking about buying a second property when we hadn't even bought the first one.

"Listen to us," I chuckled, "we sound like property magnates don't we?"

"Well, who knows Ange, maybe one day, after all, anything can happen," he said, with a gleam in his eye.

We reluctantly got back in the car. I took some Panadol and the children were packed like sardines into the back again, complete with big blue case and cool box.

"Here you are kids," I said, throwing a large bag of crisps over my shoulder. "Enjoy those."

For the next few hours, all we could hear was the rustling and crumpling of the plastic crisp bag, interspersed with a loud belch from time to time, as Blaise and Ryan took turns guzzling fizzy pop.

"This is just what holidays should be like," I said relaxing.

Fortunately we weren't more than a few hours away from Valencia. I closed my eyes and reminisced about days gone by, when my sisters and I had sat in the back of dad's car outside a pub in North Wales. Mum always appeared with bags of crisps and small bottles of lemonade, brightly coloured straws poking out of them. We would sit in the car guzzling fizzy pop through straws and munching salted crisps. In those days, bags of crisps came complete with little blue paper bags of salt. You had to sprinkle the salt over the crisps, gather the top of the crisp bag and shake it violently to disperse the salt evenly over the crisps. These were great childhood memories. Our journey to Valencia continued, while my childhood stories were relayed, fairy tale style, to an eager and enthusiastic audience.

We arrived at the villa in Villamarchante at eight o'clock. Ryan said he couldn't feel his feet or his knees because of the weight of the cool box that had been resting on them. Blaise wanted the toilet and fast. Colin and I just wanted to stretch our legs. David was at the gate to greet us. We were lucky the owners weren't there, especially as I had forgotten to book accommodation. David looked very happy to see us.

We were all extremely tired and hot, but immensely relieved that we had finally arrived. Colin pulled the little car through the gates and parked under the vine-covered carport. We flung the car doors open and the heat of the day greeted us. We were extremely stiff from the journey and were eager to get out. Colin pulled the case off Ryan's legs and we got out of the car like robots. We unloaded the car and took the cases that contained our clothes inside the villa, leaving the cases with goods for 'Bona Gent' in the boot. The heat was exhausting and I could see the children glancing longingly at the pool, its bright turquoise water glittering like someone had scattered a thousand tiny sequins on its surface.

Colin and I unpacked; the children chose their bedrooms, changed into their swimsuits and ran outside. They dived headlong into the cool water of the pool and their laughter could be heard from inside the villa. They were having a great time. Although Colin and I felt exhausted, in true holiday spirit, we decided to join them anyway.

"Let's not cook tonight," Colin said.

"We'll stay in the pool until we have cooled off, get dressed and then go out to dinner. We can head into Villamarchante and eat late when it's cooler. Well, late dinner by English standards," he added.

"Perfectly normal time for dinner here though," I commented, floating like a jellyfish in the water.

"Yes, normal for here," Colin agreed.

140

We lazed in the pool, relaxed on the sun loungers and watched the children play in the water. Colin looked shattered, his eyes heavy with the need to sleep.

"Come on Colin, let's go for a siesta," I suggested, walking into the villa.

Colin followed me and we both collapsed on the bed.

We awoke at ten o'clock, bleary eyed and hungry. We listened for the familiar sound of the children, but all was quiet.

"Where do you think they are Colin?"

Colin was finding it a real effort to open his eyes. He blinked several times before answering.

"They are probably inside getting ready to go out for dinner," he replied through a half yawn.

"Well, I suppose we should make a move and go and get ready ourselves," I said with a sigh.

The children were in their bedrooms getting ready, just as Colin had thought. We showered quickly, threw on cotton T Shirts and shorts and climbed in the car. The children held the gates open while Colin drove out, locking them securely behind them. They climbed in the back of the car and we set off to for dinner in Villamarchante Square.

An evening in Villamarchante Square in the middle of summer is like one huge carnival. Everyone talked loudly at breakneck speed. Little children tore around the square on their tricycles, their mothers or fathers running relentlessly behind them trying desperately to keep up with them. Grandmothers and grandfathers drew on their Camel cigarettes and passed the time of day. They gesticulated wildly with their hands and picked olives from the small bowls placed on the tables.

One of the bars had put a huge TV screen outside its frontage and judging by how many people were seated at their tables, an important football match was under way. Colin indicated for us to take a seat at a nearby table. Ryan who had never been to the area before, seemed mesmerized by the sights and sounds of the square. Now and again, we could hear English being spoken but we couldn't distinguish the origin of the speaker in the mass of bodies that were sat in the square.

I had never seen so many people in the village square before. Banners were hoisted on high with the sign Romano y Festes. I wasn't sure about the last word, perhaps it was 'Fiestas' and I had been too tired to see it properly. Anyway, whatever it said, the whole area was in a festive mood. Bangers and firecrackers sounded off in every direction, typical of a local festival.

I can only describe the celebration as a 'stepping out' or 'promenading' festival. All the young men and women of the town, who had finally left school (those aged eighteen) promenaded around the square. A young man accompanied each young woman. They were dressed in the most elaborate costumes. The young men in dinner dress and the young women in what can only be described as wedding dresses. Each dress was the same in design and colour, perhaps the local design of the town I thought.

The doorways to the houses of the young women were decorated with upturned Palm branches, so that they made an arch above the doorway. Before the couple left the home of the young woman, there was a huge display of fireworks. Bangers and firecrackers lit up the entire square and everybody turned their heads to see the young couple emerge through the archway of palms.

We sat at a red plastic top table and sipped our cool drinks. A strong smell of gunpowder permeated my nostrils and the loudest bang I have ever heard in my life left my ears ringing for almost twenty minutes. The hair on the back of my neck stood up as a loud banger went off directly at the back of my chair. In shock, I turned to look at the young couple. They looked stunning in their finery. The girl's dress was cream with deep coloured piping along the bodice. A dark bolero jacket fastened over the top of the dress, which could easily be removed if the young lady became too hot. They obviously promenaded late in the evening when the air was a little cooler. It was wonderful to watch them strolling arm in arm, their parents following at a respectable distance behind them.

Blaise and Ryan thoroughly enjoyed the evening, but with all the excitement of the 'stepping out' there was not a hope of getting anything other than pizza to eat. The restaurants were finding it hard to keep pace with the growing number of families congregating together. Colin suggested that we share a large pizza and then take a BBQ chicken

promenading

C. Kemp

and some ice cream back to the villa. He quickly ordered a cheese and tomato pizza, which arrived within minutes and which we ate with much gusto. We headed across the square in the direction of the car park, to the shop with the sign 'Pollos Asados.' Colin bought a hot barbeque chicken and a large portion of paella without snails and drove us back to the villa.

We sat on the outside patio and pulled chunks of chicken from the carcass. Colin spooned paella on to our plates and we devoured every morsel. It had been a long, tiring day but a fascinating one. Ryan and Blaise had that sort of glassy-eyed look that said they were exhausted and needed to sleep. The pain in my back had returned and Colin looked as if he had fallen asleep on his chair. I put the rubbish in the bin, washed up the few dishes we had used and headed towards the bedroom. It was just like a scene from 'The Waltons.'

"Good night Blaise."

"Good night Mum, good night Dad."

"Good night Dad, good night Blaise."

"Good night Ryan, good night Blaise."

"Good night Ange."

"Good night Ryan."

"Goodnight darling."

"Good night."

All that could be heard was the whirring of the fans David had kindly placed in each bedroom.

Feeling contented and happy with my life, I walked around the perimeter of the villa. I looked up at the dark blue sky and searched for the man in the moon before switching off all the outside lights. It was a beautiful night, calm and still. I thought about the sights in the town, the beautiful young women strolling excitedly with their escorts. Bangers and firecrackers could still be heard, their bangs and cracks piercing the night air. Somewhere in the distance a rocket illuminated the sky, its bright stars falling in a glittering silver cascade. I retired to bed enchanted by the evening's events with the image of hundreds of tiny sparkling lights dripping to earth like falling crystals.

Chapter 11
Pool with a View

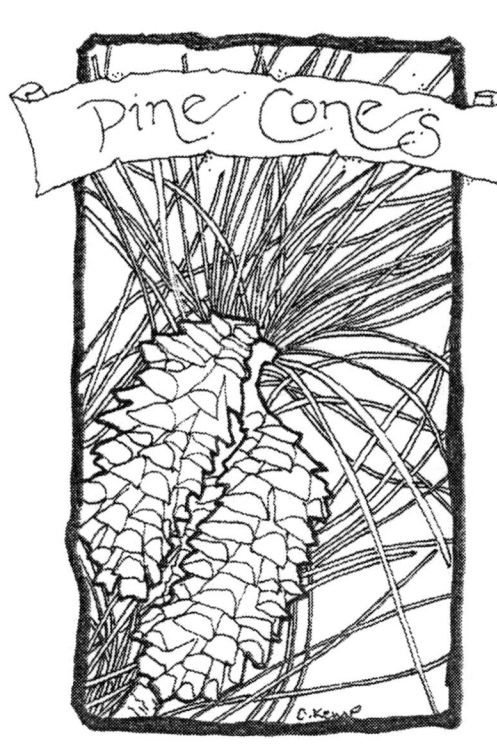

"What time is it?" I groaned my voice husky with sleep.

"Dunno, s'early," replied Colin, his lips hardly moving.

I swung my legs out of the bed and made my away across the hall to Blaise's room. Peering in, I saw the sheets heaped on the floor. Blaise was nowhere to be seen.

"OK. I'm coming to find you!" I yelled playfully, opening up a wardrobe door.

I moved the clothes about, certain that Blaise was crouching down in the corner. I couldn't find her. I walked further down the hall to Ryan's room and pushed the door ajar. He too was missing. The same sight greeted me, the bed sheet half on the bed, half on the floor, the fan whirring away. I walked from the hall to the kitchen at the end of the corridor. The children were not in there either. I walked the entire length of the hall again back to the lounge. It was in darkness but I heard muted voices outside. I opened the curtains thinking how strange this house was. The kitchen was at one end of the house and the lounge at the other. A long corridor linked the two rooms, with doors off either side of the corridor to the bedrooms and the bathroom.

I unbolted the large metal door in the lounge and stepped out onto the patio. The view was amazing. Pine trees and hills stretched out as far as the eye could see. You could easily forget you were in Spain and imagine you were in Switzerland or Austria. Greenery was abundant. I turned towards the pool and spotted Ryan and Blaise. There they were, with their swimming goggles on, swimming up and down the pool, length after length.

"Good morning kids," I shouted from the poolside.

Blaise lifted her goggles and placed them on her forehead. She reminded me of Benny Hill when he did his pilot impersonation. Her little round face peered back at me.

"Hi mummy. We didn't wake you did we?" she asked cautiously, adding "only we tried our best to be quiet and not to wake you and Dad," she added.

"No you didn't wake me treasure," I reassured her. "How long have you been in here then?"

"Oh, not long, about half an hour. Ryan's training," she replied.

"Training for what?" I asked curious.

"Oh nothing specific, just training, you know, like working out type stuff."

"Oh that sort of training," I said nodding my head.

Ryan looked up from the edge of the pool.

"Guess how many lengths I've done Ange?" he asked breathless.

"Fifty," I answered.

"No, higher," he encouraged.

"Seventy."

"Higher."

"Seventy five," I replied hopefully.

"Nope, I've done eighty up to now. I'm gonna do a hundred. That's what I'm gonna do each day for my training," he said proudly.

"That's good. I'd love to be able to do that but I can only manage ten at best. I'm OK as long as I float or do back stroke, but I can't do breast stroke, it kills my back," I announced.

"Is it still sore Ange?" he asked concerned.

"Well it's a lot better than it was, the disc has gone back in, but my sacroiliac joint is twisted so that causes pain too. But I keep swimming and walking and it's getting better."

"I bet you hate taking all those pain killers don't you?"

"Well, it's not great but it eases the pain. I only take them when I need them, usually first thing in the morning and last thing at night, to ensure I can sleep. It's when I wake up that it hurts most. I'm supposed to sleep on my side with a pillow in between my knees, but it's never there in the morning. When I wake up I am nearly always lay on my back and then my back goes into spasm. But, it will get better eventually, I'm doing everything I'm supposed to do."

"Swimming will be good for you," he stated, seeming genuinely interested.

"Yes it is. But I have to be careful how I twist or turn in the water. Overall, it's very good and it will strengthen my stomach muscles too."

Colin appeared on the patio.

"I'd best finish my lengths," Ryan stated, swimming off towards the other end of the pool.

"That sounded like a good conversation," Colin mouthed, halfway through a yawn.

"Yep, I suppose it was," I replied, reflecting on the last few minutes of conversation.

Ryan didn't really say much to anyone these days, I suppose it was that teenage stage when all anyone got was a nod, grunt or at best something that sounded like a mumble. Ryan had joined a gym and had been working out regularly. He was quite serious about keeping fit and it gave him something to talk about too. Not to be outdone, Blaise shouted over.

"Mum, come here a minute."

"What Blaise?" I asked sitting on the swimming pool ledge.

"Guess how many lengths I've done?" she asked excitedly.

"Twenty," I guessed.

"Higher."

"Twenty five!"

"Higher."

"Thirty!"

"Yes, do you think that's good mum?" she asked and before I answered, she pushed off the side of the pool and swam away.

"I'm going to do fifty if I can mum; I'm going to train like Ryan."

I laughed and praised her efforts, shouting encouragement to her as she swam away.

Colin joined me at the poolside and sat down. He watched the children doing their training and waited for them to finish their routines.

"I suppose I might as well train too," he said in a resigned tone.

"It'll do you good and you'll enjoy it," I encouraged, rubbing his hair affectionately.

As Ryan got out of the pool, Colin dived in and began a swift, strong, front crawl up and down the length of the pool. Blaise had almost finished her fifty lengths and shouted to me that she only had another two lengths to go. She asked if I was pleased with her. I told her that I was and shouted for her and Ryan to shower off the chlorine before breakfast.

I ferried croissants, fruit juice, ham and cheese to the table. It was still early at just turned half past eight. Colin, Ryan and Blaise had all done quite a substantial amount of exercise and were ravenous. They eagerly tucked into their breakfast and devoured it at lightening speed. I noticed a faint smell of Jasmine on the breeze and made a mental note to try and locate and water it after breakfast.

Colin and the children cleared away the breakfast things and I slowly descended the ladders to the pool. The pool wasn't really big enough for four serious swimmers so Colin and the children let me have time in it on my own without risk of getting knocked or kicked. Although it was early, the water was a warm 27 degrees. I went through my physiotherapy exercises and swam about ten lengths backstroke. I could get fourteen arm movements in on one length of the pool. It was all one depth and I could only just stand on tiptoe. I finished my swim and held on to the side of the ladders for support. I carefully climbed the metal ladder and got out of the pool. Of course Colin and the children got back in as soon as I got out.

Colin had rolled one of the sun loungers under the shade of the patio and put on a 'Sounds of the 70s' CD. I lay back in the sun with my holiday novel, 'Tara Road' and started reading. The CD was great, songs of my teenage era and I felt more relaxed than I had done in a long time. I rested the book on my stomach and closed my eyes as an 'oldie' came on the CD. It was Pickety Witch singing 'Same old Feeling' and I was transported back in time to my early teens, when I used to go to the local Discothèque, The Birdcage. I was dressed in my lilac, snowflake patterned hot pants, grey suede boots and a matching Maxi Coat. All the years of watching my sister Norma put eye make up on had been invaluable. I was made up like Mary Quant, with eyelashes drawn on my bottom lids and freckles painted on my nose. I laughed at the memory and closed my eyes.

It was one o'clock in the afternoon when I woke up. Colin, Ryan and Blaise were playing ball and diving in the pool. They looked like wrinkled prunes.

"Blaise, do you fancy a game of bat and ball with me?" I asked as she climbed out of the pool.

Colin and Ryan headed for the cool interior of the house and the shade.

"OK mum, but can I get a drink first?" she replied.

"Sure, there are plenty of cold drinks in the fridge, help yourself."

"Does anyone else want one?" Blaise asked.

"Coke please!" shouted Ryan.

"Bring four cans of cola please Blaise," I shouted, as she disappeared through the front door into the kitchen.

Blaise returned juggling the cans in her arms. We each picked up a bat and played on the front patio. The sun was relentless and although I really loved playing games with Blaise, it was not much fun for her. Each time one of us missed, she had to chase after the ball, as I couldn't bend to pick it up.

"Mum, I'm too hot," she pleaded, after a five minute game. "Can we play ball later when its cooler?" she implored.

"OK treasure," I answered, looking at her poor little red face.

"Ange, can I have something to eat?" Ryan asked looking sheepish.

"Ryan, you have only just eaten breakfast," I answered.

"That was four hours ago Ange," he stated.

"Four hours ago, it can't have been. What time is it now?"

"Half past one," Ryan answered.

"Blimey, I didn't realize it was that time. Is anyone else hungry?" I asked, looking from face to face.

"I am mummy," Blaise replied.

"OK. Fruit and ice cream, will that do you Ryan?" I asked, wondering what else we had in the fridge that he could eat.

"Yeah, that's fine," he answered.

Ryan and Blaise spent the next half hour munching fresh fruit and slurping melted ice cream. Blaise said she felt very hot and asked if she could go back in the pool. I told her that she could but not for long because the reflection of the sun on the water would burn her. She slipped off her towel and jumped into the pool; naked as the day she was born.

"Ryan, don't come outside for a little while," I shouted flustered.

"Can't I swim with Blaise?" he asked.

"NO!" I yelled quickly. "Why don't you sunbathe with your dad?"

"OK," he replied.

A few minutes later, both Colin and Ryan appeared on the side patio.

"Ange, come and look at Dad. Dad's nude sunbathing!" Ryan shouted, laughing loudly.

What on earth had come over my family? The sun must have gone straight to their heads.

Colin jumped up from off the sun lounger and did a funny walk around the patio, wiggling his bottom, much to my disgust. I was startled by the sound of hooves outside the villa. A man of about forty years old or so, sat atop a big dappled grey horse, a cowboy hat perched on his head. He glared over the hedge at Colin's naked bum. I laughed as Colin made to dash under the covered patio. The man must have thought we were a bunch of lunatics. Not deterred by the incident, Colin proceeded to dance in the nude, which made Ryan laugh hysterically.

Blaise screamed and I hobbled over to the pool.

"What's wrong?" I asked concerned, wondering if she had cramp.

"That man saw me didn't he?" she asked anxiously.

"No darling, he couldn't see into the pool, he was watching dad. Your modesty is intact treasure," I added, reassuring her. "Perhaps you'd better wear a bathing suit next time."

Armed with a huge bath sheet, held at arms length to form a curtain, Blaise climbed out with her modesty intact. I wrapped her up in the large soft towel and steered her towards the shower.

"Can we go and feed the dog later?" she asked coyly.

"I'll take them over to see Probenta when they have showered," Colin volunteered. "There are some bits in the fridge we can give to her. What have you got planned today Ange?"

"Well, it's just turned two o'clock. The Carrefour supermarket will be open and more importantly, it will be quiet. We could go there or would you prefer to go to Lliria? There's a Mercadona and a Lidl in Lliria."

"Let's go to Lliria, it's nearer and quicker," Colin replied.

"OK. You and the kids go and feed the dog and I'll get dressed."

I entered the house and left Colin and the children to feed the scraps to Probenta.

A quick trip to Lliria and an even quicker shopping session and we were back at the villa, all happily munching mixed nuts. There were Pistachios, Macadamias, Peanuts, Cashews and Almonds. We were relaxed and happy. Ryan and Blaise said they really liked the peace and tranquillity of the area. They agreed that everything was slower but that time seemed to go quicker. It wasn't long before Ryan was hungry again and Colin and I laughed at our inability to satisfy his hunger.

"Where's he putting it?" I chuckled to Colin.

"I don't know, look at him, there's nothing of him," Colin replied.

Dinner should have been a dish of tuna salad but the tin opener was useless. Instead, we had sausage, salad, curried rice and potato wedges. Blaise and Ryan played bat and ball for a while; taking turns who was batting and who was chasing after the ball.

"Let's go and buy a proper tin opener," Colin exclaimed suddenly, before adding, "I fancy some chocolate too. Come on, we can leave the children to play here, they will be quite safe for half an hour."

Colin picked up the car keys and called out our plans to the children.

"Can we go in the pool again?" asked Blaise, catching us on the hop.

"Yes, but be careful not to burn," I answered adding, "Put plenty of sun cream on."

The children closed the double gates behind the car and Colin and I headed towards Lliria to buy a decent tin opener and some chocolate.

On our way, we spotted a sports car rally on some waste ground at the side of the road. There were huge marketing tents everywhere and we distinguished the familiar colours of Coca Cola and Red Bull straight away. Sports cars of every shape, size and colour were parked up in the dirt car park in front of the tents.

"Ryan would love this Colin. Why don't you come back with him and take a look around?" I suggested.

"We might, we'll see what time it is when we get back. He might be tired. He's not really stopped today has he?" Colin said thoughtfully.

"He's got a lot of energy to burn," I answered. "It's good to see a young man of his age with so much energy. Can you remember what it was like to have that much energy Colin?" I asked, remembering back to when I was a teenager.

"I used to walk to the shop at the top of our road. Pat and Dennis owned it then. There was a bus stop opposite the shops and when the bus used to pull up at the stop, I would stand outside the shop, ready to start running when it set off again. I would wait for the bus driver to put the bus in gear, you could always tell because the gears were on the steering column in those days and you saw him move the stick. That was my signal and then I would set off running just as the bus would start to move. I remember how much energy I had; I could feel the acceleration and power curse through my legs as I pounded down the pavement. Sometimes, I was running so fast, I couldn't stop at our gate and ended up running past by some 20' to 30'. I often won too and always felt exhilarated. Did you ever do anything like that Colin?" I finally paused to ask.

Not waiting for his reply, I continued, "I was a great runner at school, very fast over short distances. I remember winning the 80 metres sprint in ten seconds. I enjoyed running in races on sports days, but I never fancied joining a running club."

"I ran a lot of cross country marathons at school," Colin put in quickly before I started talking again. "I was a very good cross country runner. That's how I injured my knee. Ryan's a lot like me. Do you remember when he was very young Ange, how he used to run through the passageways near Evesham Grove and then just squat until we caught up with him. Then he'd be off again!" Colin recollected.

I smiled at him. It was true; Ryan ran everywhere as a child and was never out of stamina.

"I think he will be an excellent sportsman," I said confidently.

"Well, he was good at karate wasn't he?" asked Colin. "Do you remember when he fought the Freestyle Karate champion? It was his first time in the ring and he didn't lose by many points either. That lad, the champion, said Ryan gave him the hardest fight of his life," Colin stated proudly.

"I remember. Ryan fought brilliantly didn't he?"

"He sure did," Colin said thoughtfully. "If he's not tired out, I'll take him to see the cars," he added.

We arrived in Lliria and parked up at Lidl. Colin had seen a tin opener there earlier in the day. We found them in the centre aisle baskets. They were very cheap and on inspection looked very well made. It was easy to rotate and manoeuvred well. In the past, I had often been on camping holidays where the essentials such as a bread knife, potato peeler and tin opener were provided. They were all tucked neatly into kitchen drawers but the tin opener supplied would have operated better as a pencil sharpener. I have no idea to this day how people used those contraptions successfully. They looked more like a staple extractor than a tin opener. I determined never to have such rubbish in my own place. I was delighted with Colin's find at Lidl and purchased the deluxe tin opener for €2.99. Colin stacked up on chocolate, even though we weren't entirely sure we could get it back to the villa without it melting. We double wrapped it just in case the worst happened and climbed back into the car and headed back to the villa.

We arrived home to find the children still playing in the pool. I showed them my fantastic tin opener but they weren't the least bit impressed by it. They were too busy splashing around in the water and after all, how exciting could a deluxe tin opener be to a ten and a fourteen year old?

"OK, time to get out now," came Colin's voice from the lounge. "You'll end up looking like tinned prunes," he said laughing.

"Aw! Do we have to?" asked Blaise imploringly.

"Yes," said Colin firmly.

Blaise and Ryan climbed out of the pool and sat down on the sun loungers. It was still very hot.

"Ange, when can we go back in the pool?" asked Ryan quietly.

"After five o'clock Ryan, the sun's rays wont be as strong then."

Ryan's face and neck looked very red; it was obvious he'd already burnt.

"Ryan, did you put plenty of sun lotion on?" I enquired.

"Yeah, but I suppose it comes off in the pool. My ears feel a bit tender," he added. "Have you got any of that stuff we had in Gran Canaria, that blue stuff?"

"You mean the Aloe Ice Gel from Avon. Yep, I brought some with me. Shall I get some for you?" I volunteered.

"Yes please Ange," Ryan replied, rubbing his ears.

I took the large bottle of bright blue after sun gel from the bathroom and returned to help Ryan.

"Can you put some on my ears Ange?" Ryan asked politely.

"Sure. Come over here in the shade," I replied.

I rubbed the bright blue gel over Ryan's red and tender ears. Colin shouted over for me to put plenty on. I added another dollop for good measure. Blaise took one look at him and burst out laughing.

"You've got blue ears Ryan," she teased, mercilessly.

"Have I Ange?" he asked.

"Yes, you have Ryan, it's the gel. But don't worry, it will soon soak in," I reassured him.

"Anyway, it will give us all a laugh," added Blaise.

"You look like an alien," laughed Colin.

"Yeah, like Sully from Monsters Inc.," shouted Blaise, who dodged as Ryan's towel flicked by her ear.

"Get lost yous lot!" Ryan shouted, in his thick Manchester accent and launched himself onto the sun lounger, covering his head with a hand towel.

"OK you two, stay in the shade while mum and I have a siesta," Colin instructed. "Do NOT under any circumstances go back in the pool or the sun."

"OK dad!" they chanted.

We left the children relaxed in the shade of the patio and headed indoors for a siesta. We were pleasantly sleepy.

Chapter 12
From Synchronized Buzzing
to Synchronized Swimming

They say tomorrow never comes, but it certainly did for Colin and I. I awoke to find the house deadly quiet. I hoped Ryan and Blaise hadn't moved the sun loungers out of the shade and fallen asleep in the sun. I headed down the corridor, through the lounge to the patio. Ryan and Blaise were swimming, goggles on, going hell for leather up and down the pool.

"Hey you two, I thought you'd done your training this morning," I shouted. "Dad told you not to go back in the pool or the sun. He will be furious with you both," I admonished, convinced they had burnt to a frazzle.

Blaise stopped swimming, lifted her goggles to her forehead and looked up.

"What did you say mum?" she asked.

"I said I thought you and Ryan had done your training this morning. Thought you'd do a spot more eh?" I added.

"But it is morning mum!" Blaise said with a surprised look on her face. "This is our morning training. Ryan's doing a hundred lengths and I'm doing fifty, although I think I might do more today," she added nonchalantly.

"Morning! Morning!" I repeated, confused.

"Yes mum, it's MORNING! You and dad slept through. Got to carry on now," Blaise added, pulling her swim goggles down on to her face before kicking off from the wall.

Ryan hadn't even looked up and continued to swim rhythmically.

I hobbled to the kitchen, grabbed my watch from the crystal ashtray. It WAS morning!

"Good grief!" I said aloud, rubbing my eyes, still not quite believing. "We've slept through," I remarked, somewhat breathless.

I headed into the bedroom to wake Colin up.

"Come on Colin, we've slept through!" I said, pulling the blinds up.

Daylight flooded the room and Colin buried his face in his pillow to shield his eyes from the bright sunlight.

"Morning?" questioned Colin, rubbing his eyes. "Morning? Are you joking?"

"No darling, it really is morning; the kids are doing their training in the pool. We fell asleep and slept through. Look, we are still fully dressed," I stated laughing.

"We must have really needed it then," Colin mumbled, walking to the bathroom.

I busied myself getting the breakfast things ready and took our usual favourites of croissants, fresh fruit, ham and Brie to the table. I arranged the breakfast on the side patio and returned to the kitchen for a large jug of fruit juice and mosquito nets. Colin emerged from the villa, quite giddy and dressed in his swimming trunks.

"How many lengths are you going to do?" I asked.

"About twenty or twenty-five, just enough to loosen up a bit," Colin replied.

"OK. Breakfast is ready whenever you are but it's covered so it won't spoil," I said, finishing my glass of fruit juice.

I strolled around the back of the villa enjoying the peace and quiet. The Pine forests were spectacular and covered the hills for miles around. The scented breeze rustled the long stalks of dry grass in the field that adjoined the villa. The Jasmine bush was trying desperately to flourish, putting out thin shoots, feeling its way through the wire fence as it weaved its shoots in and out of the mesh. I walked to the side of the house, grabbed the hosepipe and turned on the water, giving the vine and the Jasmine bush a much-needed drink. I concluded that Jasmine was a very hardy shrub, as no matter how neglected it got, it always seemed to pull though.

I gave the rest of the garden a good hose down and watched the water disappear instantly into the parched ground. The rose bushes looked like charred sticks. Roses in Spain! Somehow it seemed odd having Roses in Spain. In an English country garden, yes, but in Spain, it seemed weird. I finished watering the garden just as Colin got out of the pool. I rolled the hosepipe up on its carrier and told Colin I'd found the Jasmine bush.

Everyone had worked up a good appetite and breakfast was polished off in minutes. Colin and the children cleared the breakfast things away, giving me twenty minutes alone to exercise in the pool.

"Why don't you jump in mum?" Blaise asked.

"I can't darling, my disc might come out again," I replied flatly.

"Won't you be able to jump in ever again?" she asked.

"Of course I will darling. One day I will be able to jump and dive in just like before," I sighed.

That day seemed like a long way off just now. Still, I continued my exercises and swung my legs one at a time, forwards, backwards, forwards and backwards, for at least five minutes. I swam for a further ten minutes and rested at the side of the pool, holding the ladders for support. I suddenly felt very lonely. Here I was in a lovely swimming pool, surrounded by Pine trees and lemon groves with no one to talk to or to keep me company.

"Hey you lot!" I shouted. "Come over here and keep me company. I'm lonely."

"Oh poor mum. Can we get back in then?" Blaise asked, ever the opportunist.

"Yes of course you can. I feel a bit lonely here on my own. Perhaps we can play a game," I enthused.

Colin appeared at the poolside.

"Here you are," he said, tearing open a box and handing the contents to Blaise.

"Wow! That's great dad. Look mum, pool toys! Remember, we bought them at Larkfield Leisure Centre? Look mum, there's an egg with a little turtle in it. And there are other toys too. Wow, that's great, you can throw them in for me mum and I'll dive for them and bring them back to you," Blaise added excitedly.

The pool set comprised of a diving baton, a small egg with a miniature turtle in it, a hoop and a disc. They were fluorescent pink, lime green, yellow and blue. Blaise and I spent the rest of the morning in the pool. I threw the toys, Blaise dived for them and brought them back to me, then I threw them in again and she retrieved them. Funny how the simplest of games keep children entertained for hours. After some time had elapsed, I began to resemble a Gran Canaria potato. My fingertips were wrinkled and my face felt taut. Another hour in the pool and the sun would probably age me by another ten years. Making my excuses to Blaise, I got out. Fortunately for her, Ryan got in and took up where I left off. He and Blaise spent the rest of the morning making up pool games for each other. It was a joy to watch them having such a good time and I wondered how long it would last!

"What on earth is that?" I shouted above a loud buzzing noise on the patio. "It's getting louder Colin!" I remarked, putting my sun lounger in the upright position.

The children had left the pool as the heat of the day rose. They'd gone indoors to chill out with their portable CD players. I was perplexed by the high pitched buzzing and stood peering over the wire fence at the small ceramic factory.

"Perhaps it's the spray guns they use," I said thoughtfully.

"Why would they want to use a spray gun in a factory that's supposed to hand paint ceramics?" questioned Colin.

"I don't know. Perhaps it's a base coat. Anyway, they should be having a siesta by now, it's almost two o'clock."

"Perhaps they have a rush order on."

"Well Colin, if they have, I don't see many people rushing about."

"I haven't seen anyone there yet, have you?" asked Colin, rising from his lounger.

Colin collected his earphones from inside the villa and reappeared with his portable CD player. Spreading his towel over the sun lounger, he resumed his position. I stared hard at the factory. It was about 200' from the garden fence, a single storey building, with graffiti on the outside walls. It was surrounded by flat scrubland and had a small car park in the grounds. The last time Colin and I stayed at the villa; we never saw any activity and so I was utterly surprised that it had kick started into life so quickly. I never saw anyone going into the factory and never saw anyone come out of it. I never heard any cars pull up in the morning or depart at night. It seemed very strange.

"Perhaps I should have a walk down to the factory. Maybe they sell pots for the garden or something. I wouldn't mind having a browse," I shouted to Colin above the buzzing.

Colin hadn't heard a word I'd said. Not only was the buzzing so loud that you had to shout to be heard, but Colin was firmly entranced in his music. I noticed that his jaw had dropped slightly, which meant only one thing. He had nodded off.

The buzzing continued, the tone rising higher and higher. It was deafening. Colin snorted and opened his eyes. He pulled the leads from his ears and sat up.

"I must have nodded off," he remarked loudly and somewhat surprised.

"Yes you did, but only for a couple of minutes or so. I'm glad we didn't buy a house here Colin, that noise is driving me mad," I said, rising from the lounger and walking towards the wire fence.

Suddenly there was a lull in the noise and everything fell silent.

"Aha! Lunchtime, a break at last. Perhaps we can have a siesta too now that flipping noise has stopped," I said impatiently, walking back to the sun lounger.

I grabbed a cushion to support my back and arranged myself on the white plastic bed. No sooner had I lay down than the noise started up again.

"Oh hellfire!" I shouted. "It's impossible to sleep with that racket going on. Someone should report it to the environmental health. It could be dangerous," I said, spitting the words out.

Colin arose from off the sun lounger and made his way to where I stood. He looked over the fence at the factory.

"It looks empty Ange. I don't think anyone is there at all. Perhaps it's electric cables somewhere, overloading."

Colin looked skyward and the noise decreased in volume. He walked toward the lounger again, a puzzled expression on his face. He sat on the sun lounger and the buzzing started up once again, much louder than before.

"Right! That's it. I've had it," I said getting off the lounger. "I'm going indoors to lie down. At least I can stuff cotton wool in my ears and try to ignore it," I said agitated by the fact that I couldn't relax outside in the shade.

"What good is having a lovely patio with a superb view if you can't sit and pass the time of day on it? You can't even hear yourself think out here," I added and in a good old-fashioned sulk, headed for the lounge door.

Ryan and Blaise were listening to their music collection. I sat on the sofa contemplating a nap but I was so wound up by the constant buzzing that I couldn't sleep. It wasn't just the noise that had aggravated me, I was worried. What if it was electric cables? What if we were in danger? A thought hit me like a lightening bolt.

"Colin, I know what it is," I said charging through the patio door. "It's an electric fence, it must be and it's all around us. Yes, it's the fence."

Colin walked over to the fence. The buzzing stopped yet again.

"Try touching it," I encouraged.

"You try touching it!" he shouted back at me.

"But I might get hurt," I said meekly.

"Oh! So it's OK for me to get hurt but not you. Thank you very much."

"Well you're a man."

"Well what has that got to do with it?"

"Well, men are tougher than women."

"Oh are they?" Colin said, firing me a glance that said men are tougher only when women want them to be.

"And, you have a higher pain threshold than I do," I added quickly.

"Well, thanks a lot Ange; I know exactly how you feel about me now. It's OK if I get electrocuted because my pain threshold is higher. That's great!" Colin said in an amused but resigned tone, making his way towards the fence.

He looked at the concrete posts that held the wire fence in place.

"It doesn't look like an electric fence. I can't see where any current could come from. It's just a plain 2" chicken wire fence."

"Well, touch it just to make sure," I encouraged.

"Do you think I am mad woman?" said Colin exasperated.

"Well you don't think it's electric, so it won't electrify you."

"Electrocute," corrected Colin.

"Well whatever. It's the only way to find out."

"I'm not touching that fence," he replied firmly, as the noise rose again.

"What the heck is it Col?" I asked concerned.

"I don't know. We'll ask David when we see him. In the meantime, don't touch the fence and tell the kids not to either."

"Colin, if I tell the kids not to touch the fence, then they will. If I say touch it, they won't."

"What are you talking about?"

"The kids Colin. If we tell them to do something they don't, if we tell them not to something, they do."

"Well, don't tell them anything at all then just in case."

"OK. I'm going back inside; it's doing my head in!" I said, making my way towards the lounge door, heading for the sofa and my book.

Blaise and I stayed inside the villa; Ryan joined Colin on the patio. As the afternoon progressed, the buzzing continued but became less and less noisy, finally becoming spasmodic. I peered out on to the patio. Ryan was playing round the base of the lemon tree. Colin was staring at the fence. I returned to the peace and quiet of losing myself in my Maeve Binchy book 'Tara Road.'

"I know what it is!" shouted Colin excitedly. "Ange, come here, I know what it is!" he repeated.

I walked to the patio door and Blaise followed behind me.

"Well?" I said expectantly.

"It's insects," said Colin calmly.

"Insects!" I repeated, pulling a face.

"Insects!" Colin stated.

"Insects?" Blaise repeated.

"Yes, everyone, listen to me, it's insects. I N S E C T S!" he said, slowly spelling out the word.

"Listen to them, can you hear the buzzing? It's not as loud as before but it's still buzzing. Now Ryan, walk over there to that lemon tree," Colin commanded.

Ryan did as he was asked. The buzzing stopped and then slowly started again, reaching a crescendo.

"Ryan, stamp your foot," Colin ordered.

Ryan stamped his foot down hard. The buzzing stopped again. Slowly, with no further movement, the buzzing started over again. One by one, we took it in turns to test out Colin's theory. Each time one of us walked near the tree or bushes, the buzzing stopped.

"It's crickets," said Colin triumphantly. "I've read about Crickets and saw a David Attenborough TV documentary about them too. When they get too hot, they vibrate their back legs to cool themselves down. That's what we can hear."

"Amazing," I added, shaking my head in disbelief. "Who would think they could make a noise that loud?"

"I sat and watched Ryan running around outside and sure enough, each time he went near the bushes or trees, the noise stopped.

"There are shrubs growing all along the fence border, around the entire circumference of this plot. That's why you thought it was an electric fence. The insects are in the shrubs," Colin said triumphantly.

"Well who'd have thought it?" I said relieved. "I was beginning to feel quite unsafe Colin. Fancy that. Crickets!"

We all felt a lot more relaxed after Colin's discovery. I was pondering where we could stay if the villa had developed an electrical fault. So, the discovery put all our minds at rest. As the sun cooled, the crickets became less and less noisy. We slipped into the pool once more for a nice cool dip, swam a little and watched the children dive for the pool toys.

"Let's leave the pool to the kids," Colin said, climbing the ladders. "Time for a snooze."

I climbed out and rested on the pool ledge while the children started a new game, 'Blaise and Ryan's Olympic Games.'

Our children's imagination never ceased to amaze me. Ryan and Blaise were acting the parts of several people. They were fascinating to watch. But just as the real Olympic Games have an edge of competitiveness, so did Blaise and Ryan's version. I could hear them disagreeing with each other, becoming argumentative. I sat quietly and listened to them for a while. They were obviously in a huff and not speaking to each other, as they left the pool and went their own way.

After some considerable thought, I decided to ask each of them for their version of what had happened. It unsettled me when they had a falling out. They saw each other little enough as it was and I wanted them to treasure the time they had together, not argue, but I guess that's what normal everyday family life is like. Asking a ten and fourteen year old not to argue is probably something of a tall order. I asked each of them if they would write an account of what had happened in their version of the 'Olympic Games.' As always, Blaise was happy and eager to oblige and I passed her my journal and pen. She sat for a moment with the end of the pen resting on her bottom lip, and then began to write:

Blaise's version:

'Me and Ryan had a small fall out and decided to play are own games. I didn't watch Ryan that much but I did see him pretending to be the fastest swimmer in the champion ship. He was also pretending to be a common tater. I was a butiful world champion dancer in the water. I was a bit noisy when I jumped in. I splashed water every where but I ignored that. I did flips, handstands, legs in air while swimming, turns and loads more. I WON. I also pretended to be a common tater. I remember saying "She has some elegent moves and she's won." I thought they were elegent but Ryan didn't. After a while, Ryan came over and asked me if we wanted to play with each other again I said YES then I asked him if he wanted a race and he said YES. So we did two lengths. Ryan won but I did a butiful turn then spun back from it. I then stopped playing Olympics and played a different game till bed. This is my version. By Blaise.'

Ryan's version:

' . . . .'

It was obviously something Ryan didn't want to talk about. Eager to lighten everyone's mood, I suggested that Colin and Ryan drive into town to see if the sports car rally was still on. We ate a simple meal on the patio in relative silence. Blaise didn't want to talk to Ryan and Ryan didn't want to talk to Blaise. After our meal, Blaise and I relaxed inside the villa. We listened to music, read magazines and wrote our journals. Colin and Ryan drove to the rally. About an hour later, I heard the car pull back into the drive, as Ryan and Colin appeared, bleary eyed. They said they had seen some very nice cars but they were both very tired and decided to return.

It was ten o'clock, still relatively early. The combination of fresh air, sunshine, swimming and outdoor activities made us relaxed and ready for sleep. After a treat of ice cold bars of chocolate (that almost broke what few teeth I had left,) and a fizzy drink, we went to our beds. We could see fireworks in the distance. Perhaps another village was celebrating their Romano y Festes and the young women and men of the village were strutting around the town like proud peacocks and peahens. I checked all the fly screens were in place before opening all the bedroom windows. I turned Ryan and Blaise's fans on to the maximum speed before turning off the remaining lights. The evening breeze rustled through the Pine trees and perfumed the air.

The heat was oppressive and I expected a storm to break. The air was heavy and humidity was high. It reminded me of a holiday I took on the island of Majorca one August. I had gone with my friend and her three-year-old son for a fortnight's holiday in Palma Nova. I had never travelled abroad in August before, preferring to take a break in May or October, when the temperature was cooler. Nothing prepared me for what I experienced. It was so humid it felt tropical. I caught tonsillitis on my second day there and spent most of my two-week holiday in bed. My fever took five days to break and it was the worst holiday I ever remembered taking abroad. The doctor forbade any sudden changes in temperature. Why she thought I was going to experience this I really don't know. There was no let up from the heat. She did however ban me from the swimming pool. It had been a great shame because the pool was the only thing that cooled me down.

The worse flood I had ever seen occurred while I was there. There was a terrific storm and rain drops the size of tangerines fell. Within two hours, the entire road at the front of our hotel was under water, all the pool areas flooded and all electricity in the hotel failed. The sound of the rain on the balcony was frightening and it continued for two whole days. This was the first time since that holiday in 1988 that I had ever been abroad in August and I hoped a similar storm was not about to let loose on us.

Colin turned our bedroom fan up to maximum speed and with a sigh, I lay atop the bed, thinking about whether or not to find a synchronized swimming club for Blaise. She looked quite elegant pirouetting and making large swirls in the turquoise pool. Perhaps I would check it out on the Internet when I returned to England and see what I could find.

Chapter 13
Pork and Plastic

Lord, but the fan was so noisy! It was still dark outside. Colin tossed and turned in bed beside me. I too found it hard to sleep and tossed and turned along side him.

"No, that's not going to work," I said, getting out of the bed and feeling my way along the corridor to the bathroom.

I pressed the light switch and fumbled along the lounge mantelpiece for Colin's mobile telephone. At least it had a time display on it. According to the mobile, it was half past two in the morning. I remembered that Colin hadn't set the clock for Spanish time, which made it half past three. Goodness, it was unlike me **not** to be able to sleep. Had I forgotten to say my prayers? That must be it. I never settled until I had said my evening prayers.

"Is that you Angela?" Colin called from the bedroom.

"Yes, go back to sleep it's the middle of the night."

I turned off the bathroom light, felt my way along the wall for our bedroom door again, sat on the edge of my bed and said my prayers. Feeling relieved, I flopped back into the bed making a mental note to explain to God why I couldn't get on my knees just now to say my prayers. Colin continued to toss and turn for most of the night. I tried counting sheep but it didn't work. I just couldn't drop off and felt wide-awake.

Determined not to get up, I lay there for ages, staring into the darkness. There was nothing I could do at such a ridiculously early hour of the morning, it was pitch dark outside and if I watered the garden it would set off the Villamarchante dogs version of the midnight call from Walt Disney's '101 Dalmatians.' I padded along the corridor again to Colin's mobile telephone and touched the display, waiting for the luminescent glow. It was half past four and only the constant whir of the fan in our bedroom broke the eerie silence.

The kitchen was at one end of the villa, down the corridor to the left of our bedroom. I put the light on, hoping it was not intrusive and wouldn't disturb anyone and poured myself a glass of milk, hoping it would make me feel sleepy. I read somewhere that milk was supposed to induce sleep. Draining my glass, I picked up the long handled soft brush and swept the floors of the villa. I started in the kitchen and swept my way methodically through the porch, hallway, bathroom and lounge. There was an awful lot of dust and although I couldn't really see how clean the floor was, judging by the amount of dust I had collected, the floor must have looked much better for the sweep. I took another quick peek at Colin's watch. Half an hour had passed. Great! What to do for the next two to three hours!

Thankfully at that moment, a huge yawn crept up on me and contented with my housework, I made my way back to the bedroom and lay down on the bed to the sound of the cockerel crowing. Daylight wouldn't be far away now. I closed my eyes and felt an overwhelming sense of gratitude, thankful for so many blessing in my life.

I awoke to sunlight streaming in through the bedroom window.

"What time is it?" Colin asked stretching his limbs.

"I don't know, I'll take a peek at your mobile phone," I replied, padding yet again down the corridor to the lounge.

"Half past eight," I shouted down the corridor.

I walked back up the corridor and peeked first in Ryan's room then Blaise's. They were nowhere to be seen.

"The children must be in the pool again," I shouted, making my way to the lounge.

I looked out onto the patio and there they both were. The morning training sessions had begun.

I busied myself with the usual breakfast preparation, putting a generous amount of bacon in the frying pan. I transferred croissants, fruit and drinks from one end of the villa to the other, armpits and hands full, three mosquito nets clamped firmly in between my knees. My walk was somewhat strange and would have qualified me for a star role in 'Monty Python.' It must have looked quite weird. I continued through the lounge door onto the patio and admired the magnificent view. I carefully placed the food on the table, took the mosquito nets from between my knees and covered up all the food before the flies got to it. Colin appeared at my side and gave me a quick good morning kiss.

"Come on kids, time for breakfast," he boomed over the rim of the pool.

"Did you see me walking like a Geisha just now?" I asked, taking a seat next to him.

"What's that smell?" Colin asked, ignoring my question, his nose sniffing the air. "It smells like burning plastic. Can you smell it Ange?"

"Not really, I can only smell the bacon. The BACON!" I shouted rising as quickly as I could, setting off like an Olympic power walker, down the corridor towards the kitchen.

The smoke that drifted down the corridor told me that all was not well. I took the smouldering pan off the heat, grabbed a nearby tea towel and frantically wafted the air, my eyes stinging from the billowing smoke. I opened the front door to the villa in the hope that the breeze would blow it through.

"Breeze, huh! That's a stupid idea!" I shouted to myself, frantically wafting the tea towel to and fro, this way and that.

"Mum, are you playing bull fighting?" Blaise asked, peering at me from the front door, as she sniffed the air, her nose twitching like a rabbit's.

"What's burning mum?"

"Your breakfast!" I answered curtly, removing the pan from the cooker ring.

I peered at the pan. It was black and smouldering.

"What on earth happened to the bacon mum?" she asked innocently.

Don't children just ask the silliest questions? They have the knack of stating the obvious and asking the ridiculous. I glared at her.

"What do you think happened to it?" I replied, still wafting the tea towel.

"It looks burnt to me mum."

"Angela, can you smell burning plastic, it's really strong," Colin added.

I poked around the frying pan with my fork. Black bits of bacon crunched and shattered in the pan. Although I like my bacon crispy, I wondered if I could actually salvage any of the black mess in the pan.

"Crispy but not like cinders," I whispered.

A huge sigh escaped me.

"Never mind mum, you can always cook some more," Blaise reassured.

I discarded the burnt bacon, tossing it into the rubbish bag and started to clean the pan. There were burnt remnants of bacon all over the pan base and it was very hard to scour off. After using about a quarter of a bottle of washing up liquid on it and having finally resorted to using a Brillo pad, I managed to clear most of the charcoal. Slowly, after much elbow grease, the pan came clean and I was ready to start over again.

"Can I help you mum?" Blaise volunteered.

"Oh sweetheart, that's very kind of you. But the pan will get very hot and hot oil spit's a bit. Better if you just watch mum for now."

I took the opened packet of bacon and lifted it out of its wrapper ready for transfer to the frying pan. I placed a couple of slices in the hot oil and was just about to put the third piece in when I heard Blaise shout.

"Mum, you have to take the plastic off it first!"

She rushed over to the worktop and grabbed the packet of bacon.

"What plastic?" I queried, my brows furled.

"This plastic," said Blaise, peeling a wafer thin layer of plastic film from a slice of bacon.

"Good Lord!" I exclaimed surprised.

I picked up a fork and flicked the two slices of bacon from the pan onto the work surface. The plastic had melted into the bacon and it resembled a waxwork image.

"I didn't even see the plastic. How on earth did you spot it Blaise?"

"Well mum, your eyes aren't so good are they? Remember, we used to play a game when we went on holiday, you used to be my legs and give me a piggyback and I used to be your eyes. Remember mum?"

"Yes I remember," I replied, smiling as I reminisced about our holiday in Estartit.

"Mum, I'll take the plastic off the bacon and then I'll snip the bacon edges for you, so they don't curl up."

"That would be fantastic Blaise," I replied, grateful for her help.

I could just imagine another batch of bacon and plastic filled croissants.

"Good heavens, I could have poisoned you all!" I shrieked in horror. "Plastic poisoning! I wonder what the anti dote for that is." I chuckled.

"Never mind mum, you didn't know, it's not your fault," said Blaise, as supportive as ever.

Suffice to say, Blaise carefully took the wafer thin strips of plastic from the bacon, snipped the edges and passed the slices back to me for cooking. Between us we finally produced a mouth-watering plate full of crispy bacon. We delivered it to Colin and Ryan, placing it on the patio table and feasted on it. It was scrumptious.

"I wonder what the burnt plastic smell was," I said, winking at Blaise across the table.

"Oh it was probably from the ceramic factory," said Ryan, oblivious to my kitchen catastrophe.

I smiled at Blaise willing her not to tell.

"It probably was," I agreed, winking at Blaise, who immediately winked back.

Breakfast over; we sat surrounded by the green Pine forests and hills of Villamarchante. The dogs in the valley stirred, barked and howled to greet the new day. We swam, played bat and ball and watered the garden. Blaise held the hosepipe and I directed her to some of the more treacherous parts of the garden, where it was too rocky underfoot for me to tread. I didn't want to run the risk of a twisted ankle but Blaise was nimble footed.

The vine that covered the carport was heavy with luscious green grapes. They hung down from the metal carport in huge bunches. There were so many of them, you could have eaten a kilo every day and still not made an impact on them. There was only one vine but it had spread to cover the entire carport frame. After watering the Jasmine, we rested for a short while and discussed what to do for the rest of the day. Tomorrow was going to be quite stressful for us. We were going to sign for the house.

"Let's go to El Osito or Heron City," I suggested.

"Heron City, hurray, yes!" cried Blaise with glee.

"OK, Heron City," Colin agreed, adding "El Osito won't be open today Angela, its Sunday."

"Oh yes, I forgot. Well Heron City is fine with me," I replied.

"Go get showered and changed kids, last one in the car is on gate duty," Colin said, racing them to the bathroom.

"That's not fair," Ryan laughed. "We always have to open and shut the gates anyway."

Colin made it to the shower first and as usual, the kids had to open and shut the gates before climbing in the car for a trip to Heron City.

We drove down the CV35, past the huge giant panda logo of El Osito. As expected everything at El Osito was closed. It was Sunday and not a supermarket anywhere would be open. Colin continued further down the CV35 to Heron City. The car park was almost full, indicating that it was definitely open. It was Ryan's first trip to Heron City and we were glad there was something for the children to do.

Ryan was impressed by the multi coloured lights of the fountains and even more impressed by all the pretty girls that seemed to be milling around, with their long shiny black hair, skin tight jeans, studded belts and stiletto heels. I'm not sure if he ever really saw anything else at all there, but from the smile on his face, he was happy and, as every parent knows, if the children are happy, the parents are happy.

Although Heron City was aimed at luxury spending and the pursuit of pleasure (not for any serious necessity shopping,) there was one small shop that seemed to sell a multitude of oddments for the home. There were scented candles, teapots, coasters, place mats, tea towels and other bits and pieces. One particular item caught my eye. It was a lovely blue linen laundry bin, the colour of a summer sky, supported by a very shiny metal frame, which folded neatly together when not in use. It would be wonderful for 'Bona Gent.' Having made a note of the price, I herded my family from the shop. Blaise spotted some small soft toys and was making pleading noises in my direction. I gave her the same familiar reply that had been played over and over again like a favourite record that loses its impact after a certain length of time.

"You know the rule Blaise!" I replied sternly.

"I know mum, one toy in one toy out. I promise mum, if I can buy this, I will definitely sort a toy out when I get home."

"Hmm, will you though?"

"Honest mum, I will, honest," Blaise pleaded.

"We'll see."

"But mum, I will really, I will."

"I said we'll see Blaise. I'll think about it and next time we are here, I'll let you know my decision."

"But mum, someone else may buy it if I don't get it now," she sulked and her whole body creased as if she had been struck a mortal blow."

I stood and stared at the other thirty or so identical small soft toys that lined the shelf.

"Look Blaise, there are plenty of them, it's highly unlikely that they will sell out."

Blaise recognized defeat looming and tried one last appeal.

"But mum, they are not the same as this one. This one has a cute face and its eyes are different."

I looked at the toy Blaise was holding in her hands and then looked at the other toys on the shelf. They seemed identical in every way possible. It was time to play my trump card.

"It's the Sabbath Blaise. We don't buy things on the Sabbath."

"No mum," she replied, realizing there was no way she was going to get the toy on this particular visit.

She placed the toy back on the shelf.

Thank goodness I knew my daughter well. In a few days, another toy would have taken the place of this one and the next one would be just as impossible for her to live without and so on and so forth. I looked at her sad little face, as mother guilt crept over me. I needed a diversion.

"Come on everyone, let's have a look in the sports shop," I suggested.

"That's a great idea," added Colin, "I think we could all do with some new swimming goggles. Mine have about had it."

"So have mine," added Ryan.

"And mine keep breaking all the time mum, you know at the side, the strap keeps coming undone," Blaise quickly added.

"OK, over to the sports shop then," I conceded, glad of the diversion.

Inside the shop was heavenly. It was fully air-conditioned! Quickly looking around, the shop was split into sections for each hobby or sport. Within each section was displayed all manner of clothing and equipment appropriate to that particular sport or hobby. There were running shoes, tops, cycling shorts, swimming trunks, tennis skirts, tracksuits and everything was conveniently under one roof.

Colin priced four sets of swimming goggles, made a note of the prices and lazily browsed the rest of the shop.

"I'm getting hungry," Colin said, looking longingly at the kebab counter.

"So am I Colin, but it' Sunday," I replied.

"We've nothing at the villa Ange; we only have enough for a quick breakfast tomorrow."

"Oh please mum, can we have a kebab? Ryan do you want a kebab?" Blaise quickly asked.

Ryan knew better than to answer immediately. He had spent a lifetime learning to judge the mood and tone before making any reply. He remained silent.

"We will get something here Ange; it will cheer the children up. We really **don't** have a lot to eat at the villa."

We made our way to the kebab house and sat down at the nearest table while Colin ordered huge kebabs for us. The food arrived quickly and our ticket number was called out. Colin took the ticket to the counter and collected the food. He placed the food down on the table in front of us and we tucked into the meat and salad enthusiastically.

"It's alright here," Ryan said in typical teenager response mode.

He continued to stuff the kebab in his mouth like he hadn't eaten for a week. Colin and I laughed and wondered where he put it all.

We finished the delicious kebabs and headed back to the sports shop to buy the swimming goggles. I chose a cheap pair while Colin, Ryan and Blaise opted for brand names. The children were delighted with their goggles and gave Colin and me a big hug. I said a silent prayer.

"Please Lord, don't let Blaise remember the soft toy, please let her be so happy with the goggles that she forgets the duck."

As always, my prayers were answered and not a mention of the soft toy was made. Feeling satiated and happy, we made our way back to the car ready for home.

"Let's show the children Pedralba on our way back to the villa," Colin whispered. "We can show them the stream running through the village," he added excitedly.

The children, having overheard Colin, cheered at yet another bedtime delay.

"The houses are extremely old," I explained, painting a verbal picture of the tiny crumbling houses, each house with its miniature bridge from the front door over the stream into the street.

"If I had the money, I would buy those properties and develop them. In fact, I would buy the village and make it a perfect place, just like the man did in the film 'Big Fish.' Do you remember Colin?"

For some reason, Colin and the children thought this was extremely funny and laughed at me.

"You can't buy a whole village mum," chided Blaise.

"Why not?" I quickly replied.

"Dad could make them an offer they can't refuse," joked Ryan.

"You make it sound like your Dad's in the Mafia or something."

"Yeah mum, but he's always saying that back home, about his favourite Oast house."

"Well you have got a point I suppose," I replied, remembering the many times Colin had said those words each time we drove past the enormous Oast house.

I laughed and looked at Colin's face, the corners of his mouth creased in a smile, his dimples clearly visible.

"And then I would write a book about it. I would call it 'The Good People of Pedralba.' Wouldn't that be great?" I added, still in my daydream.

"Yeah and then they could make a film of it," added Colin.

Carried away by my fantasy, I had bought the village, lovingly restored it and left the inhabitants to live there rent free, in return for olives, oranges and the odd crop of vegetables. I bought the new agricultural machinery needed by the people's co-operative and brought wealth and wonder to the tiny village of Pedralba. The sight of the weary, old, crumbling buildings of Pedralba shook me back into the present as quickly as I had wandered from it.

"Mum, it's so old!" gasped Blaise in disbelief, as she looked at the narrow cobbled streets.

There was something about Pedralba that made it totally enchanting. It was the very fact that it looked old, with its crumbling walls and buildings that endeared it to everyone. It was like the faded pair of denims that you had the best of times in, threadbare and torn; you simply can't bear to detach yourself from them, even though you know they should have been cast off a long time ago. You cling to them like a faithful dog. That was the way I felt about Pedralba.

"One day, I am going to park up and walk every single street in this village," I said purposefully and determined that one day I would.

A movement ahead of us on the dusty road caught our attention. A man appeared from a doorway in front of us to the left. He was carrying a baguette. Like eagles, we fixed our gaze upon him. We spotted a small sign above the doorway that read 'Pan y Dulce.'

"Bread and sweets," I translated slowly.

"Let's take a look," Colin added, pulling the car up alongside the very high-sided kerb, what I considered to be one of the true trademarks of real Spain.

"It's Sunday Colin, surely it won't be open."

"Well, someone just came out of there, so let's take a look."

Colin parked the car and we walked across the small road to the door. Colin was right. The sign 'abierto' clearly showed in the window.

"It's open," we said in unison somewhat surprised.

I was more than a little relieved since we had no bread whatsoever for tomorrow's breakfast. Once inside, we saw the most delicious looking cakes on display. I spoke in my best 'Spanglish' and enquired about the price of the cakes.

"€18," the young Spanish man replied.

What a bargain, a gateau that would keep four of us going for at least a week!

We chose the orange cheesecake and asked for two baguettes. Summoning my best knowledge of the Spanish language, I enquired if the shop was open every Sunday. The young man behind the counter said it was. He grinned and apologized for not being able to speak English very well. We assured him that we understood him perfectly well and that it was us who should be apologizing for not being able to speak Spanish. Once again, Colin and I discussed learning Spanish in readiness for our next visit to Spain.

I looked around the tiny shop. It was quite dark and the walls were nicotine stained. There were about four or five square tables dotted around the floor space, some with dirty espresso cups on them and some with ashtrays overflowing. I supposed it was a typical Spanish Salon de Te. The glass counter was sparsely stocked and I wondered if this was to prevent flies from landing on the pastries and cakes. Or, was it more likely that on a late Sunday afternoon, most people had already purchased their tasty treats? Whatever the reason, there was not a lot left. We thanked the young Spanish assistant and left the shop.

"We'll have to bring the children here for a hot chocolate and a cake," Colin remarked, crossing the road towards our car.

"It's lucky we found somewhere open for bread, especially on today of all days. Very unlike Spain isn't it, you know, to be open on a Sunday?"

"Well, there's nothing open anywhere else, we were fortunate to find it really," Colin finished.

"That's what I was thinking," I added, feeling a little guilty that I hadn't planned forward sufficiently to have provisions in for Sunday.

I had been making a great effort back home, preparing everything on the Saturday for Sunday evening. Sundays had been much more relaxed and restful for the little extra effort it took me on a Saturday. But, things on holiday always seemed different and we never really planned too far ahead. One of the pleasures of a taking a holiday was not being organized all of the time. Feeling happier with myself for at least having found provisions for Sunday, we headed out of Pedralba, slightly more in love with it than when we entered.

We arrived at the villa hot and tired. The sun was shining, the Pine trees scented the air and we all had new swimming goggles. Colin and I headed indoors for a siesta; we were weary and tired out from the previous night's disturbed sleep. The children of course, headed straight to the pool.

"What time is it Colin?" I screeched through a yawn.

Colin picked up his mobile telephone and stared at the display, his eyes screwed up trying to read the small numbers.

"Six o'clock," he answered placing his phone down.

"Wow, that time already. Where are Blaise and Ryan?"

"They're still in the pool."

"No, you're joking?"

"I'm not. You know the kids, give them a swimming pool and they will entertain each other all day."

"I'm going to put a chicken in the oven to roast and we can have it with salad and fresh bread for tea."

"And orange gateau for dessert. Fantastic!" Colin added, licking his lips.

I put the oven on and prepared the chicken, liberally sprinkling it with olive oil, fresh rosemary, sage, salt and pepper. Colin put a CD on and turned up the volume. Another 'Sounds of the 70s,' great! I felt incredibly happy and cheered as the first song boomed out.

'I'll keep working my way back to you babe,
With a burning love inside,"

I started to sing as loud as I could. The song always put me in a good mood and before my disc slipped, I had performed step aerobics to it. Exercising to music somehow seemed easier. Colin had set up an exercise play list for me on the PC and I used to work out in the kitchen each night after work. It was great and an hour's step aerobics always passed at lightening speed.

"Shall we go and join the children then?" I shouted from the kitchen, pausing at my favourite bit …

"Forgive me girl,
Come on, give me a chance,
Won't you forgive me girl,"

I continued the song, wiping sweat from my top lip. It was very hot inside the villa and the heat from the oven added to the soaring temperature inside.

"Shall we take a dip in the pool then Col?"

"Sounds good to me," he replied, his footsteps echoing down the corridor as he made his way to the lounge door.

I sprinkled a little more salt, pepper and herbs over the skin of the chicken, added another drizzle of olive oil for good measure and then slid the roasting tin into the hot oven. I quickly put on my costume and went to join the others in the pool.

Colin dived in as I approached. I slowly trod the pool steps, taking hold of the pool thermometer on my way. The water was warm and I screwed up my eyes to read the temperature. It looked like 28 degrees. I slowly felt for the last step and dropped silently into the pool. I put on my new swim goggles and swam the length of the pool. On my way back to the ladders, I felt an uncomfortable pain jab my lower back. I stopped and slowly brought my legs down in the water. I made my way, tortoise-like, toward the ladders and made a grab for them. Breaststroke was still out of the question. I trod the water and looked at the stunning scenery surrounding the villa. It didn't matter how many times I looked at the view, its simple beauty always made me catch my breath and count my blessings and in so doing, the pain of my injury subsided and eased off.

Colin and the children were fooling around and playing games with each other. I kept to the outside edges of the pool, well out of their way. I finished my exercises and left them to their raucous play, while I relaxed on the sun lounger. I turned the pages of a Mills and Boon romance while their tomfoolery continued. However, it wasn't long before their high spirits progressed to outside of the pool. This entailed Colin and Ryan running off with each other's shorts. They laughed hysterically at each other. I made my way into the kitchen to check on the roast chicken. I saw Colin stark naked, carrying Ryan to the pool. I watched as Colin threw him in, the shock waves spilling over the edges of the pool as Ryan's body made contact with the water. Blaise shrieked and said it was gross to be running around stark naked. I totally ignored them, grabbed a handful of salted nuts, took my fizzy bottle of Fanta lemon and headed back outside to the patio. Colin and the children were laughing so hard; they had to hold their sides. It reminded me of something I'd recently heard on Radio 2. Apparently, if you had a good laugh, a real belly laugh, the sort that made you cry, for every minute that you laughed it was supposed to add nine minutes extra to your life. If that was true, then we were all doing just fine. I watched Colin run naked around the pool, Blaise shielding her eyes in disgust. Ryan rolled around in laughter. Finally, Colin launched himself into the pool, with a magnificent belly flop that had us all holding our sides in laughter.

Chapter 14
A Tale of Two Chickens

'Dear Diary,

Today is **THE** *day! Today we are going to sign for the house, today we get the keys and today, Bona Gent becomes ours! Hurray!*

I arose very early, feeling on cloud nine. The whole day is going to be spent rushing here there and everywhere and the children, bless them, have offered to clean Ann and David's villa from top to bottom. They promised Colin and me that when David comes to check us out, everything will be spit spot and we have nothing to worry about. Ryan assured us, all would be OK. He and Blaise would leave no stone unturned and no corner unswept! Even the fridge would be emptied, the garden watered, the cooker cleaned and all our bags would be packed and ready to go on our return. It's such a relief because Colin and I know that today is going to be one of the most important days of our lives. It marks the realization of a dream for both of us. We have come through such a lot together and the past couple of years have been hard. Colin has put up with such a lot from me. I don't know how he's managed to keep sane because I've certainly had stages of pure insanity. I blame hormones of course, but it must have been hard for Colin to understand (if he ever did understand.) I remembered years ago, when mum was still alive, there was a

big argument going on in the kitchen. My sister Linda and I had gone to bed.
The argument was about lots of things. I had never heard my Mum and Dad
argue as bad before and I hid under my blankets trying to blot out the noise.
But it didn't work. I didn't understand any of it of course, I don't even know
to this day what it was about but I do remember dad saying quite clearly,

"I can't do right for doing wrong Marian. Tell me what I am doing
wrong."

*Of course having begun the menopause myself, I now know or at least
understand a little of the situation they must have been in. Colin had said the
exact same thing to me. I recalled a time when I hated the whole world and
his dog and didn't know why. But there's no point dwelling on it. At least
not today. Not today of all days. Today is THE day. A landmark and an
historic day for Colin and me.*

Colin and I dressed soberly befitting a day in a notary's office in the
city of Valencia. Our first stop was VSI's office in Villamarchante. We
greeted Sally, who informed us that Jose Antonio would be driving us to
the CAM Bank. She told us Alfredo was on holiday and that his mother,
Masie would be at the notary's office to represent VSI. The proceedings
would all be in Spanish but there would be an interpreter in attendance.
Colin and I were both relieved. Only idiots would sit through the whole
proceedings in Spanish, sign and commit themselves without a word of
English being spoken. And Colin and I were not idiots!

Jose Antonio drove us to the centre of Valencia. I sat in the back,
content in my own little dream world, while Jose Antonio drove us
through all the back streets and short cuts to the city. We arrived at the
CAM Bank about half an hour later and Colin and I went inside and
withdrew some money, just in case of emergencies. We were not sure if
we had to hand over any more cash for fees or anything and Alfredo who
had arranged everything with the bank, was on holiday. I didn't want
anything to go wrong so we agreed to go laden with cash just in case. We
probably had about €5000 with us, just in case of emergencies. We got
back into the car and Jose Antonio drove us to the notary's office. He
parked in the buildings basement car park and the three of us climbed
the stairs to the notary's office.

We were shown into a room with a large oval table with eight chairs placed around it. Colin and I sat down next to each other and Jose Antonio sat with us. Masie arrived next, followed shortly after by the sellers, Juan and Julia, who had brought a family friend along with them as a representative. A member of staff from the CAM bank arrived next, a dark haired woman, probably in her late twenties. She was very friendly and smiled at us, shaking our hands in turn. We sat around the large oval table staring at each other for what seemed like a long time. The door opened, its slight creak breaking the silence. A gentleman in a dark suit appeared.

"This must be the notary," I whispered to Colin.

"I don't think so Angela, he's not carrying any papers," Colin replied seriously.

Jose Antonio went to fetch some more chairs, as those around the table were now occupied. He passed three more chairs into the room and we all squeezed up closer to each other. The man in the dark suit was also from the CAM Bank.

"What's happening?" asked Colin under his breath.

"I don't know!" I hissed, through clenched teeth.

"This is ridiculous Angela. We have been sitting here for fifty minutes. I feel stupid just sat here."

"I do too, but there's not a lot we can do about it."

"I thought we were having an interpreter."

"So did I."

People bobbed in and out of the room like yo-yos and I wondered what was going on. Colin was getting more and more anxious by the second and I was beginning to feel out of my depth. I decided to say something. I would count to ten and then demand an interpreter. I took a deep breath.

"One, two, three," I whispered.

I took another deep breath.

"Four, five, six, seven," I murmured, wondering why everyone was acting like nothing was happening? Why was it only Colin and I appeared bothered?

"Eight, nine, nine and a quarter, nine and a half, nine and three quarters, ten!"

"Where is our in.." I was just about to say 'interpreter' when the door was positively thrown ajar and in walked a very erect, smart looking gentleman in a navy blue pin stripe suit. Chairs scraped on the tile floor as everyone stood to attention at his entry.

"Perhaps he's a judge," I whispered to Colin under my breath.

"Why would he be, we are not on trial," Colin answered anxiously.

Introductions were quickly made and the door opened yet again. In walked a very pretty blonde haired girl. She introduced herself as 'Socorrista' the interpreter. I mouthed her name slowly,

"S o c o r r i s t a."

"Si, yes," she answered politely, showing a beautiful set of evenly spaced brilliant white teeth.

The notary sat down and unfolded his files, turning over the pages of the paperwork inside. Documents were handed out and it was very much a case of "Sign here" and "This is this and that is that," and so it went on.

The proceedings went so fast that I lost track of what was being said and who said what to whom. We signed and signed again. This continued for what seemed like ages. The notary proceeded to hand over various cheques. One was handed to Juan and Julia. Another to Masie and yet another to the bank representative and finally a cheque was kept by the notary himself. Suddenly, everyone was smiling. We listened intently to the interpreter, waiting to hear her say 'Free from all debts and all services fully paid.' Socorrista confirmed this to be true and everyone smiled again, shook hands, kissed each other and within two minutes, everyone except Colin, Jose Antonio and Socorrista had disappeared. Socorrista gave us her business card and told us to call her if we needed help in the future. I thanked her and looked at the small white card. The blue lettering was typically business-like, printed on both sides. I studied the writing.

"This isn't your card," I stated, handing it back to her. "You must have picked up someone else's card from your office. Look, it has someone else's name on it," I said pointing to the writing on the card. "No es Socorrista. You are Socorrista."

"Yes, I am Socorrista," she said, turning the card over to reveal the words clearly written on the back, "Socorrista. Helper," she added with her lovely smile.

"Oh I am so sorry, I thought Socorrista was your name," I said, turning scarlet with embarrassment.

"It's not a problem, don't worry. Enjoy your life in Pedralba," she answered before she too vanished.

Colin and I stood looking at each other in disbelief.

Jose Antonio gestured for us to follow him to the car park. On the way, he showed us some huge trees and told us they were famous in Valencia. They were over a hundred years old. They were magnificent looking with trunks broader than I had ever seen. He asked if we minded stopping off at his home while he collected a letter he had to post. He said he lived in the city and it was not far away. We agreed and climbed in the car ready to set off for his apartment. Jose Antonio parked up outside his apartment block and gestured for us to get out of the car. Colin and I both looked confused as we got out.

"There," he said pointing to a tiny café bar and ice cream shop.

He gestured for us to go to the Heladeria and get an ice cream while we waited for him. We took seats outside on shiny chrome chairs and discussed what flavour ice cream we wanted. I opted for a tub of chocolate and vanilla, while Colin chose mango and vanilla. Colin ordered and paid for the ice cream tubs and we sat on the pavement chairs of the Heladeria celebrating our property acquisition with ice cream. It was delicious.

"That was bizarre wasn't it?" I remarked in between slurps of ice cream.

"It was. I didn't have a clue what was going on at one point. I was getting fed up with all the waiting around. What did you think?" Colin asked.

"I'm not sure. It was all very anti-climatic. Yes, definitely anti-climatic. I don't know what I was expecting, but I wasn't expecting to be sitting around a table for hours. And what about all those cheques! Blimey! I wonder how much we paid in commission to all those people. Did we pay **all** the commission do you suppose Colin?"

"Yep, we did. It was about £4,000."

Colin and I both sat there and ate our ice cream in silence. The meeting wasn't at all as I had imagined it would be. I had even thought of taking some very English treats for Julia, like Thornton's toffee or Branston fruity sauce. I even considered giving her some cheddar cheese.

Thank goodness I hadn't. It would have been so out of place. Still, we had the keys to 'Bona Gent.' 'Bona Gent' was ours at last!

Sitting in the sunshine on the side of the very busy road, I wondered if Colin had the keys to 'Bona Gent,' as I couldn't remember picking them up. I panicked. What if we had lost the keys already? Reading my mind, as Colin so often did, he placed the bunch of keys on the metal table and smiled.

Jose Antonio appeared from the doorway of the apartment block and waved to us. He crossed the road and joined us at the Heladeria and politely asked if we had enjoyed our ice cream. We told him that we had and asked if he also liked ice cream. He said he did and so Colin offered to buy him one in the flavour of his choice. He declined but said that he would accept an iced lemon drink instead. Colin handed him the lemon slush and we chatted for a few minutes. He told us that his apartment was over sixty years old and that it covered three floors. It sounded like a very big apartment. He finished his drink and gestured for us to get back into the car. He said Alfredo was on holiday in Argentina and the Audi he was driving belonged to Alfredo. He had loaned it for business use while Alfredo was away on holiday. He explained that his own car was very old and not very reliable.

"You can sit in the front if you want Angela," Colin said, opening the door for me.

"Thanks Colin," I replied gratefully, sliding onto the passenger seat.

"Back to Villamarchante to get our car. Vamos a Villamarchante por mi coche," I said confidently.

Jose Antonio and Colin smiled and the engine started.

The journey back to VSI's offices could only be described as something from 'Whacky Races.' No wonder Colin let me sit in the front. I clung on to the door handle with all my might. The whole journey resembled the 'Rock and Roller Coaster' ride at Euro Disney. In fact, it was faster and scarier. I was as white as a sheet when we got back to VSI's office.

"Are you OK?" Sally asked, as I entered the office.

My knees trembled and my hands shook.

"Yes fine," I lied, holding on to the desk for support.

My knees felt weak and my arm muscles ached from clinging on to the car door.

"Congratulations on your purchase," Sally said, in her friendly manner adding, "please call in to see us from time to time."

"Yes of course we will," I reassured her with a smile.

We said farewell with the usual three kisses, thanked her again for all her help and exited the office.

"Good luck!" she shouted, as we left.

Colin and I made our way hand in hand across the faded zebra crossing to the dusty, pot holed car park. It was half past two.

"Time for the afternoon Bull Run," I commented, as we climbed into the car. "Shall we go and get the children and bring them back to see it?"

"Yeah, let's do that," Colin answered. "Let's get the children and luggage, drop everything at 'Bona Gent' and come back and watch the bulls."

Excited as school children playing hooky, we drove to the rented villa.

We arrived feeling very excited and ready to tell the children that we were now the proud owners of 'Bona Gent.' Colin tooted on the horn and we waited for the children to open the gates. They dutifully opened them and closed them again behind us and we followed them into the kitchen. They had been busy cleaning the villa. It was spotless just as they'd promised. Even the fridge had been cleaned. The patio had been swept and the whole place sparkled. We gave Ryan and Blaise the biggest of hugs, smothered them with kisses and thanked them. The luggage had been placed in the kitchen ready to be loaded into the car. They looked at us sheepishly.

"OK. What is it?" I asked.

Years of experience in identifying sheepish looks meant one thing only. TROUBLE!

"Nothing, well nothing really, not really," Blaise spluttered.

"It's just that we dropped a vinegar bottle and the washing up bowl split," gushed Ryan.

"No problem kids, we can easily replace them," Colin replied calmly.

I watched them both sigh with relief. I had already purchased a new washing up bowl because it had begun to split when we first arrived. Its demise came as no surprise to me. I held up the replacement bowl ready to place it in the sink.

"How did you know it was split?" Ryan asked, his eyes wide with disbelief.

"Aha! Mums know everything!" I responded, winking at Colin.

"Come on Ryan, help me load up," Colin said, motioning for him to help.

The car was loaded quickly and we were ready to depart.

David arrived on time to check us out. We explained about the washing up bowl and vinegar bottle and agreed to replace the vinegar bottle, suggesting we leave it with Sally at VSI for collection. He returned our deposit and said we were very honest to even bother mentioning it. I showed him the new washing up bowl and he thanked me for taking the trouble to replace it. The villa was sparkling fresh and the smell of polish and disinfectant scented the rooms. Blaise and Ryan had quite obviously worked very hard and had successfully transformed the place. There was nothing for us to do whatsoever but to thank them once again and dole out more hugs.

We thanked David for the use of the villa and said that if we ever needed an overspill for family and friends, we would make contact with him. David said he expected his wife's family to move to Spain for good, although he didn't know exactly when that would be. He was confident that they would make the move though. He also said he wasn't sure if the villa was going to be let out in the future, as he had experienced a nightmarish rental just weeks before we had arrived. I asked him to recount the tale for us, our faces eager in anticipation of an exciting story. He said it was about a man and two chickens and he slowly began his tale.

David had received an enquiry from a Spanish man who wanted to rent the villa for a week. The enquiry had come from what David thought to be a reliable source, an estate agent; therefore there he was happy to accept the booking. He decided to check on the property to ensure that the guest was satisfied and that there were no problems. Upon his arrival at the villa, he said there were seven people staying there, the man, the man's wife, the man's children and his grandparents. The beds had been moved outside under the patio. David noticed that there were eggs in the garden and at the rear of the patio and a huge amount of feathers were strewn over the garden. Fearing the man had brought his own poultry with him to slaughter and concerned that the man had lied about the number of occupants, David asked him, in no uncertain terms, to leave. He later found chicken poo on the furniture and had been extremely worried incase it marked it permanently. He believed the man had killed one of the chickens, plucked it and then cooked it. The feathers strewn all over the garden behind the patio were al the evidence David needed. When the family had vacated the villa, David returned to check the property more thoroughly. To his surprise, he found a Bantam chicken up one of the trees. The poor bird was terrified of coming down. It had probably seen its companion killed and plucked before its very eyes. No wonder it didn't want to come down from the tree. Gradually, over a period of a few weeks, David and one of his friends managed to coax the Bantam down. Suffice to say, David was now the proud owner of the rescued Bantam. Compared to the previous tenants; we were the ideal guests and David assured us that we would always be welcome there. We thanked him for his story, which prompted exclamations of "You've got to be kidding!" and "No, they didn't kill and eat the chicken did they?" from the children. We explained to Ryan and Blaise that people in Spain lived differently from the way we did. They sat in the street and watched TVs through their open front doors. They brought their tables and chairs out and ate in the street. Rearing their own food and killing it when they needed it was no big deal for them. However, the children were stupefied by the tale and Colin and I tried to imagine the scene that must have confronted David.

We shook David's hand and bid him farewell. He in turn wished us the best of luck with our own place and said he looked forward to bumping into us in Villamarchante square at some time or other. With our car fully loaded yet again, we set off for Villamarchante to catch the end of the Bull Run. Unfortunately, by the time we had parked up and walked to the square, there was only about ten minutes left for the bulls to run. From the safety of the barricade, we glimpsed the rear of a bull heading round a street corner some 100' away, before we heard it being loaded into the livestock carrier. We promised Blaise and Ryan we would come back and see the bull run before we went back to England

and thankfully, we were all so excited about getting to our own villa, that everything else was soon forgotten. We drove straight to 'Bona Gent,' through the wonderful little village of Pedralba.

"Look kids, do you see the stream running in front of the buildings? That's spring water. People come with their empty plastic carriers to fill from the natural spring," I said, trying to make it sound like one of the 'seven wonders of the world.'

Finally, we showed them the seemingly endless columns of orange groves that filled the surrounding countryside for as far as the eye could see. They were quietly transfixed by them. Ryan, having never seen orange trees before in his life, thought the landscape incredibly beautiful.

"Are we nearly there yet?" Blaise asked, bringing us all back to the here and now with a bump.

"Yes Blaise, we are nearly there now," Colin and I chorused.

On we drove through the village, past open fields and finally into the road that led to our villa. We turned left at the 'Generalitat Valencia' sign and slowly drove along the narrow road. The pale terracotta wall of 'Bona Gent' came into view. Recognizing the wall, Colin turned left and we pulled up to the double gates.

"OK Ryan, it's the key with the green plastic cover on it. Unlock the gates and open them please," he instructed, handing Ryan the keys.

Ryan and Blaise sprung from the car and Ryan unlocked the gates in record time. They pushed the heavy metal gates open, holding them ajar while Colin drove in. Entering slowly to negotiate the gates, Colin pulled up to the lounge window and turned off the engine. We had arrived at our villa, 'Bona Gent.' Colin and I saw the gleam of excitement in the children's eyes, as they surveyed the pool and garden.

"Is that our pool?" asked Ryan excitedly.

"It sure is," Colin confirmed, walking over to help Ryan close the gates.

Blaise was jumping up and down with glee.

"We love it don't we Ryan?" she cried, jumping with joy.

Ryan was still taking everything in, the pretty front patio with its bright striped coloured Dutch awning, the swing sofa and the lovely turquoise tiled pool. I followed Colin to the door while he carefully tried keys in the lock, searching for the right one. Finding the correct key, he pushed open the sturdy double glazed door and we trooped in behind him, like baboons. The cool of the dark interior was welcoming and for a moment everything was quiet, each of us lost in our own thoughts.

"This is our Spanish home, 'Bona Gent' and we have endured a lot to be here in this house," I spluttered, tears pricking my eyes.

Colin disappeared through the opened front door and shouted to the children to help unload the car. Ryan and Blaise ran in and out of the bedrooms, deciding which room to claim as their own. Colin and I watched as Blaise showed Ryan around the house.

"So much for them leaving all the furniture," shouted Colin, as he made his way down the hallway, peering from bedroom to bedroom.

I sensed unease in the slight tremor of his voice. I wondered what could be wrong and whether it was something major.

"Well, they've taken the double beds, both of them have gone. We've got three singles and no double. Great!" Colin barked angrily.

"Let's go to the Carrefour, I need to pick up some bits and pieces, you know crockery, cutlery and extra pillows. I am sure we can order a double bed there and most things seem to be very reasonably priced," I answered, eager to ease the tension.

Sensing Colin's mood of displeasure and for the second time in the same day, our wonderful children assured us all would be well and they set about unloading the mountains of things I had brought with me for the villa. The car was emptied and Blaise and Ryan stood like centuries at either side of the iron gates, as Colin reversed the car out of the drive.

"See you soon kids, we won't be long!" I called back, waving to them as we headed down the road, bound for the Carrefour supermarket.

The Carrefour supermarket was a fifteen-minute car journey from 'Bona Gent.' It was situated in L'Eliana, just off the CV35 in the direction of Valencia. There were plenty of parking spaces and judging by the amount of cars in the car park, it was very busy.

"We'd better take a trolley each Col," I suggested, thinking of the bulky items we needed.

We each took a trolley and entered the store. I looked around for a store assistant and spotted one in the household section. I walked towards her and smiled.

"Is there anyone here who speaks English?" I asked.

"Ah si, si, uno momento," said the dark haired assistant, as she disappeared in the direction of the stock room.

A couple of minutes later, another dark haired lady appeared and greeted us in English. We explained our predicament.

"Can you help us to get a double bed?" I asked.

"Can we have it delivered?" Colin asked.

"And how soon can we have it?" I enquired.

"First you must choose a bed," she instructed.

"We already have," Colin said, pointing to the large double bed in front of us.

"And a mattress?" she enquired.

"Oh, we forgot that," I said wondering where the mattresses were kept. "We'll take that one," I added pointing to the nearest one I could see atop the bed.

"That is not possible madam, that mattress is for the display only," she answered politely.

She carefully pulled out a catalogue from the cupboard beneath her computer screen and thumbed forward to the mattress section. We looked at the symbols for medium soft or medium hard.

"This one," I said, pointing one out on the page.

She looked at us in amazement.

"That will do fine," I said convincingly, while she keyed in information on her PC ready for our order.

"How are you paying?" she asked politely.

"With my credit card," I said, delving into my handbag for my credit card and passport.

I handed the passport and the credit card to her.

"OK. Now it is processing," she said, tapping the numbers of the credit card in. "It will be possible to deliver on Thursday."

"Can't you deliver it before then?" Colin pleaded, his brow furled and forehead lined with worry.

"I'm sorry that is not possible. Thursday is our earliest for Pedralba. Give me your contact number and I will ask the driver to telephone you when he is on the way."

Colin called out his mobile number and the assistant wrote it on the delivery pad. She promptly handed us a copy of the order sheet and wished us a happy time with our new purchase.

Colin and I stifled our laughter.

"What on earth does she mean?" I giggled, pushing the large supermarket trolley to the household goods section.

Colin laughed and followed me into the crockery aisle.

Two hours later, the car was filled with crockery, cutlery, glassware, pillows, kitchen utensils, washing up bowls and cleaning stuff. Colin loaded the car and drove us back to 'Bona Gent.'

"At least we will have a bed soon," I chortled.

"That's three nights on the sofa for me then," Colin stated, a look of resignation on his face.

I laughed at his misfortune. Still at least we had two sofas for him to choose from. Thankfully, Juan and Julia had left us a three-seater and a two-seater sofa. Sadly, they had taken the lovely mosaic patio table from the front patio. I was particularly disappointed that Juan and Julia had taken it, as the colours of the mosaics were an exact match of tiles on the patio exactly. Still, the table was their property and after all, you didn't leave all the furniture when you moved house in England did you? We were lucky to have been left anything at all.

"We did well really Colin, three single beds and fitted wardrobes in two of the bedrooms, free standing units in the other two bedrooms and plenty of storage, the dishwasher, washing machine, microwave and cooker. We are very lucky indeed," I finished.

Colin just nodded his head and said "Hmmm."

We arrived home and found the children had unpacked and were celebrating. They had picked their own rooms and had arranged them to their liking. The air-conditioning was on full pelt and the rooms were cool. Colin and I made a start on the luggage. We unpacked mountains of things from the ugly green suitcase, ferrying them from room to room.

"I'm hungry Colin," I said, rubbing my stomach as it growled fiercely.

"Me too, let's eat," he replied.

It was quite late and not wanting a huge meal so late in the evening, I prepared a very simple dish of cold meats, fresh bread and cheese, which we thoroughly enjoyed. The children cleared the pots away and I placed bed lined on the single beds. I gave Colin a sheet for the sofa and we retired to our bedrooms. I was so tired, I didn't even hear Colin or the children say goodnight. I mumbled a quick "Thank you Lord for everything," yawned, wished everyone a good night and settled on top of the bed for a much needed sleep.

Chapter 15
'Bona Gent'

I awoke feeling elated, cool and refreshed, having slept peacefully and contentedly.

"This house is so wonderful," I said aloud, listening to the echo down the corridor.

I had no idea what time it was. Perhaps I had woken up in the middle of the night, I really couldn't tell, as the metal shutters were down. I walked down the hallway, feeling the cool terracotta tiles under my feet. I peered into the lounge to find Colin still asleep on the sofa. Turning back, I retraced my steps and quietly tiptoed into each of the children's

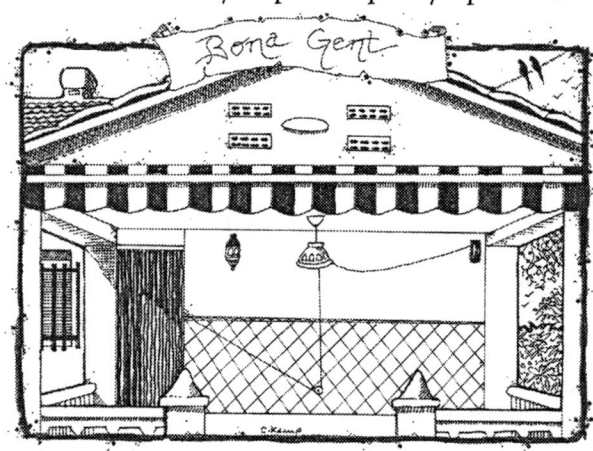

rooms. They too, were sound asleep and unaware of the new day. They were usually up and in the pool at the crack of dawn, but after such a late night, they definitely needed to sleep late.

'Bona Gent' was a wonderful villa. It stood on a rectangular shaped plot of some 527m². The villa itself was built on one level and consisted of a covered entrance porch, with access to the front door, leading into a large room with open plan dining area to the right and lounge area to the left. There was a double bedroom on the right, (a square some 12' x 12' had been allocated from the living space and had been walled off to create a bedroom.) An ornate wood and glass door led to a central corridor style hallway, with modern kitchen, modern bathroom and one double bedroom off to the left and two further double bedrooms off to the right. At the end of the corridor was a heavy-duty iron door, with reinforced glass panels.

The whole of the house had a terracotta tiled floor; cool under foot in the heat of summer. The house was double glazed throughout, with a white UPVC front door and white windows. Every window was fly screened, shuttered and protected with thick black metal window guards.

The dining area was sufficient in size to accommodate a dining table and ten chairs comfortably. Being totally devoid of furniture, this was where we put our bursting suitcases.

The lounge had two old sofas, a three-seater and a two-seater. They had blue nylon covers and had the appearance of something from the 1950s era. A huge open fireplace adorned the corner of the lounge, complete with mousetraps and ashes. The mantelpiece was made of red and black glazed bricks. I supposed this was the Spanish equivalent of an Inglenook. The lounge and dining area walls were painted lemon. There were black metal curtain rails, which looked quite modern against the lemon paint. A Calor gas heater stood in one corner of the lounge and an old pale beech effect TV stand stood against the wall to the left of the fireplace. A matching pale beach effect coffee table and bookcase had also been left behind. On the inside wall that divided the lounge from the kitchen, the huge air conditioning grill blew cold air with gusto.

The kitchen was a modern American kitchen. It had wall and base units in medium oak. It was equipped with a huge fridge freezer, microwave, dishwasher, electric oven and gas hob with extractor fan over. The unit tops were black and grey marble, with two deep round sinks and a very old brass tap that must have cost the previous owners a fortune. It reminded me of an old-fashioned water pump I had seen at Styal Mill in Cheshire. The kitchen was fully tiled in light grey, blue, green and terracotta. All the kitchen equipment seemed to be in working order.

The bathroom was undoubtedly my favourite room. It too, was fully tiled. On entry, the sink unit was on your right. a huge white porcelain sink set in a marble top, placed over a chestnut wood cupboard unit. Hand towel rails were fixed to both sides of the sink in the same rich chestnut wood. The white porcelain sink had cobalt blue leaf patterned border around the inside perimeter. It was exquisite. A chestnut framed mirror hung on the wall over the sink unit, the glass bordered by a blue and white check tile border to match the sink. A spotlight on the centre top of the mirror completed the unit. Next to the sink on the right was the bidet, with a matching chestnut flannel holder. Next to the bidet was the toilet with integral toilet brush and base and matching toilet roll holder. Along the far side of the room was a white bath, with telephone taps and wall fixing for the shower head. A blue shower curtain on an expandable white plastic pole hung the entire length of the bath. The bottom half of the walls were tiled in pale terracotta and the top half tiled white A blue, green and white patterned border tile divided the two colours. In all my life, I had never had a house with such an ornate and opulent looking bathroom.

Blaise had claimed the double bedroom off the lounge and dining area. It was painted pale blue and had a large, cream, built in wardrobe in the corner. There was a pink and white checked curtain hanging on a wooden curtain pole and a single Pine bed occupied the space under the window. A floating wooden shelf and two pictures in matching wooden frames hung on the wall adjacent to the shelf. The pictures looked like cartoon toddlers and Blaise really liked them.

Walking down the hallway, the next double bedroom on the right had been claimed by Ryan. Also painted in blue, it had similar built in wardrobes, a Pine coloured bookshelf and a fold up chair. A cream, tab top curtain hung on a wooden pole above the window.

The next door along on the right was also a double bedroom, painted in a slightly brighter shade of lemon than the lounge. There was no curtain rail and consequently, no curtains, but there was a light oak double bedroom unit that filled an entire wall.

The door opposite (the last door on the left on the hallway) was the fourth double bedroom. It was painted in the same bright lemon and contained a single wardrobe unit and a large Pine storage box. A wooden curtain pole held a cream muslin curtain that flapped gently in the breeze.

Every room had air conditioning, even the bathroom and the kitchen. The vents were placed above the doorways in each room, creating a vacuum when the air conditioning was in operation.

The villa was well laid out and it reminded me of Dr. Who's tardis. It looked quite contained from the outside but once you stepped through the front door, the full size of the house could easily be seen.

To the rear of the property was a separate concrete building, divided by a brick wall to make two rooms, each room with its own door. One room housed the Paellero (complete with wood store, grate and chimney breast for cooking paella and barbequing.) It had two huge white pot sinks (Armitage Shanks style) with chrome mixer taps, a double gas hob and oven and a front load washing machine. The floor was laid to grey and black marble effect tiles. There was a small double glazed window, an electric light switch and a double electric socket. There was also a small wooden kitchen utensil unit, which housed a variety of frying and paella pans. The adjoining room had shelves along the whole of one wall and there were a variety of toys and old bits of rubbish heaped in the corners. It needed a good clear out but would make a very useful storage room. The floor tiles were the same as in the Paellero.

Coming out of the back door and turning left along the rear of the villa, a further path turned left again along the side of the house. High up on the wall hung the air conditioning unit. It was colossal. Further along the path was a black metal door to a long and narrow tool shed. It was filled with all sorts of spanners, wrenches, saws, trowels and screws. Three rows of shelves stretched from one end of the wall to the other, each shelf about 8' or 9' in length. Colin had a safe place to store his tools and he was extremely happy about it.

Retracing my steps to the back door, I continued and passed a concrete table and bench set. The tops of the table and benches had been tiled. You could cook your paella and bring it straight to the table. Turning right to walk along the full length of the house, (the side nearest the road,) the tall cypress hedge, covered in cones, was broken at intervals by mature Jasmine shrubs, their white star shaped flowers falling to the ground like confetti as I passed by. The scent from these delicate pale flowers was heavenly.

At the front of the house, black railings and a matching gate separated the front patio from the pool area. I particularly liked the railings because you could lock off the pool area for child safety. Stepping onto the ornamental grey and terracotta patio, I pulled the lock back on the metal gate and entered the pool area.

The pool measured 14' x 28' exactly and was sunken into the ground. The pool ladders were situated to your right as you entered the pool area. The swing sofa, with its brightly coloured parasol, was to your left and an old green circular plastic patio table and four green chairs was next to that. At the bottom end of the pool, steep steps led to the pool under build, where the pump and the pool cleaning equipment was housed. The steps were very, very, steep. I would have to take great care going down them if I ever needed to adjust the timers or sort out the pool pump. The under build was filled with cobwebs and flaking whitewash. Thank goodness I wasn't afraid of spiders!

At the bottom of the plot was the pool house, flanked on each side by mature trees. The pool house was a separate concrete building and inside was a fully tiled white shower suite, which comprised of a toilet, washbasin and shower. A large white cupboard stored toilet rolls, soap, shower gel, bleach, cleaning fluids and shampoos. Above the sink was a large wooden framed mirror. To the right of the mirror, inset into the wall tiles, was an electric shaver point and an electric socket. The light switch was on the right by the door as you entered and overall, it was very impressive for a concrete hut. Sally at VSI had told us that it was common for people to swim and then shower and change in the pool house rather than leave a trail of water through their own home. .

To the right of the pool house was a huge fig tree, dripping with ripe, purplish black figs, the size of small pears. The ground was stained black and purple as the figs fell from the tree, hit the ground and burst open. The sticky and syrupy pulp stuck to the soles of my flip-flops. I felt like I had trodden in glue. Behind the fig tree in the corner was a small box made from wood and chicken wire. Inside it were the remains of some very large snails. About six large snail shells lay amongst the rotting leaf debris. I wondered if the owners had used snails in their paella. Yuck!

Walking along the other side of the pool, I arrived at the orange tree, heavy with deep green baubles of unripe fruit. I wondered whether we would be back to see them as ripe and juicy oranges.

The entire plot had a 3' wide border garden. Along the bottom and the roadside was the cypress hedge, interspersed with Jasmine and small ground covering plants with tiny red flowers. These tiny red flowers opened and closed with the sunrise and sunset. They gave excellent ground coverage and kept most of the weeds at bay. I had seen these tiny flowers in Gran Canaria the previous year and had remarked to Colin how pretty they were. Two hibiscus plants situated either side of the double metal gates, each put out a single red flower.

In the border garden along the boundary wall of our neighbour's plot, were bright red and yellow oriental lilies, a rubber plant, a rose tree, a rosemary bush, carnations, wild onions and more of the ground covering plants. The concrete wall was topped by more green wire fencing and lined with a green canvas covering on our neighbours side.

Large privet like shrubs in black plastic tubs had been placed at intervals along the entire perimeter of the villa's hedge. The leaves were very fleshy, smooth, but firm to the touch. A solitary pink geranium flowered in a black rubber pot at the front of the house and an ornamental tiered, cast iron plant stand, stood to the right of the patio.

Looking head on at the villa, the pretty covered patio with white balustrade gave much needed shade. A lovely blue multi coloured china light shade hung from the middle of the ceiling. There were two hooks on the wall, each holding a plastic fly swat. To the right was an old fashioned electric mosquito zapper. The patio had two electrical sockets. The covered patio was tiled from ground level to half way up the back wall in pale peach, trimmed with a narrow multi coloured border. The 2'6" high white balustrade, supported at two corners by white concrete pillars, bordered the patio and gave it real holiday villa appeal.

Attached to the wall above the covered patio was the striped peach and white Dutch awning. It wound out to about 9' and was at least 12' in width. Above the Dutch awning was an oval house plaque in 'French Script' lettering. It read 'Bona Gent.'

The balustrade gave way to a central entrance flanked by another two white pillars. At either side of the entrance were two white metal sun chairs. To the left of the covered patio was the lounge window. I took a seat on one of the metal chairs and found it surprisingly comfortable.

"Bona Gent!" I said aloud. "What are we going to do today then?"

I surveyed my dream home. I sat on my chair looking out on to a turquoise pool, surrounded by fruit trees. I felt that awful tightening and constricting in my throat, as tears pricked my eyes. This was a dream come true and I was overcome with emotion.

"Bona Gent. Good people," I whispered and closed my eyes, feeling the hot sun on my face, arms and legs. As my tears subsided, I wiped my eyes, blew my nose and sought the company of my family.

I spent the rest of the morning pottering around inside the villa, putting bits and pieces away and taking stock of all the household items. I found the huge, ugly green suitcase and unzipped it. It was so tightly packed that the zip practically sighed with relief as I unfastened it. It was crammed with all manner of items, place mats, table cloths, dish cloths, chopping boards, sheets, pillow cases, cork screws, ornament mats, coasters, clocks, batteries and an assortment of newly bought bed linen. I wandered around the villa, placing things here and there, pleased with the mountains of things I had brought with me. There were bath towels, hand towels, tea towels and face cloths. I had bought eight sets of bedding from Ikea and some lovely chopping boards with pictures of cats on them from a lovely little shop in Chatham Dockside Retail Outlet. They were terracotta coloured, with white and blue patterns border patterns and they matched the kitchen perfectly. The cobalt blue Ikea tea towels made the kitchen look fit for feature in any of the glossy 'House and Home' type magazines.

I had asked Colin, Ryan and Blaise to bring old T-shirts, shorts, swimwear and other clothing that they could leave at the villa, without being missed too much at home. Thankfully, we all had sufficient room in our inherited wardrobes to accommodate them. On my last trip to France, I had bought some anti-slip floor matting and Colin had cleverly rolled it up and packed it in the case. I laid it around the pool, happy that we had taken safety measures into account. Ryan and Blaise had a bad habit of running round the pool area however, having watched hundreds of children at the swimming baths, I came to the conclusion that all children run when they get out of a swimming pool. I don't know why they run, they just do. I had often heard a mum or dad shouting, "Don't run!" their hands over their mouths in worry, half expecting little Johnny or Jane to fall and crack his or her head open.

Having emptied and put away quite a lot of the case contents, I heard the children stir. They appeared sleepy and dishevelled and headed straight for the swimming pool.

"We're going for a swim before breakfast," they said excitedly, running towards the pool.

From inside the villa, I could hear their cheers and laughter as they splashed around. I smiled as I watched them jump in the pool, surface and climb out, only to jump in and repeat the process all over again. Colin opened his eyes slowly from his makeshift bed in the lounge.

"What time is it?" he asked sleepily.

I glanced at the clock on the wall. Its batteries had obviously run out.

"I have no idea Col," I replied, folding more bedding and throwing it over the back of the unoccupied sofa.

"Col, we have to get some money from the bank today. We can go to the branch at Riba Roja."

"OK, shall we say in about an hour?" Colin asked, pulling on his swim shorts. "I'm just going to join the children in the pool for a few minutes."

"Yes that's fine. We'll have a quick breakfast and then we'll go. The children will be OK here for a while. I don't think we could drag them away from the pool even if we tried," I added.

"OK. After breakfast then," Colin shouted.

I watched as he dived headlong into the deep end of the pool.

My usual morning ritual began once again, as croissants, cheese, ham, melon, peaches and all kinds of fruit jams were laid on the patio table. I placed two jugs of sweet Valencia orange juice at each end of the table.

I sat down and admired the wonderful colours on the table before me.

"Breakfast is ready!" I shouted and as if by magic, my family appeared, took their places at the table and folded their arms ready for prayer.

I could usually tell by the length of the prayer how hungry the person saying it was. This morning, Colin was in a very jovial mood.

"Into the mouth, over the gums, watch out tum, here it comes!" Colin joked, much to the amusement of Ryan and Blaise, who burst out laughing.

I giggled at his moment of lunacy and kicked him under the table, keeping my eyes closed. I waited for the laughter to die down and Colin began the prayer again.

"Amen!" we all chanted and reached for our favourites.

We munched our way through the food like hungry caterpillars and Colin gave the children their instructions for the day in between mouthfuls of ham and croissant.

"Clear the table, stack and turn on the dishwasher. Swim in the pool but come out of the sun at one o'clock. We should be back by then," he instructed soberly.

Colin and I got in the car and waited for the children to open the gates.

"Do you think they will come out of the pool at one o'clock?" I asked.

"Yes, their quite sensible Ange. They have learned their lesson I suppose. Ryan doesn't want a repeat of his Gran Canaria experience and Blaise has never forgotten when she burnt her shoulders in Turkey. They'll be fine, so don't worry."

Colin and I drove through the narrow cobbled streets of Pedralba, on to Villamarchante and finally on to Riba Roja. Fortunately, one of the ladies at the bank spoke a little English and she told me that I could use either my passbook or cash card to withdraw money. I stared at her blankly.

"Oh dear, we don't have either as yet. We are supposed to go to Valencia to collect them some time this week," I exclaimed, hoping she understood me.

The lady was most helpful and after completing papers for a manual transaction, I signed the necessary paperwork and she handed the euros to me. We thanked her for her assistance and left the bank with our supply of euros. We crossed over the road to a rather large Ferreteria. Judging by the window display, this one seemed to have a good supply of just about everything. We were introduced to Danny, who spoke excellent English. He told us that he could order anything for the pool or garden that we wanted. Colin was delighted as he eventually wanted to buy a pool cover. Danny advised us to measure the pool, telephone him with the sizes and he would make enquiries and get us a price. He handed his small white business card to Colin with a smile. Colin explained that we spent most of our time in England however Danny said he would simply order one ready for delivery to us when he knew we would be back at the villa. He reassured us that it wouldn't be a problem and we should just telephone him with the measurements. Danny seemed to be one of those people who would go the extra mile for you and we drove back to the villa feeling very pleased.

We pulled up at the gates to 'Bona Gent.' I got out of the car and after unfastening the inside lock on the gates, pushed them open and waited until Colin had driven in. I closed the gates, locked them again and listened for the children's voices. It was quiet. Too quiet! I wondered where they were. It would be far too hot inside the villa. Colin and I unloaded our bits and pieces from the car and changed into our swimwear as quickly as we could. Colin dived in the pool and I made my way slowly down the ladders, sliding gently into the cool water. The children were conspicuous by their absence.

"They must be in the play house," Colin called to me, having obviously read my worried expression.

"What play house?" I enquired.

"The room next to the Paellero. They asked me if they could clean it out and use it as a playroom. I said yes. Haven't you noticed that the green patio table and chairs have disappeared?" he said laughing.

I looked over to the patio at the poolside. Sure enough the table and chairs had vanished.

"I hope so Colin. If they are, well at least they were sensible enough to come out of the sun in the hottest part of the day, we can be thankful for that. Do you know they have never got sunburned the whole time we have been here?" I added.

"Well that's because they have both suffered in the past and I guess by now they have learned their lesson!" Colin answered, ducking his head under the water.

Worried by the unaccustomed silence, I decided to check on the playhouse. I climbed out of the pool and slid my feet into my orange plastic flip-flops. I walked slowly down the side of the house, past the Jasmine bushes to the back of the villa. Slowly and quietly I opened the playhouse door.

"Hi mum, you're back; can we go back in the pool?" Blaise yelled, rising from her plastic chair to greet me.

"Wait another hour Blaise, and then you won't get burnt."

"Oh mum, please, please," she pleaded, widening her large brown eyes at me.

"In half an hour then, I'll shout you when it's OK," I replied, pulling the door closed behind me as I left.

"Yippee!" she shrieked, as I walked back towards the pool.

"Satisfied now?" beamed Colin from the pool.

"I feel better now I know they are in the playhouse. We've got half an hour before they descend on us," I grimaced.

"That's fine; at least we've had time to cool off before we start sorting more things out for the house."

Half an hour later to the minute, the children appeared, all grins and smiles. Toys were thrown back into the pool, swim goggles were placed on foreheads and two very excited children leaped high in the air and launched themselves into the water.

"OK time for us to get out I guess," I shouted, over the sound of splashing, as Blaise and Ryan hit the water simultaneously, sending a huge shock wave rushing over the sides of the pool.

"We'll have to refill the pool at this rate," Colin muttered, heaving himself up the gleaming chrome pool ladders.

Colin and I dried off at the poolside and sat on the white chairs at the entrance to the patio. I thought I heard Colin say something about a 'DVD' and 'special offer.'

"I am simply not having a DVD in the villa Colin. What on earth would I want to come to Spain to watch DVD's for?" I bristled angrily.

"If we want to hire out the villa, we will need a DVD," Colin firmly replied.

On hearing the words DVD, Ryan shouted over from the pool.

"Dad, are we getting a DVD?"

"No we're not!" I shouted back.

"Please mum," Blaise added.

"No. I am not spending all my time in Spain waiting for you lot to finish watching your DVDs. It will be just like back in England. I can see it now, you lot sat watching some stupid film while I am swimming alone in this beautiful pool. I will not have a TV and DVD here, do you hear me?"

Colin, Ryan and Blaise eyed me sadly before I stormed off to the cool of the villa. A few minutes later Colin appeared in the front doorway.

"There's no need to get so grumpy about it," he said sheepishly. "It's just that if we want to rent the villa out over the winter, you can't expect people to just sit in the house twiddling their thumbs. They will want to watch TV and stuff, just like we do back home."

I knew he was right but I was determined not to give in without a fight.

Colin and I spent the rest of the afternoon and evening pottering around the garden and sheds, before finally adjourning to the lounge, hot and exhausted. It had been a long day and every hour or so, the children mentioned TV and DVD, which triggered a steely glance in their direction. Eyes were averted, lips were sealed and Colin fidgeted in his seat.

"Have YOU put them up to this?" I enquired solemnly.

"Up to what?" Colin meekly replied, over the top of his 'Biker' magazine.

"This whole TV thing. It's a conspiracy! I feel like the big bad wolf!" I said crossly.

"It's not my fault if everyone wants a TV and DVD and you don't."

"That's not the point Colin. You know how much I dislike TV. I get tired enough of it at home. It would be ghastly if it was like that here."

"It wouldn't be like that here; it's just that if it was bad weather, you know, winter or something, then all I am saying is that it would be nice to be able to watch a film or something."

"OK. I get the point. I guess I need to think about it, but I am not happy about it Colin, not at all happy. What did people do before TVs and DVDs? Tell me that? I'll tell you what they did. They played cards and board games, ate salted crisps and drank fizzy pop. They went for walks and sang songs."

"Well that was long before my time Ange," Colin joked.

"You cheeky sod!" I retorted, clipping him over the head with my notepad. "I am not THAT old Colin!"

"Oh mum, tell us about the olden days," pleaded Blaise.

Colin and I laughed and I shuffled around the lounge singing...

"In olden days a glimpse of stocking was thought of as something shocking, now heaven knows, anything goes!"

My family troupe, sensing my mood had lifted, followed behind me in a conga line and we made our way to our beds in a cheery mood.

I awoke in darkness, pitch black all around me. I fumbled my way down the corridor to the kitchen. It was so hot. I felt like I was going to pass out. I dripped with sweat and thought about opening the front and back doors to let the breeze pass through. Then I remembered it was the heart of summer in Spain and there was not a breeze to be had anywhere.

"I can't possibly sleep in this heat," I heard myself saying.

I felt ill. I opened the refrigerator door and stood naked in front of it. I simply had to get cool somehow and the fridge provided instant relief. I thought about turning the air conditioning on but it would have been too noisy in the stillness of the night. It would wake everyone up and keep me from dozing off again.

"Well, my first mistake was a good one," I said aloud. "I should never turn off the air conditioning before the house is freezing cold."

I stood looking into the refrigerator, its small blue interior light illuminating the kitchen. I drank half a litre of cold water, grabbed the cold fresh wipes from the shelf, shut the door and headed back to bed.

Angela Love

I laid the wipes on my feet, head and legs and waited for sleep. It didn't come. I headed for the refrigerator again.

"More water, wonderful. And oh, what's that? Ice cold chocolate, yummy! That will certainly take my mind off the heat," I said aloud.

I grabbed another handful of fresh wipes and headed for the bedroom, the chocolate in one hand and fresh wipes in the other. I laid the wipes over my body once again and munched on the chocolate. I felt much better and closed my eyes to let the cool wipes and melting chocolate take full effect. The most delicious comfort blanket anyone could wish for had to be Chocolate.

I awoke to sunlight streaming through the tiny square holes in the metal shutters of the bedroom window. The rays made such a pretty pattern, like golden streamers. I wondered what time it was. I heard Colin opening the lounge shutters but there was no sound of children though.

"What a night! I feel dreadful. I've got such a headache," I rambled.

"Perhaps it's got something to do with all that chocolate you ate," Colin answered calmly.

I headed for the bathroom to check my watch. It was twenty past eleven. I had slept late. I looked at my reflection in the mirror.

"What on earth is all that black stuff on your chin and right shoulder?" Colin asked addressing me through the bathroom mirror.

I rubbed at the dark marks on my chin.

"Dunno, it feels slightly crusty and powdery. I must have dribbled in my sleep and chocolate saliva's stained my chin. It must have dropped on to my shoulder too."

I quickly wiped it off before the children could see me. They were bound to make fun of me. I grabbed my dressing gown and walked wearily to the front patio. I felt very grizzly. I sat on the patio chair staring into the sunshine and wondering at the brilliance of the banana yellow sun. I rested for a few minutes enjoying the peace. Feeling slightly better, I commenced my motherly duties and brought the usual assortment of food to the patio table.

"Grubs up everyone! Come and get it," I called, watching as everyone appeared on queue. We chatted as we ate, made plans for the garden and added bits to my shopping list. I felt much better after I had eaten and made my way to the pool. Ryan and Blaise had already taken a dip earlier and retreated to their playhouse to cool off. I looked at my new rubber ring, flattened and filled with water, draped over the back of the patio chair.

"Blaise has broken my rubber ring. It's a shame because I only had about fifteen minutes play with it. Never mind, I suppose we can always get another," I finished, grabbing the ring and placing it in the black refuse bin next to the pool house.

"You must be feeling better now. You look much better," said Colin, studying me.

"Yes, I do. Sorry I was a bit ratty earlier on. Broken sleep plays havoc with me," I explained reticently.

"I know. Why do you think I never wake you up when you have gone for a nap," laughed Colin. "I'll keep to the far side of the pool while you do your exercises."

"Thanks Col, I shouldn't be too long."

"No problem, don't hurry them. Just take your time and enjoy yourself. After all, I can swim anytime I like."

I set about my exercises, calm, relaxed and happy. Having your own pool was simply terrific!

Ryan and Blaise appeared from the side of the villa. They waited patiently for me to finish my exercises and busied themselves looking for insects, searching the crevices in and around the perimeter of the pool.

"Mum! Mum! We've found a pixie!" Blaise shouted, excitedly.

"I found the pixie you mean," said Ryan, proudly.

"Mum it's lovely; she's tiny and red with a yellow buttercup pulled over her head for a bonnet."

"Oh she sounds wonderful Blaise," I remarked, looking over the pool ledge.

I had hidden three tiny pixies (or fairies, not quite sure what makes them one or the other) in the garden. There was a red one, a purple one and a green one. They were very cute and I knew the children would love them once discovered. It was part of my plan to make the garden magical. I looked around to see if Ryan had found the others, but he had vanished into thin air, or so it seemed.

"Blaise, where's Ryan gone?" I asked.

"Don't know mum," she answered, too engrossed in the little red pixie to care.

"I'm here!" rang his voice from the bottom of the garden.

"Where?"

"Here, up here, in the fig tree. I thought I would pick you some figs."

"Thanks Ryan, that's really kind of you. Be careful you don't fall though."

Ryan handed Colin the syrupy figs. They were so ripe that some of them burst in his hands, as he passed them to Colin.

"Put them in a container in the fridge," I shouted, as Colin carried handfuls of deep purple figs into the villa.

"Well, you definitely deserve a swim," I called to Ryan.

"Can we mum?" Blaise asked joyfully, ever the opportunist.

"Yes, of course, come on in, I've finished my exercises now."

Not needing a second invitation, Ryan and Blaise jumped into the pool and swam its entire length underwater. Not wanting to get in their way, I hastily waded towards the steps. The heavy scent of Jasmine greeted me as I pulled myself slowly from the pool and drew up a chair from the patio table. A light breeze wafted the heavy scent through the Jasmine tunnel down towards the pool. I thought about starting on the day's jobs and wondered where my 'to do' list was.

Colin went to see Sally at VSI's office in Villamarchante. We needed our pool instructions translated from Spanish into English. I checked on the washing I'd put in the machine earlier and realized I must have put it on the wrong programme. The clothes were still wet, however, they did look clean. I set about sweeping and mopping the house and patio, but after what seemed like no time at all, I felt droplets of sweat creep down my spine and cleavage. I pulled my T-shirt off and wiped my forehead with it. It was far too hot to continue and I returned to the pool for another cooling dip. The joy of having your own swimming pool!

The children joined me in the pool for about half an hour. It was fast approaching mid day and they would soon adjourn to their playhouse to keep cool. Within half an hour they both climbed out and made their way through the Jasmine tunnel, to the back of the house. I had the pool to myself at last and floated aimlessly, blinking as the sun beat down.

It was lovely to relax and so peaceful, not a sound anywhere, no dogs barking, cockerels crowing or car stereos belting out bass at a thousand decibels. However, it was short lived. No sooner had I thought about the peace and quiet than the crickets drummed their back legs creating an almighty din.

I ascended the pool ladders and showered off in the pool house. I put on my towelling robe and strode through the garden and house to the kitchen. I grabbed a handful of ice cubes, dropped them in a tumbler and poured myself a long cool drink. I watched the ice cubes crack and chink the glass, as the cola cascaded over them. I carried my cold drink to the patio, sat down and took a long slurp from the tumbler. The scent of Jasmine filled my nostrils and I inhaled its strong scent. It was hard to believe that all that I surveyed belonged to us. It had always been our dream to have a house in the countryside, somewhere warm. We now had a house surrounded by orange groves and our very own orange and fig trees. The weather was fantastic, the climate had to be good of course to support such an abundance of fruit trees. I felt truly blessed and inspired. I picked up my pen and opened my journal and began to write. The tranquillity of 'Bona Gent' fed my soul and I was truly happy with my lot. The toot of a car horn outside the gate announced Colin's return. He brought good news, Sally was going to translate the pool instructions for us.

"Hurray!" I cried gleefully.

"Sally mentioned a huge retail shopping outlet called Bonaire, just off the A3. It has a huge supermarket called Al Campo, a garden centre and lots of designer shops too. Do you fancy a ride out to find it?" Colin asked excitedly.

"OK, why not. I can make us all a quick sandwich and then we can go. We can turn on the air-conditioning just before we leave too. It will be lovely and cool when we get back," I rambled.

"I'll go and tell Ryan and Blaise then. Are they in the back shed?" Colin enquired.

"Yes I think so," I answered, preoccupied with ensuring the plastic was peeled off from between the slices of Gouda cheese.

We ate quickly, dressed and headed off in the general direction of Cheste, where Sally said we could pick up the A3 motorway to Bonaire. The route from Pedralba to Cheste was quite spectacular. Cheste was better known for its motorcycle racetrack, the Ricardo Tormo Circuit. We drove past neat little rows of vines along the way, heavy with ripe black grapes. They looked delicious and I was sorely tempted to stop and pick some.

"Perhaps I could look for a vine at Bonaire's garden centre Col and we could grow our own grapes," I suggested, with images of freshly picked grapes on the breakfast table flashing through my mind.

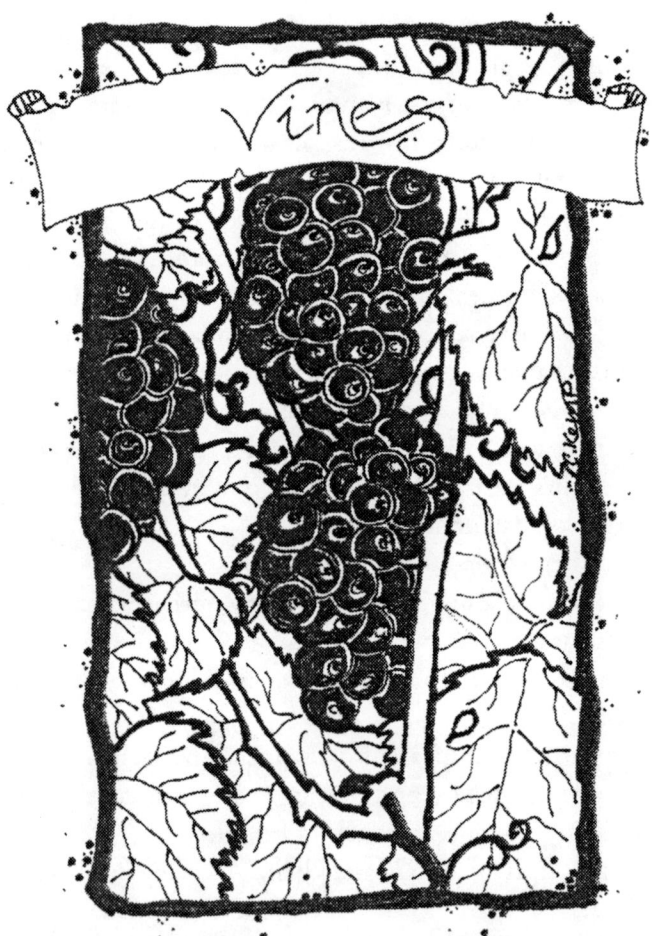

Bonaire was a huge retail outlet, comparable to Bluewater in Kent, or The Trafford Centre in Manchester. It consisted of a huge supermarket called Al Campo, various electrical retailers, sportswear retailers, IT retailers, restaurants, a cinema and lots of small designer retail outlets. I took my shopping list with me, eager to browse the 500 or so shops!

There was also a large garden centre called Leroy Merlin that sold household goods and doubled up as a DIY Superstore.

Colin looked for road signs for Bonaire and spotted a large billboard indicating that we should take exit 345. We left the motorway at the appropriate exit and wound our way through a maze of driveways and roundabouts towards the hub of the retail park. We parked the car in the biggest car park I had ever seen. I wrote the nearest car park reference grid on an old cinema ticket and slipped it into my pocket. It would be awful if we got lost and couldn't find our car. Colin led the way towards the bright neon lights of what looked like an entry point. We followed behind, fascinated by the thousands of fairy lights that hung along the perimeter of the car parking areas. The entrance was located behind an American Burger House and colourful children's carousels lined the tree-lined avenue entrance.

There were hundreds of shops. We browsed the boutiques and bought new outfits for Blaise and Ryan. Leroy Merlin's was a huge Homebase type store with interior and exterior aisles. We trudged around the outlet for hours. I bought an iron and ironing board, six patio chair cushions and a large square patio table, which was a snip at a mere €21.95. We bought new green, plastic fence lining, cable ties and a shower curtain. We finally arrived at Al Campo hypermarket, very tired and weary after our marathon shopping spree. Colin and Ryan entered the store with instructions to purchase mosquito nets and fly dollies, while Blaise and I sat on a bench in the mall, exhausted. They returned at ten o'clock. I had obviously sat for far too long on the wooden bench and my back was unforgiving. I struggled to get up, my joints as stiff as concrete posts and the pain in my back was most excruciating. Blaise helped pull me to my feet and I staggered like a wounded deer towards Colin.

"I'll come back tomorrow and get the step ladders," Colin announced.

I winced at the thought of another session at Bonaire and hobbled to the car.

"Where is it all going to go?" I asked, eyeing all the 'stuff' we had bought.

Although I had every confidence in Colin's ability to make things fit where they shouldn't, I couldn't quite see how he was going to fit the patio table and us in the car.

"Leave it to someone who knows what they're doing!" Colin said confidently, with a huge grin.

I laughed. Colin and his packing skills would save the day, yet again.

We set off back to the villa through the town of Cheste and the vineyards. The children were tucked safely in the back seat, trapped by a huge white plastic patio table. We were such an hilarious sight, people we passed along the way stared at us and scratched their heads. We looked like something from a cartoon scene. Finally, after many stares and strange glances, I saw the funny side of it and began to laugh at the people laughing at us. Wild laughter quickly filled our tiny car as we chugged home, each of us radiating happiness.

We arrived home just before eleven. Ryan and Blaise, firmly trapped by the table in the back seat, were unable to open the gates. I found the key with a green cover on it, exited the car and unlocked the gates. I pushed them ajar and Colin drove in and parked up in front of the lounge window. We pulled the large white patio table from the back seat of the car, so that the children could get out and help us unload. They stretched their limbs and carried the goods from the car boot to the villa. We emptied the car quickly and watched as the children carried their designer bags to their rooms.

"Hey, don't forget you have to work off what you owe us for the clothes!" I shouted, as they passed me. "You can start tonight if you like," I added.

"OK mum, what shall we do?" Blaise asked happily.

"How about watering the garden," I suggested.

"Fine," answered Blaise and made her way to the hosepipe.

Blaise and Ryan took turns watering the garden. We heard them laughing outside. They were having a good old-fashioned water fight and we decided to leave them to it. After all, it would cool them down before bed.

Inside the house was cool and fresh. The thought of the previous evening's heat made me shudder. Thankfully, we had been out long enough for the house to have substantially cooled and I was looking forward to getting under the crisp, cool, sheet on my bed. I wrote the children a small task list and stuck it on the wall with Blue Tack.

"Fancy a midnight swim Col?" I asked, grabbing a towel from the back of the sofa.

"Sounds good to me, I'll get my shorts," he replied, making his way down the corridor to the bedroom.

I peeled off my clothes and put on my bikini. The children were at the bottom of the garden watering the fig tree.

"Come on kids, midnight swim!" I called.

"Hurray, hurray!" they shouted, making their way to the house.

"Just going to get changed mum," Blaise shouted.

They reappeared in their bathing suits. Colin turned on the pool lights and the four of us swam up and down in the cool water. Our neighbours Francisco and Mercedes, called over to us from the other side of the fence.

"Good night Colin, good night Angela."

"Buenos noches," Colin and I called back over the garden fence.

"Be quiet now kids, Francisco and his family have gone to bed," Colin said in a low voice.

"We will dad," they answered sincerely.

We swam quietly under the light of the moon and the stars and eventually made our way back inside the house. Chilled by the pool and the cold air of the villa and feeling utterly contented, I fell into a blissful sleep.

Chapter 16
The Bull Run

I awoke to find that the children had already done most of the chores. The house was spit spot. Outdoors had been swept and breakfast was laid out on the patio table. I met Colin in the hall, dressed in his swim trunks and swim goggles.

"We are waiting for the croissants to thaw and then the children are going to cook bacon and eggs for us all," he stated.

"Have I got time for a swim first?" I asked.

"Sure, you've got about fifteen minutes or so."

I checked my watch. I had slept very late again, but in my defence, I hadn't gone to bed until about one o'clock in the morning. I relaxed in the pool, did several yoga exercises and swam a few lengths. Blaise insisted that I mount Colin's inflatable chair. She held it still while I positioned myself to get on it.

"It will be comfortable for your back mum," she stated, grasping it firmly.

Balancing on the pool ladders, I eased myself on to the chair. She was right. It was extremely comfortable. I floated around the pool while Colin, Blaise and Ryan ferried food from the kitchen to the patio. I relaxed my head and rested it on the back of the inflatable cushion. I was just drifting off to sleep when I heard Colin's voice.

"You look very chilled out!" he called from the patio, watching me through the viewfinder on the video recorder.

For once, I didn't try and pull my tummy in and stick my chest out, or cross my legs and pout. I continued dozing on the chair, while it drifted slowly around the pool.

"The bed should arrive today Colin," I called.

"Yep, it should. I'm going to Al Campo after we've eaten to get those ladders. You can stay here, just in case the bed arrives early."

"That's fine by me Col," I answered. "I really don't fancy another session at Al Campo just yet. It's exhausting walking around in this heat."

Blaise and Ryan tidied up, eager to pay off their clothes bill and we spent the late afternoon swimming, dozing and listening to music. I cut some length off Blaise's new trouser legs, as they were long enough to fit a giraffe. I telephoned Candice, asked her to come at eight o'clock and settled down to read my book.

Colin arrived back just after seven o'clock. He had bought two sun loungers, a pair of aluminium ladders, two pool thermostats (one as a gift for our friends Dave and Jackie back home,) some fresh fruit and a pack of frozen pizzas.

"How does he fit it all in?" I exclaimed to Ryan and Blaise.

"He's just used to doing it mum," Blaise answered thoughtfully and added, "because you always buy too much stuff."

I laughed heartily. She was so right. Out of the mouth of babes!

Colin started to assemble the new patio table and just as the last bolt went in, Candice and her husband Ben arrived. I busied myself showing her around while Colin poured drinks. Our long-term let enquirer wanted more than a twelve-month rental agreement. Candice was not happy about it and had declined the offer on our behalf. We agreed to meet again on the following Monday, to take photographs for the website. We concluded our business and waved Candice and Ben off. I returned to the villa and busied myself preparing our evening meal. I turned the oven on and put the pizzas and potato wedges in to cook. I chopped some lettuce, cucumber, tomatoes, onions and peppers and put them in the salad bowl. Using some of the finest Olive Oil I could find in my cupboard, I mixed a dressing made with lemon juice, black pepper and mustard and poured it liberally over the salad. At least I would be in the children's good books tonight. They loved pizza!

"Hey, the bed hasn't been delivered," I announced, remembering that it was supposed to have been delivered.

I had forgotten to tell Colin the bad news and quickly made my excuse of taking the food to the patio, beating a hasty retreat. Colin had been looking forward to sleeping in a proper bed and would be tetchy to say the least. Placing the pizzas to the table, I sat down, closed my eyes and folded my arms, avoiding Colin's glare. Colin said grace and we all took a slice of pizza.

"I did telephone them this afternoon but there was no-one who could speak English," I explained, between mouthfuls of pizza.

Colin was furious and announced that he was going to go back to the Carrefour first thing in the morning to give them what for!

"Ben has lost two and a half stones in twelve months," Colin stated. "Apparently, the weight just dropped off him once he started working here."

"Well it will I suppose working in this heat," I replied in a matter of fact tone.

The children and I had a long cool drink and retired to our beds, leaving Colin to the sofa, yet again. I felt awful and offered to swap for the night. But Colin being a perfect gentleman declined my offer and settled down on the sofa for the night.

I awoke in the middle of the night feeling roasting hot. I tried standing in front of the fridge several times, but it didn't work. I wandered around the villa feeling utterly miserable. I kept my footsteps soft so as not to start off the dogs' dawn chorus and sat on the patio and watched the stars. I saw no point getting upset or frustrated about it. I would cool down sooner or later. I watched the new day dawn and finally returned to bed at five o'clock.

"Ange, it's time to get up. Come on Ange, if you want to come to the Carrefour with me, you have to get up."

After only four hours sleep, I was not feeling very sociable.

"I'm coming, for goodness sake Col, give me chance to wake up!" I shouted angrily.

I dressed with eyes half closed and shuffled along the corridor to the lounge.

"Ready!" I sighed.

Colin grabbed the keys from the basket next the TV and followed me out.

We drove to the Carrefour in silence, both of us in a bad mood. Entering the Carrefour, Colin headed straight to the desk where the assistant had taken our order and asked for an English-speaking assistant. After much commotion, we were assured that the bed would be delivered without further delay. We were asked to telephone the deliveryman at four o'clock to see where he was and get an estimated time of arrival. We headed back home tired, frustrated and hot.

The children had been angels yet again. They had cleaned the house and tidied up outside. It improved our mood considerably. Colin declared playtime in the pool to cheer us up and lighten our mood and we quickly donned our swimwear. It certainly cooled us and left us feeling more at peace with the world.

Colin assembled our newly bought sun loungers and placed them proudly by the poolside. I collected a few fresh figs from the tree for Blaise and I to eat and decided to change into my new pink bikini. The less clothing I had on in this heat, the better. I changed quickly and reappeared at the poolside. Blaise gave her seal of approval, as I got back into the pool. Colin let out a long wolf whistle.

"Nice bikini Ange. I'm just going out to stand on the main road so the Carrefour man doesn't miss us," Colin called, as he made his way through the gates and closed them behind him.

"OK. Stand in some shade if you can Colin, it's awfully hot," I shouted over the hedge, concerned.

"I will, don't worry," Colin responded.

Blaise joined me in the water and we used two polystyrene toggles we'd found in the pool house to water cycle. They were superb and it was a comfortable way to exercise without my back hurting. We cycled the water, treading round and round the perimeter of the pool. Blaise with her vivid imagination, made up a game for us to play. She pretended we were riding sea horses.

"Let's say all the Spanish words we have learned," she suggested.

"OK. You start," I said, trying to recall all the different Spanish words I knew.

"Uno, dos, tres, quatro," Blaise counted.

I was just about to carry on when I heard a large delivery van toot its horn.

"Quick, it's the bed!" I exclaimed in panic. "I don't want the men to see me in my pink bikini."

"Mum, why are you fussing so much? It doesn't matter if they see you, they don't know you."

"That's not the point Blaise."

"Well, what is the point?" she asked typical of a ten year-old daughter who thinks she's a teenager.

"The point is they will **see** me Blaise."

"Yes, but they will see you when you put your clothes on too."

I sighed, worn out by Blaise's powers of reasoning.

I climbed out of the pool and reached for my towel, securing it tightly around me. I walked quickly inside and put on my bathrobe. I was wrapped up like an Eskimo but at least my modesty was intact. I reappeared to welcome the deliverymen and in my best Spanish accent shouted, "Hola!"

They nodded silently.

"Soy muy contento," I beamed at them.

They nodded silently.

"Mi cama es aqui," I said, pointing towards our bedroom.

The two men trooped inside the house silently, dropping all the base bits and pieces on the floor before returning to the van for the mattress. I was so delighted that we finally had a double bed that I gave them a generous tip before they left.

Colin busied himself sorting out the legs, frame, bedstead, screws and bolts. I felt like a little child, silly and excited. As the last screw was tightened, Colin smiled his dimpled smile and winked at me.

"OK, last one in the pool is a sourpuss!" he shouted, laughing as he ran to the pool.

I de-robed in an instant and followed him to the pool, singing …

"We've got a bed, we've got a bed, ee I adio, we've got a bed,"

We laughed at my silliness and I mounted my toggle and water cycled around the pool perimeter. Colin grinned from ear to ear.

"This will be our first night in a double bed in our Spanish home," he said winking.

"I better make a special meal to celebrate having a double bed then," I replied.

I dried off, put on a clean T-shirt and shorts and prepared a meal of roast lamb with freshly picked rosemary, skewered peppers, mini roast potatoes and left over pizza for Ryan and Blaise.

"Let's take the children to the Bull Run tonight. It will give the house chance to cool down before we go to bed," Colin suggested.

"OK. Sounds like a good idea to me," I replied enthusiastically.

Two nights of heat hell was the most I could stand and any method of cooling down the villa was more than welcome.

We tucked into our roast dinner, talked about the day's events and planned for the evening ahead. We wondered what it would be like and the children asked us questions, clearly nervous but excited. We were all excited and I had to admit, I was slightly worried. I was terrified Ryan would want to run with the bulls. I didn't want to have to be the bearer of any bad news to his mum. He would never be allowed to come away with us again. Perhaps I was being over anxious, but I knew Ryan had a great spirit of adventure. I needed to be worried.

The children stacked the dishwasher, collected their money and cameras and we piled into the car. Colin drove to Villamarchante giving out safety instructions to the children on the way. It was ten o'clock in the evening. We had been told that the Bull Run started at about eleven o'clock, possibly as late as midnight.

Arriving in Villamarchante, everything seemed normal. We parked the car in the usual place, crossed to the square and took a seat at one of the pavement cafes.

"Perhaps we have got it wrong," I said quietly, hoping the children wouldn't hear.

They would be terribly disappointed if there were no bulls.

"Let's just walk around the streets and see what's happening," Colin suggested, heading off into the first small street off to the left of the square.

We all followed Colin expecting to see a ferocious bull at any moment. People ate at long trestle tables that were spread the full length of the narrow streets. Children played matadors on the street corners. One youth, probably no more than twelve years old, held a set of horns and pretended to charge the toddlers. The younger children ran excitedly and shrieked with delight. They dived behind metal bars and barriers into shop doorways and houses.

"Look Colin! All the house doorways have metal bars in front of them. I never noticed that before, did you?"

"No I didn't. It's obviously for protection," he answered, looking thoughtful.

We walked the narrow streets of Villamarchante, watching the people feasting, Spanish flags hung from upper floor windows, gently wafting to and fro in the breeze. Everyone had a smile on their face and looked very excited. Young men and women collected at one end of a table while the older citizens gathered at the opposite end, tearing handfuls of garlic bread, passing bowls of salad and calamari and gesticulating wildly with their hands, while the conversation gradually got louder and louder.

"Dad, I'm still hungry," said Ryan. "Please can we get something to eat?"

"OK. Let's get a table in the square. There won't be any bulls for a while because everyone's still eating."

Obediently we made our way to a very small table in the square. Ryan ordered a steak, bacon and onion baguette with chips. Blaise ordered a cheese and ham toast. Colin ordered drinks for us and we sat watching everyone around us, as the excitement grabbed the population of the square in a mini frenzy and whirlwind of anticipation and activity.

Angela Love

The square was packed and more people arrived by the minute. A group of toddlers played matadors outside the town hall entrance.

"Here come the bulls," shouted Colin.

A large cattle truck pulled into the lay by and the strong scent of manure filled the air. The truck had metal sides and swayed from side to side as the bulls made their presence known. We heard snorting and banging on the sides of the wagon, as the bulls kicked against the walls of the cattle truck. The crowded square buzzed with excitement at its arrival. The atmosphere was wonderful and people sizzled with anticipation. Blaise jumped up and down as she watched the cattle wagon sway. I wondered if she was a little worried. If she was, she wasn't the only one! I too, was a little concerned about bulls being let loose in the square. But everyone around me seemed to be having such a great time, I felt reassured. After all, wouldn't everyone be running for cover if they were about to let the bulls out of the cattle truck?

The truck started to move a little and parked up almost blocking the narrow street where we had walked ten minutes previous. We finished our meals and made to leave the cafe, our chairs scraping the stone patio as we made our way from the table. We walked toward the little street where the cattle wagon had parked. As we were parallel with it, we heard a huge thump as the bull inside the wagon kicked out. Blaise and I almost jumped out of our skins and grabbed hold of each other's arms for security!

"That doesn't sound very friendly," said Blaise concerned.

Colin got the video camera ready as the truck started to reverse up the street.

A young man wearing spectacles sat atop the wagon, holding two thick ropes. At the entrance to the narrow street was an 'A' frame barrier. Heaving with all their might, men young and old, pushed the barrier in an effort to create an opening, so that the truck could reverse and release the bull. The frame hardly budged.

"Here Angela, hold this a minute while I give them a hand," Colin instructed, handing the video recorder to me.

Colin and Ryan joined the men and pushed the wooden barrier back to form an opening. The truck reversed slowly through the gap. In what seemed like an instant, the bull was released into the narrow street, to the cheers of hundreds of people. The truck drove forwards out of the narrow street and the men pushed the huge wooden frame back into place, to seal off the opening.

The 'A' frame barrier was built with several rows of planks acting as seating or standing platforms. Within seconds of the barrier being put in place, men, women and children climbed up the frame. The bull ran up the street away from the barrier. Blaise and I could only peer from behind the 'A' frame, our view broken by dangling legs and feet. I looked around me. There were young women with newborn babies, old women with grandchildren, youths and old men. In short, the whole population of the town seemed to have turned out for the Bull Run. Colin and Ryan climbed to the top of the barrier and were sat at the highest point. They had climbed the 'A' frame quickly to secure the best view. The tension and suspense was electrifying. Nervous excitement surrounded us. Blaise and I continued to peer through dangling legs, trying to catch sight of the bull. And suddenly there it was, about 100' away from the barrier. It looked awesome even at a distance.

The bull's horns had been dressed with what looked like huge pompoms and these had been set alight. No wonder the bull kicked the side of the cattle truck; it must have been very angry and frightened. I'm sure I would be if my head was set alight! I wondered how they'd managed to light the pompoms, but instantly forgot about it as the bull charged towards us, horns aflame. Singed hair and petrol scented the night air. The pompoms had obviously been soaked in petrol. The barricade was about 8' high and I wondered if Colin and Ryan would come tumbling down if the bull charged it. Blaise and I saw people running down the street, diving in between the doorway barriers for safety. The bull stopped short of the 'A' frame, turned and ran in the opposite direction back up the street. Those behind the bull now found themselves in front of it! They ran quickly, the bull hot on their heels. Blaise jumped up and down in excitement and I tried to unclench my hands. For some reason, my fists were clenched in a tight ball and my knuckles were white. Rather a strange reaction I thought. It was such a wonderful and exciting experience, like nothing I had ever felt. We heard the bang and crackle of fireworks up the street. Young men lit bangers and firecrackers and threw them at the bull's feet. This served to make the bull even angrier of course, which was obviously the objective.

For about two hours, we watched with awe as the huge bull, horns alight, charged people along the streets of Villamarchante. We saw people taunting it with flag poles draped in red material, their hands waving the pole to and fro from the safety of their upstairs balconies. Colin shouted something. The bull had something on the floor, about 80' away from us. Blaise and I couldn't see clearly enough to determine what it was, but I guessed the bull had got its own back on at least one person. A lady standing nearby told us that there had already been three deaths that week and that the ambulance crews were parked in the lay-by round the corner, ready to deal with necessary aid for the injured. Behind us, we heard the wagon start up its engine again.

"Looks like a second bull is going in," shouted Colin from atop the frame.

"Colin, it's half past two in the morning, I am really tired," I shouted back to him, pointing to my wristwatch.

Colin nodded to me and he and Ryan descended the barrier, their places instantly taken by others.

"Shall we go before they put the other bull in? I don't want to see this bull exhausted and distressed and I don't want the children to see it either," I reasoned.

"OK Ange, let's go then. I have enough on video anyway," Colin responded, putting his arm protectively around the children.

We pushed our way through the gathering of people back towards the square. We passed the wagon holding the second bull, our senses alert as it rocked from side to side. The bull tried desperately to avoid having its horns lit and we thought at one point that the lad atop the truck might be dislodged. It was definitely time to go home. I worried that as more alcohol was consumed, false bravado would prevail and more risks would be taken. It needed only one mistake and the outcome could be disastrous. And those under the influence of drink **would** make mistakes. Alcohol definitely lessens one's ability to react quickly. Two bulls running around the streets were just a little too much for our first time at a bull run, with no experience of what to expect. It would be awful if the children saw something like a goring. And with two bulls loose, that could very well happen. We sat in the car and Colin pulled out of the car park, homeward bound.

The children chatted all the way home, reflecting on the events they had just seen. This had been a new experience for them, something they had never seen before in their young lives and they were full of stories and tales.

"Did you see the bull charge that man?" Ryan asked.

"No, but I did see the bulls horns on fire. Did you see it when the bull turned round and then chased the people who had been behind it up the road?" she replied enthusiastically.

"Yeah, it was dead funny," Ryan answered, giggling.

And so the conversation continued all the way back to the villa. Colin and I chuckled at their excitement.

We arrived back at the villa tired but happy and still on a high from the evenings entertainment. The house was as cool as cucumber when we entered. It was blissfully cold! Colin connected the video recorder to the TV and we all watched, totally mesmerized by the footage of the Bull Run. It was amazing.

"Looks like the bull caught an elderly man. I wonder how many more will get hurt tonight?" I asked.

"I don't know Ange but judging by the amount of people there, the chances of someone getting hurt are very high. There could be as many as four bulls in there before this night's through. And there'll be someone who's had a bit too much to drink that thinks he can outrun it, or outfox it and they'll probably get badly hurt," Colin answered.

"Four bulls! Cool!" exclaimed Ryan, grinning from ear to ear and not at all phased by our talk of getting gored.

The video finished.

"OK everyone, I think we could all do with a rest now. Time for bed," said Colin.

The children brushed their teeth and Ryan said our evening prayer.

"Amen!" we all chorused and headed for our bedrooms.

"Colin, it's your first night in our new double bed," I said, smiling.

"Yeah, I am so glad I don't have to sleep on that sofa again," he sighed.

"Me too Colin."

I climbed in the bed and snuggled up to him, in what was now a very well chilled bedroom. Tired and exhausted once more, we fell asleep.

Chapter 17
The Melon Man

I awoke at eleven o'clock. I called to Colin and the children to get up as we had a lot to do. There were lots of jobs that needed doing and today was our designated 'jobs' day. Colin and Ryan were going to repair the covering on the driveway gates. Blaise was going to prepare breakfast and I was going to water my beautiful garden.

I grabbed the hosepipe and started to unravel it. It was about 80' long and easily reached the far end of the garden. One of the oriental irises had flowered yellow but most of them had died in bud, ravaged by the sun. They stood about 6' tall and were most impressive. I turned on the hose and made sure they were well soaked. They revived instantly, the dark olive green and red stalks standing to attention as the water fed into them, their foliage stiffening as the moisture was transported through the veins of the leaves.

The orange tree was heavy with unripe fruit. The oranges were a good size but were still a dark lime green. Two of the branches were so heavy they looked as if they were going to snap under the strain of the heavy fruit. One branch already had a wooden support, but I made a mental note to tell Colin we needed to make two more supports, to help it bear the weight of the fruit. I needed some string for the oriental irises too as they desperately needed tidying up. The fig tree dripped large ripe figs, the ground was stained purple with their splattered pulp. I collected another large Tupperware bowl full of them and placed them in the refrigerator. We could eat them for breakfast. One by one, my family awoke and appeared on the patio.

Blaise asked if she could set the table and prepare breakfast. I gave her my permission and wondered what wonderful delights Blaise would bring to the table. There were fresh figs, melon slices, grapes, peaches and apples. There was a bowl of freshly baked croissants and a pack of Brie. There were two jugs of fresh orange juice too. The table was laden with food fit for a king. Blaise had obviously taken a lot of time and trouble and had put some thought into making the table look scrumptiously appetizing.

"Blaise, the table looks wonderful. Thank you," I said, giving her a big hug.

"It's OK mum, I enjoyed doing it," she replied, returning my hug. "I want to do what I can to help today. Everyone has jobs and so I thought this would help."

"Well, it does help Blaise and everyone appreciates it. Thank you my little treasure," I grinned.

Colin and Ryan had repaired the damaged part of the gate cover. It looked very neat and tidy; they had made a superb job of it. It looked too good really and the remaining sections looked old and tatty. Colin was a perfectionist and if I had noticed, he would too.

"Food's ready," I shouted, over the sound of the radio.

We sat and feasted on the fresh fruit and food Blaise had so lovingly prepared. We sat for a while, happy for yet another perfect sunny day and grateful for the peace, quiet and comfort of our Spanish home.

I helped Blaise clear the table and found my 'to do' list. Somehow, my list had grown longer over the week instead of shorter. I added 'remove broken glass from dishwasher,' before a huge yawn escaped me. I felt exhausted. It must have been three o'clock before we all went to bed. I couldn't remember the last time I had stayed out until half past two in the morning. It was probably when I was in my thirties. I cleared the breakfast dishes, tidied around the house and picked up my pen and pad to record the day's events. Within quarter of an hour of sitting down to write, I heard great excitement outside. A voice boomed out in Spanish through a loud haler.

Colin and Ryan were busy repairing the exterior gate covering. Colin had noticed how tatty the rest of the covering looked and had set about renewing the whole lot.

"Mum!" Blaise shouted loudly from the gate, "Ryan and Dad want you to come outside."

"What for Blaise?" I asked.

"Something to do with a man selling melons," she sighed.

"Ange, dad wants you!" Ryan called running through the open front door. "There's a man selling melons, but he can't talk English and we can't speak Spanish."

"But I'm not dressed Ryan," I shouted, standing up.

Dressed only in a white T Shirt and bikini bottoms, I grabbed my sarong and flip-flops and made my way slowly to the gate.

"Soy Ingles!" I shouted, as I strode towards them.

"What is it Colin?" I asked inquisitively.

A white transit van had parked up outside 'Bona Gent.' A very stocky, olive skinned, dark haired gentleman gesticulated wildly to Colin, his arms flailing around him. Colin looked on puzzled.

"Come here a minute," Colin shouted.

I walked to the back of the white van.

"He obviously wants us to buy some melons Ange but I don't know how much money he wants for them. Can you find out?" Colin asked.

I looked at the dark haired man. He had a huge plastic bucket of melons ready for us. There were enough melons in it to fill a small cart!

"Blimey, Colin, there must be over a dozen melons here. We're leaving in three days, what on earth will we do with them all?"

I explained our predicament, mustering my best Spanish accent. I said that we only needed two melons because we were leaving for England in two days. The man sighed and looked into the back of his van. I looked into the darkness through the open rear doors. In the front seat were his wife and children. They all looked at me, their eyes pleading. I felt awful.

"How much do you want for the bucket of melons?" I said feeling guilty.

"Quince euros," he replied to my astonishment, in a thick guttural accent.

"€15 Col," I translated. "But we can't possibly eat them all."

"But €15 for all those melons is dead cheap Ange," Ryan put in, adding "I will eat two of them all to myself easy."

What a dilemma! It was a very cheap price for such a lot of melons. I looked at the man and his family again. Four pairs of pleading eyes fixed on me. What could I do but give in!

"OK. We'll take them," I announced, watching as Colin pulled his money from his shorts pocket and handed it over.

There were seventeen honeydew melons in the bucket and the man added a huge green watermelon for good measure. He then gave a tiny little honeydew melon to Blaise. Ryan and Colin carried the two handled, soft sided, rubber bucket to the patio table, tipped the melons on to the top of the table and returned the bucket to the melon man. Much back slapping and hand shaking took place, the man's gruff and gritty voice booming out, as he slapped Colin's back.

"Hey hombre!" he shouted in his thick gritty voice.

He grabbed Colin's hand and shook it furiously.

"Si, mi hombre!" Colin responded and together they stood slapping each other's back and shaking hands in the street.

The man eventually let go of Colin's hand and jumped back into his Transit Van.

"Ta lluego!" we all shouted, as the man and his family drove off.

They waved to us, smiled and blasted the horn as they went.

I laughed at our situation. The large yellow melons covered the entire top of the table.

"I think we can eat two at most and possibly take two melons home with us," I sighed. "That leaves thirteen melons, plus the dark green watermelon and Blaise's tiny melon," I laughed. The simple act of buying a bucket of melons made the melon man, his family and my family deliriously happy. Filled with good feeling, we all chuckled at our plentiful melon supply. I grabbed a sharp knife from the kitchen and sliced one into quarters. Colin, Ryan, Blaise and I each grabbed a slice and devoured it within minutes, our chins dripping with sweet melon juice. We wiped our chins with the backs of our hands and set about the day's jobs once more. Unfortunately, the sun was almost at its hottest and my concentration faltered. It was time to cool down. I half filled a large jug with ice cubes and poured fresh pineapple juice over them, hearing them crackle as the liquid made contact with them.

I headed to the pool, jug and plastic cups in hand, to cool off and do my back exercises. I placed the juice and glasses on the table and grabbed my polystyrene toggle. I slowly cycled the perimeter of the pool and hummed to the tune of *'Have you seen the Muffin Man?'* Making up my own words as I cycled, I sang ….

> *"Have you seen the Melon Man, the Melon Man, the Melon Man?*
> *Have you seen the Melon Man, he's coming here today,"*

Of course Blaise joined in enthusiastically.

> *"Have you seen the Melon Man, the Melon Man, the Melon Man?*
> *Have you seen the Melon man, he's coming here today."*

Colin laughed at us and said we were crazy. He continued lining the gates, shaking his head and 'tutting' at our silliness.

Having finished the gate, Ryan and Colin joined us in the pool. We all had a well-deserved dip and lazed around the patio with drinks of ice-cold pineapple juice. We had worked very hard and after such a late night; we were still very tired. I dried off, finished my drink and stood up.

"I'm going to do something very Spanish!" I shouted, as I walked towards the villa.

"What's that?" Colin asked.

"Are you going to make Paella mum?" Blaise asked, as she lifted her swim goggles on to her forehead.

"No. I am going to have a siesta!" I drawled, yawning as I went. "Keep the noise down everyone please."

I closed the metal shutters, pushed the bedroom door to and climbed on top of the new, comfortable double bed. Time for a well-deserved snooze.

"What time is it?" I asked, nudging Colin who lay next to me on the bed.

"Twenty past seven," he answered, groggy with sleep.

"Goodness, I've been asleep for two hours," I said, swinging my legs over the side of the bed and stubbing my big toe on the wardrobe leg.

"Ouch, that hurt," I spluttered, hopping towards the door.

"Well, don't worry about it. That's what having a holiday is all about. Resting, relaxing, having fun, leaving your troubles behind you and stubbing your toes," Colin sniggered, as he stretched the full length of the bed.

"It must be all the late nights that have caught up with me. Where are the children?" I enquired, crossing the hall to the bathroom.

"Asleep. They were plum tuckered out Ange!" Colin replied, calling out from the bedroom.

"Aw, bless 'em. Well, I'll start cooking dinner then. The smell might revive them. What you want to do this evening?"

"Well, I need more cable ties and gate cover from Leroy Merlin. I want to pull the old covering off and renew the cover on both gates. It looks odd with just the repaired pieces."

"I know what you mean. I thought you'd want to do the whole gate once you put the new piece on. Shall we go after tea then? After, we could carry on up the motorway and try and find El Puig beach. Anita said it's easy to find and really nice."

"OK. I'll wake the kids while you get dinner. But make it something quick or Leroy Merlin will be closed by the time we get there."

I fried some pork loin, using the juice for a peppercorn sauce. I put a stack of potato wedges and mixed vegetables in the oven and turned up the heat. I quickly showered and changed. I could smell the cooked pork as I entered the kitchen. It smelt wonderful.

"Come on everyone, food's ready!" I hollered, taking dishes of pork and vegetables to the table.

Colin followed behind me with a bowl of potato wedges. We ate slowly, savouring the pork and the children complimented me on the peppercorn sauce. I thanked them and was glad I had remembered to bring several Colman's packet sauces with me. We cleared the dirty dishes away, turned on the air conditioning and climbed into our little car, bound for Bonaire.

The roads were quiet and the drive picturesque. The vines were heavy with bunches of grapes. Colin remembered the route easily and we parked up quickly. Thankfully, Leroy Merlin was still open. Colin made his way to the fencing section, while I looked at shower curtains. We made our purchases quickly and returned to the car. We had gate covering, six citronella candles, a couple of coffee mugs and two frying pans. Colin packed everything in the boot, and we headed off to see if we could find El Puig beach.

We drove up the A7 towards Barcelona and five minutes into our journey, saw a sign for El Puig. Colin flicked the car indicator on and took the appropriate exit. There was a massive firework display in the distance. It seemed to come from the direction in which we were headed. The sky was alight with millions of red, green, purple, blue, orange and yellow stars. It was a marvellous display of colour.

El Puig looked like quite a nice town but after completing two complete circuits of the ring road around the town, we still couldn't find the beach.

"Perhaps we can't see it because it's dark!" I sighed looking out of the passenger window, desperate to see something that looked like a beach.

"Whatever the reason, I've had enough Ange. Let's go back. We can drive through Valencia on the way home. We need to come back when it's daylight."

"OK. You're right, there's absolutely no point driving round and round this ring road. We can come and find it another day. Let's go and see Valencia by night then," I finished, beaten but not defeated.

I turned my head and looked at the kids in the back of the car, seeking their agreement. They were both fast asleep; their heads lolled against the windows.

"Aw Colin, look. They're fast asleep. Let's just go home shall we?"

"That's fine by me Ange. To be honest, I don't really fancy driving through the centre of Valencia. I'm not as alert as I should be. I think I'm still tired after our late night last night," Colin admitted.

We arrived back at the villa just after midnight. The children practically slept walked into their bedrooms. The house was cool and I thanked the Lord we had bought a house with air-conditioning. I lit three vanilla candles and sat in the lounge with a cup of herbal tea. The cool air was refreshing. It was still 25 degrees outside. I covered myself liberally in after sun cream and retired to bed. Colin and I were asleep before our heads hit the pillow. Bliss!

I awoke at ten o'clock in the morning. Colin was already up and about. I opened some of the windows and doors and woke Blaise up very gently. I cooked eggs and bacon while everyone sat bog-eyed at the patio table. We looked like zombies. Perhaps we had been managing on reserves and everything was now catching us up. Whatever the reason, I was sure we would all feel much better after a good breakfast.

Colin and Ryan were going to finish lining the gate. The whole area around the house had definitely responded to a bit of TLC. Colin was going to trim up the cypress hedges. I wished I was better at art so that I could accurately draw the scene from the patio. The fig tree was very heavy with dark purple fruit. At least twenty-five figs had fallen off overnight and there were still hundreds of figs left on the tree. The orange tree was so heavy with fruit that its branches were threatening to snap under the strain. The wild blackberries at the back of the house were huge and the Jasmine bushes needed a frame to climb on. Colin suggested erecting two pergolas so it could climb freely and form a tunnel down the side of the villa. The scent was so pleasant; it was like walking through a perfume tunnel every time you walked down the side of the house. I never ceased to be amazed at the beauty I was surrounded by in my small garden. Trees, flowers, butterflies and small lizards abounded. Yesterday, while Blaise and I swam, a tiny lizard, a Gecko, just over an inch long, ran along the pool edge. It stopped in between the pool ladder handles and lapped water from the cement crevices. Colin managed to capture it on his video recorder. It was sand coloured and perfectly formed. I only hoped that the wild cats didn't find it and eat it.

Finally, the gates were finished and the lining was complete. Colin stepped back to admire his work.

"Well done you two, you've done a real professional job. Why don't you jump in the pool and celebrate!" I suggested.

Colin, Ryan and Blaise took me at my word and jumped into the pool. After a few minutes, Colin climbed out and left the children to play. I coated his back in sun cream and spread a dry towel on the sun lounger for him. I delivered cold drinks at regular intervals and watched my family at play. I lay on the sun lounger, thinking about nothing in particular. Colin sat on his pool chair and the children jumped in and out of the pool several times, almost knocking Colin off his pool toy on several occasions. Still, they all seemed to be happy and were obviously enjoying themselves.

"I'm going to clean the pool after Ange," Colin replied sitting down on the sun lounger next to me. "It needs a good clean."

"OK. I'll do some sweeping where the ornamental tree keeps shedding its leaves. That shouldn't be too strenuous for my back. I'll brush out the pool house too," I added.

We closed our eyes and listened to the children playing tag in the pool.

"I suppose we should go and say hello to the English people down the road," I suggested.

"What for?" Colin asked.

"Out of politeness. We should really Colin. It's neighbourly. I'll have a wander down there I think. I won't be long."

I walked into the house and changed into my shorts and T-shirt.

Blaise decided to accompany me and we set off walking down the road. A little way down the road, we met two girls, probably about Blaise's age. I asked them their names and they said their names were Tasmin and Rose Ann. Rose Ann said she was going back to England soon. Tasmin and Rose Ann were cousins. Blaise and I introduced ourselves and continued our walk. Tasmin directed us to her house and we walked the perimeter of the plot. It was a very big plot with a two-storey house on it. Grape vines tumbled over the wall around the house. Blaise spotted a toddler and an older gentleman, probably the toddler's grandfather, near the swimming pool. Tasmin had told us that her mother and father had gone to Valencia for the day. Realizing no-one was likely to be home, Blaise and I decided we would return to 'Bona Gent' and call back the following day. On our way back, I noticed that Blaise looked very flushed. The temperature had soared and it was the hottest part of the day. I suggested a dip in the pool to cool her off and she cheered up instantly.

We arrived back at 'Bona Gent' and stopped outside to admire the new gate liners. They looked perfect. Colin was busy cleaning the pool. He held a long sky blue metal rod with connecting hose in his hand. On the bottom of the rod was a palette, which cleaned the bottom of the pool. This was called a 'pulpo,' which is the Spanish word for octopus. Suckers on the bottom of the pulpo took the dirt from the bottom of the pool up the rod and through the hose to the filter. It was a bit like an under water Hoover. I watched carefully incase I ever had to clean the pool myself.

Ryan and Blaise wanted to clear out the back shed. Colin suggested they use it as a cool or shade room as it would give them somewhere to go out of the midday sun. They wanted to organize it so that they had their very own private games room. Carrying brushes and cleaning cloths, they made their way to the shed at the back of the house.

"It's siesta time for me Colin," I shouted.

"OK. Just finishing up the pool," he replied.

"Hasta lluego," I shouted back at him and made my way to the bedroom.

I awoke three and a half hours later. I went back to the poolside, equipped with nuts, crisps, chocolate digestive biscuits and melon. This evening, we were going to eat out at a Chinese restaurant in Lliria. We had driven passed it many times. It was called the Hong Kong Restaurant. I was thankful that I didn't have to cook and was looking forward to an evening out. The children helped themselves to drinks and nibbles and we lazed quietly around the pool. Candice was due to visit us the following day to complete the paperwork for managing the property. I took my 'to do' list from my glasses case and crossed several items off the list.

After an afternoon of doing nothing in particular, we all made a little extra effort with our appearance. We seemed to spend the whole day in swimwear or T. shirts and shorts. It was good to dress up for a change and we were happy to be eating out in a restaurant instead of eating at a pavement cafe. Blaise and I wore pretty dresses and Colin and Ryan wore three quarter length cotton trousers and short-sleeved shirts. We piled into the car and Colin drove us to Lliria.

The restaurant was not particularly busy and we were seated immediately. The waitress greeted us warmly and seemed very polite. She handed us an A4 sheet of paper with a list of dishes in English. It was very badly typed and just about legible. We ordered rice, noodles, sweet and sour chicken, chicken curry and roast pork. The main dishes arrived with prawn crackers and our drinks but no sign of the rice or noodles. We each picked at the food, which actually tasted very good. However, most of the main courses had gone by the time the rice and noodles appeared. Feeling too tired and laid back to complain, we finished off the remaining main dishes with the rice and noodles. Not brilliant, but OK. Finally Colin asked for the bill and we were presented with four thimble sized glasses and a bottle of liqueur.

"Sin alcohol?" Colin asked, pointing to the bottle.

"Ah, uno momento Señor," the waitress replied, removing the honey coloured bottle from our table.

She returned quickly with another bottle.

"Sin alcohol," she stated and with a huge smile poured each of us a glass of the golden syrupy liquid.

"Hmmm that's lovely," said Blaise, emptying her thimble in one gulp.

I quickly picked up my thimble sized glass and dipped my tongue in. The taste was very sweet, like melted sugar but there was definitely another taste, nut flavoured. I asked the waitress what it was and she brought the bottle over to us.

"Avellana," I mouthed slowly, looking at the picture on the bottle for clues.

"What is it Ange?" Colin asked, taking the bottle from me.

"I think it's hazelnut syrup Col," I answered.

We looked at the picture on the bottle again. It was definitely hazelnut and we thoroughly enjoyed it. Colin paid our bill and we made our way home to 'Bona Gent.' The moon was full and the stars bright in the sky.

"Are we going to have a midnight swim again mum?" Blaise asked, inwardly willing me to say yes.

"No, not tonight darling. We need a reasonably early night after all the late nights we have had recently," I replied, hoping she wouldn't make a fuss.

I flicked down the sun visor and looked in the courtesy mirror. Blaise yawned and rubbed her eyes. She looked so tired, I was happy with my decision.

We arrived home ten minutes later and entered the cool villa. Colin volunteered to stay up for an hour or so, to let the air conditioning run a little longer. I was much relieved as it gave me chance to fall asleep while it was still cold. We wished each other goodnight and the children and I retired to bed.

Chapter 18
A Little Snip Here!

I woke up wondering what day it was. I had completely lost all sense of time and couldn't remember either the day or the date. We were supposed to be going to Valencia to collect our bank cards. There was just one problem though. Candice was supposed to be coming over. I telephoned her and told her our plans. She was happy to postpone her visit until later but warned us that it was a bank holiday and nothing in Valencia or the local town was likely to be open. Colin telephoned VSI to speak to Sally.

There was no reply. After several attempts, we realized that there was no point going to Valencia. We ate a leisurely breakfast and pondered what to do for the day.

"Perhaps we could telephone Candice and ask her to come earlier," I suggested.

Colin punched her telephone number into his mobile phone. There was no reply. She had most likely gone out for the day. With the whole of the day to ourselves, Colin and I debated whether or not to cut the hedge and clear some of the rubbish. The rubbish could be burned in the paellero, as we had lots of cardboard packaging waste from all the products we had bought. Colin decided to burn it while we considered what to do for the rest of the day and began tearing up the cardboard into small pieces. He lit the cardboard mountain and returned to the patio.

Colin had bought a super powerful hedge trimmer at Bonaire, which I referred to as a chainsaw! Concluding that the hedge definitely had to be trimmed, he went to fetch it. Blaise and I agreed to collect the trimmings while Colin and Ryan did most of the heavy work.

Colin started at the bottom of the pool area. A pair of shiny new step ladders had been put out ready for use. We would have a fabulous new box cut hedge that I could stare at proudly. Colin asked me to plug the extension lead in to the pool house electric socket.

"There. That's a cinch!" I said to myself, fixing the plug securely in the socket.

"You are ready to rock 'n' roll!" I shouted, leaving the pool house to hold Colin's ladders for him.

The motor started up and Colin applied the razor sharp blades to the hedge in an upward sweeping motion. The shorn branches and foliage fell like lead confetti onto Blaise and I below. I spat out a mouthful of foliage and shook my head vigorously in an attempt to dislodge the bits from my hair. Blaise ran off up the garden, shrieking as she pulled the twig lets from her hair! I must have looked a frightful sight. There were bits of twigs and hedge in my hair and down my T-shirt. I felt very uncomfortable and dreaded what I would find inside my T-shirt. My skin crawled.

"Hey Colin, wait up!"

"What's up?" he called, above the whir of the motor.

"Can't you see? I'm covered in hedge trimmings?"

"Well it won't do you any harm."

"It might do if there's a scorpion in there!"

I was sure there were hundreds of creepy crawlies in the hedge and about my person and wondered what might be nestling in my cleavage. Brushing the bits off as best I could, I looked up at the hedge. The glare of the sun was strong and in my temporarily blinded state, a piece of cypress hedge caught me full pelt, just to the side of my right eye.

"Ouch!" I shouted.

By now, shorn hedge cuttings surrounded me. Everywhere was covered in debris. Assessing the situation quickly, I realized that we needed a plan and a well coordinated one, if we were going to do the job successfully. I could see that the task was enormous. Colin dripped sweat from his forehead. It trickled down his nose and his back glistened with beads of sweat. He would need to drink lots of water to stop from dehydrating in the intense heat. I shouted for the children to come and help us and fresh from resting in the shade of the playhouse, they appeared.

"You're just in time," I yelled, above the sound of the chainsaw.

"Can you bring us some drinks please Blaise," I asked, feeling more than a little hot and sticky.

"Ryan, you grab the bin liners please."

I quickly rolled out my plan to the children. I would sweep all the bits together and they would start putting some of it into the plastic bin bags. The children, realizing playtime was well and truly over, looked very depressed.

"Come on, if we all muck in, it will be done twice as fast," I urged, trying to motivate them.

It seemed to work. They grabbed handfuls of hedge cuttings and stuffed them into the bin liners. It was dreadfully hot, progress was good but the work was arduous. I glanced up at Colin. His face was wringing wet with sweat. He reminded me of Bruce Willis in Die Hard. The children were hot too and I was thankful that they were working in the shade of the pool house at the bottom of the garden. Colin had progressed to the gates, when Ryan had a brainwave. It was clear from the number of bin liners we had already used that we were going to run out of them and fast!

"Why don't we use the wheelbarrow?" Ryan suggested. "We can fill it up and take it to the big bins down the road."

"Good idea!" said Colin, perched on his new ladders.

The task of filling the wheelbarrow commenced and Ryan and Blaise dropped armfuls of hedge trimmings into it.

Meanwhile, at the back of the house, the paellero was still burning, the billowing smoke tainting the air. We continued working on the hedge for another hour and a half, loading the wheelbarrow and emptying it. Ryan worked extremely hard, pushing the full wheelbarrow to the bins, emptying it and pushing it back again. I brought out more drinks and we emptied our glasses in seconds. I refilled them and we sat for a minute in the shade of the patio, drinks in hand. Colin had cut two thirds of the hedge and the end was in sight. We finished our drinks and Colin resumed work with the chainsaw. As the chainsaw continued its destruction, a wave of anxiety flooded over me. What about the Jasmine bushes? Surely Colin wasn't going to hack it to pieces. A shiver ran down my spine. I needed to think quickly and take action. Shouting over the noise of the chainsaw, I asked Colin to down tools. The children brought out more drinks and placed them on the patio table. I felt like I had swallowed sand! I thought about how best to put forward my case for the Jasmine bushes. We had a substantial Jasmine arch next to the front patio. Further along the side of the house were two more Jasmine bushes. They were all growing well and the three bushes between them were forming a perfect tunnel. The scented air was a real tonic to the senses and I couldn't imagine 'Bona Gent' without the Jasmine tunnel. I broached the subject as diplomatically as I could under the circumstances.

"Colin, these Jasmine bushes are really very well established. They make a wonderful Jasmine tunnel. It's wonderful to have somewhere for us to sit in the shade with our drinks and a good book. I can read Hello magazine, you can read Biker magazine. I can just see us growing old together, sat under a wonderful scented Jasmine covered pergola. Do you think you could make a wooden pergola for it?"

"Yeah, there's no reason why I couldn't."

I grinned happily, but too soon my calm was shattered.

"But I'll have to cut it back for now Ange. Next year though, I don't see why not. I could fix a wooden support here," Colin indicated, pointing to the main bush and the cypress hedge.

"Even some sort of plastic trellis would do," I added, trying desperately to think of something else to say that would save the Jasmine.

I walked along the Jasmine tunnel, trying to imagine Colin and me growing old at 'Bona Gent.' The star shaped Jasmine flowers, pure white and heavily scented, floated to the ground like feathers. The breeze caught them and sent them swirling around my feet. On further inspection, I noticed that the third bush was also very well established and bigger than I had originally thought. Determined to protect them, I walked back towards Colin.

"Colin, those bushes need trimming with consideration, otherwise you'll kill them. If they are trimmed back too far, they may not recover," I said, my voice trembling with concern.

We both strode down the side of the house to inspect the second and third Jasmine bushes.

"OK. I will do my best. But the main one will need cutting back flush with the hedge. It's much larger than these two and will be able to stand it."

I smiled triumphantly.

"Thank you darling," I said, planting a kiss on his sweaty cheek.

Feeling much happier, I continued sweeping the bits of hedge trimmings for the children to collect and put into the wheelbarrow.

Blaise had become far too hot to accompany Ryan to the bins. She had now taken up drinks duty and was staying in the shade. Ryan said he would cope and that he would drink plenty of water. I stepped through the gates to see how much of the hedge clippings had fallen into the road. I exited the gates to assess the state of the hedge. I stood in the gateway, peering back and forth, outside, inside, outside and inside. The hedge on the outside looked awful compared to the inside view. The first thing guests would see when they approached the property would be the outside hedge. I looked at my watch. It was half past two in the afternoon and we had been working solidly for four hours. No wonder we were exhausted. But how was I going to tell Colin that the outside hedge needed doing too? It would take another three hours at least. I was sure he would object but I decided there was nothing for it but to wade in there.

"Col…" I said quietly, leaving a silence and elongating his name.

"I know that tone Ange. What now?" he replied with a sigh.

"You will have to cut the outside hedge too," I said quickly, trying to make it sound like a quick job. I watched Colin's face for signs of fury.

"It looks awful out there now you have made such a good job of the inside."

"Stop creeping Ange," Colin replied curtly.

"You have done such a fantastic job Colin, honestly, if you look outside, you will see how messy it looks now."

I was not sure if this sentence qualified as 'the iron hand in the velvet glove' approach. Colin's response made it clear that it certainly wasn't! Suffice to say, Colin made it plain to me that he thought I was always looking for ways to give him more things to do. Of course, I vehemently denied it! We were all hot, dirty and smelly and this obviously reflected in our fractious mood. Blaise appeared on cue with a large jug of cool fruit juice. Ryan rounded the corner, entered through the double gates, wheelbarrow in hand and yelled in his Manchester lingo, "Hey dad, y'no wot'd look really good was if yer did the outside too. It's tat compared to this now!"

'Brilliant Ryan!' I thought to myself, suppressing the urge to do a victory chant.

"OK," Colin sighed. "You wont be satisfied will you until it's done?" he mumbled.

"Dad, it will look great," beamed Ryan enthusiastically.

I grinned triumphantly from ear to ear.

"More drink mummy?" Blaise offered, handing me a bottle of water.

"Thank you treasure," I replied, taking the bottle from her.

Blaise looked non-too happy at the prospect of being drinks maid again for the next three or four hours. In contrast, Ryan was in his element, snapping twigs in half, loading the wheelbarrow, pushing it a quarter of a mile to the bins, tipping the contents and pushing the empty wheelbarrow back again. No wonder he was as fit as a fiddle. Colin trimmed the last bit of hedge, turned off the chainsaw and joined me on the patio.

The front door buzzer sounded and a loud voice shouted over the hedge, "Hola. Hola!"

I walked to the gate and opened it. A blonde haired, middle-aged lady, stood in front of me, waving her arms and talking at breakneck speed. Her voice rose higher and higher and became louder and louder. She gesticulated wildly, throwing her arms this way and that. I wondered at first if her husband had suffered a heart attack and she wanted help, she looked so anxious. I caught the word 'paellero' several times. With my limited knowledge of Spanish and having asked her most politely to slow down, I concluded that she was from the villa to the rear of 'Bona Gent.'

"What's she saying mum?" Blaise asked, looking slightly alarmed.

"She's saying something about lots of smoke," I replied calmly.

The lady grabbed my wrist, looked at the hedge cuttings, pointed her finger at them and made an angry face. She mentioned her husband, the paellero again and looked pleadingly at us. Then she mentioned the wind and the smoke and I realized what she was saying.

"I think she's saying that smoke is coming from our paellero and into her house or her husband. I am not sure which. She says it's OK to cook meat or paella for an hour or so, but nothing else. I don't know what the word she's saying means. Ah, wait a minute. Colin, she thinks you are burning all the twigs from the hedge in the paellero," I said aghast.

I tried to reassure her that we were not burning our hedge and that it was only a few bits of card and paper. I suddenly realized that the fire had been smouldering all day! I felt awful. And of course, at about five o'clock every day, the wind blew up out of nowhere.

"Colin, they must be choking with the smoke out there," I stated.

Colin looked at me confused and frustrated. The lady was still gesticulating at the hedge. Suddenly, we heard Francisco's friendly voice over the other side of our garden.

"Angela, what is it? Can I help in some way?"

"Oh Francisco, thank goodness you are there, I think this lady thinks we are burning our hedge in the paellero and smoking her out of house and home! But we have only been burning bits of paper and cardboard."

Francisco gestured for us all to come nearer the fence. The blonde lady began her tale of woe all over again and Francisco confirmed what I thought the lady had said. She did indeed think we were burning our hedge and both she and her husband were quite literally being smoked out of their home. We assured both Francisco and the lady that it was not the hedge. Francisco, ever helpful, said he would come round to our house to help explain.

The whole situation had become slapstick and Blaise and Ryan were holding their sides with laughter, which did nothing to pacify our blonde neighbour! We stood on our driveway; talking in turn, while Francisco translated. I suspected that the blonde lady didn't believe us, we could not placate her and finally, she asked if she could see the evidence for herself. Colin decided to take a 'hands on' approach. He grabbed the lady's hand and pulled her through the Jasmine tunnel towards the paellero and Francisco followed. Ryan, Blaise and I followed single file behind Francisco.

"She thinks we are mad cutting our hedge in 37 degrees centigrade," I whispered to the children.

I creased up with stifled laughter and made a hasty retreat to the front of the house to compose myself. Meanwhile Colin dowsed the smouldering pile of cardboard with water and apologized profusely. Not to be outdone, the blonde haired lady grabbed hold of Colin's wrist and pulled him through the gate. I was sorry we had caused so much trouble and didn't want to be labelled a social nuisances. I urged Colin to accompany the neighbour down the road to her home and my last image was of Colin and our neighbour marching hand in hand down the road to her house. Colin turned and waved to us then disappeared from sight.

"Remember, her husband is a very good singer," I shouted. "Don't forget to compliment him on his singing."

Meanwhile, Francisco said if we needed his help at any time, he would be very happy to oblige. Thank goodness for Francisco. Ryan, Blaise and I made the most of the opportunity to have a break and we sat and waited for Colin to come back with the tale of his neighbourhood adventure.

Some minutes later, he reappeared at the gates.

"It's not him who sings, it's her brother who lives next door but one," Colin informed me, as he strode through the gates.

"Did you mention how we enjoyed his singing? I asked curious.

"I mentioned that you said he had a nice voice and she seemed pleased," Colin answered.

"So, my little bit of useless information came in helpful after all, you know, to calm troubled waters, so to speak?"

"Yes it did. Everything is OK now so come on you lot, let's get back to work."

Obediently, we got up from our chairs and took the equipment we needed outside the gates, ready to start collecting the trimmings from the exterior hedge. Our mini adventure over and filled with renewed vigour, Colin picked up the chainsaw and attacked the hedge once again! The exterior was a lot easier to trim as there was a narrow concrete path running all the way around the villa. It wasn't really broad enough to call a pavement but it was broad enough to walk along and stand a pair of stepladders on. Blaise poured more drinks, Ryan wheeled trimmings to the bins, I swept the bits up as best I could and Colin expertly applied the chainsaw to the hedge. Colin's upward thrust on a particularly thick part of the hedge, sent a mass of branches and twigs tumbling onto the path. Pausing for breath, I noticed something move out of the corner of my eye. Something had tumbled from the hedge and at first sight I thought a twig had caught on the wall. I was amazed when the twig moved! I squatted to take a closer look and examine it and found to my amazement that I was eyeball to eyeball with a large and brightly coloured Preying Mantis. It was about 4" to 5" in length and was the brightest lime green colour I had ever seen. It was practically fluorescent! Its long spindly front legs bent forward, poised to catch any passing insect. It was fascinating.

Having read about a Preying Mantis a long time ago, I knew that it was a formidable predator. It rocked backwards and forwards unsteadily, like the breeze catching a leaf. I shouted for Colin to stop the chainsaw and come and take a look. I shouted Blaise too and watched for Ryan returning with the wheelbarrow. We all stood mesmerised by its mechanical swaying, backwards and forwards.

"I've got to video this," said Colin, returning to the villa for his video recorder.

Blaise and I squatted on the path and examined its every little detail. We were totally fascinated by it.

"I know about this insect," I announced smugly.

"Where did you learn about it mum?" asked Blaise.

"At senior school Blaise. We read the book 'My Family and Other Animals' by Gerald Durrell. The book formed part of my English literature 'O' level material and I thoroughly enjoyed reading it. I laughed from start to finish."

"What was it about mum?" Blaise enquired.

"Well, it was about a one parent family, a mother and her four children that moved to the Greek island of Corfu. It was about their move from England to Corfu and their life there."

"Why did they go to Corfu?" Blaise asked interested.

"Oh, for many reasons Blaise. The daughter, Margot, had terrible acne. The youngest son had a bad chest. He kept getting colds and chest infections. The middle son, Leslie, had a passion for guns and was always shooting. And the eldest son, Larry, was a writer. Gerald was the youngest son and he loved animals. He collected all sorts of things, insects, mice, and snakes. He loved nature. He and his wife are the patrons of Jersey Zoo."

"Is Corfu good for acne then?" Blaise asked.

"Yes, I suppose it is. All sunshine is good for acne, but England doesn't get much sunshine does it?" I said laughing.

"What exactly is acne mum?" Blaise questioned.

"It's when you get really bad spots, you know, when you go through puberty," I replied.

"Do you have to go through puberty to get to Corfu then?" she asked thoughtfully.

"No not really Blaise," I replied, wondering where the conversation was leading.

"Well, where exactly is puberty then?" she said, her face screwed up in a frown against the sun.

"Puberty isn't a place darling, it's a time of life when your body changes, you know, when you start to grow and stuff."

"Oh, so you can grow a puberty anywhere then."

I looked at her thoughtfully, wondering how best to explain.

"Puberty is when you start to develop a bust Blaise."

252

"Oh, I get it! Margot was growing a bust. Will Ryan grow a bust then and go through puberty?" Blaise asked.

I laughed and ruffled her hair.

"No darling. Ryan won't grow a bust, but he will go through puberty soon and that means he will get hairy armpits and a hairy chest. You know, stuff like that."

"Will he get acne too?" she asked.

"Possibly, some people do and some don't. Everyone gets teenage spots but some people develop really bad acne because of all the hormones in their body. Acne is not very nice," I added thoughtfully.

Colin arrived with the video recorder and Ryan appeared with the empty wheelbarrow.

"Come and look at this Ryan," Colin shouted.

Ryan squatted with us, transfixed.

"What is it?" he asked.

"A Preying Mantis!" shouted Blaise. "They come from Corfu," she added and I chortled to myself at her comical conclusion.

Colin touched the record button and began to video the insect.

"It's like a wildlife sanctuary here isn't it Ange?" Ryan chirped, with his eyes still transfixed on the insect.

"Well, yes. I suppose it is," I answered. "We did see a Gecko yesterday and we've got wild cats. Dad and I saw a Barn Owl on the telephone wire last time we were here too."

The Preying Mantis began to sway unsteadily on its spiny, spindly, lime green legs.

"OK that's it for now!" said Colin, standing up and walking back to the villa with his video recorder.

"Back to work everyone," he shouted, lifting the chainsaw and climbing the ladders.

The whirring of the saw commenced and once again, we set about our work. Ryan walked listlessly along the path, placing bits of newly trimmed hedge into the wheelbarrow. He followed Colin's trail of debris along the narrow path.

"Ryan looks exhausted mum. I think I'd like to help him. It will be finished sooner if I do," Blaise said, springing into action.

Fortunately, the path was in the shade and as long as Blaise could work in the shade, she would be OK. Finally, the last wheelbarrow full of clippings was loaded. It was twenty past six. When Ryan returned with the empty wheelbarrow, Blaise and I were already in the swimming pool, cooling down and chilling out. It was heavenly.

Colin and Ryan threw down their tools and showered under the outside shower. They pulled off their work shorts, climbed on to the pool rim and dived headlong into the pool They must have been so hot! I floated in the pool, luxuriating in its cooling depths. Colin, Ryan and Blaise took turns leaping from the poolside, a look of sheer delight on their faces. It was a pleasure to watch them. Never was a cool dip in the pool more appreciated than after seven hours

of hard labour. I lay on my back in the water and floated like a giant lily pad, reflecting on the day's events. It had been full of excitement, elation, determination, frustrations, negotiations and discoveries. We were privileged to be here. I said a silent prayer of thanks and contemplated what a life in Pedralba would be like.

An hour later, I climbed out of the pool and towelled down. Colin followed me out and we sat together on the patio, admiring his handiwork. The hedge looked magnificent. I thanked Colin several times over. All the family had worked as a team to get the mammoth task finished. It had given us plenty of time together as a family and I felt contented I felt tired too, in fact very tired, but mostly very contented.

Our new property manager, Candice, was due to arrive at any time, in order to complete our paperwork. We sat, proud of our days labours. I glanced at our orange tree, heavy with fruit. Already another plan was hatching but I decided not to spring it upon Colin just yet. I made yet another mental note of where the additional supports needed to be, smiled at the sheer beauty surrounding us and tried to imagine what the tree would look like in December, when the fruit was ripe and orange.

The sound of Candice's car outside interrupted my thoughts and Colin and I stood up to greet her as she entered through the gates. Colin poured drinks for everyone and I opened a large bag of mixed salted nuts and seeds. We chatted about our families, the latest news in England, the weather back home and gradually broached the subject of fees for the property marketing and maintenance service. The contract seemed to provide good value and I was happy to sign up for the service. We completed the necessary paperwork and Candice intimated that the chance of renting the villa out were very good, as it was ultra modern by Valencia standards. She suggested we get a TV and DVD, explaining that these would be necessary if we wanted winter lets. We thanked her for her time and as her car pulled away from outside 'Bona Gent,' we waved her off. I wrote 'buy TV and DVD' on my 'to do' list, crossed off 'trim hedge' and made my way to the shower.

There was no way I could bring myself to stand near a hot cooker. Colin said there was a TV and DVD on special offer at the Carrefour supermarket. Luckily, there was a Chinese restaurant just down the road from the Carrefour. We would be able to get something to eat after buying a TV and DVD. Everyone would be happy and we could stop worrying about guests having nothing to do in winter. After all, just because 'Bona Gent' had a TV and DVD, it didn't mean that we HAD to watch it, did it?

Chapter 19
A Fantastic Day

I awoke at a reasonable time, considering the previous day's exertions with the hedge. The simple pleasure of breakfast on the patio filled me with joy. I took the fruit and fresh figs from the refrigerator, arranged the croissants in the breadbasket and grabbed the mosquito guards. I padded along the cool floor tiles to the front door, arranged everything on the table and smiled as one by one, my family appeared.

Blaise had obviously modelled herself on Cathy from 'Wuthering Heights.' She plodded across the tile floor, blinking like a chameleon in the sunlight, her tousled hair and fringed sarong trailing. She looked truly bohemian. If Blaise could leave her hair unwashed and unbrushed for months on end she would. I pondered whether it would form dreadlocks if I left it alone. I would probably be locked up by the social services and I consoled myself with the thought that when she reached sixteen, she could decide the fate of her own hair. But as she was still only ten years old, I had to intervene.

Blaise had been in the swimming pool so much that I had not bothered brushing her hair until her last dip of the day had taken place. As this was sometimes midnight, I had at times, just resorted to combing plenty of conditioner on it before she went to sleep, in an effort to lessen the damage. The daily onslaught of chlorine and ultra violet rays had already turned some strands wheat coloured. The combination of sun kissed hair and a golden tan added to her 'boho' look.

"Blaise definitely got all the best bits of us both," I commented, as Colin tucked into his croissant.

"What?" he replied, still bleary eyed.

"Well, she's got my olive skin and brown eyes and is solidly built like I was at her age. She has your hair texture, nice and thick with a wave here and there. She's sociable too, just like us. I'm glad she got your straight nose though; it's lovely and straight, her side profile is pretty perfect."

A plastic chair grated on the floor tiles of the patio as Blaise plonked down wearily. The previous day's hard work had tired her out. The combination of hard work and the intense heat had affected us all, but as this was our last day at 'Bona Gent,' I wanted to make the most of it.

"I've invited Francisco and his family to dinner tonight Colin," I casually stated, between mouthfuls of croissant.

"That's nice. What time?"

"About nine o'clock, more supper I suppose really. What shall I cook?"

"Well make it something easy Ange; it's our last evening here."

"I will. I thought about lots of little bits like, omelette, potato wedges, pizza, salad and stuff."

"Yep, that sounds good to me and at least the children will love it."

Colin and I set about planning our trip to the bank. The day was bright and beautiful as we sat down, my pen and pad at the ready.

"Let's go to Valencia first and shop on the way home," Colin suggested.

"Dad, come and look at this, there's all brown stuff floating on the top of the swimming pool," Ryan shouted.

We strode purposefully in the direction of the pool and peered over the side. Hundreds of blobs of brown algae floated on the surface. Ryan and Blaise took turns with the huge pool net and tried desperately to sieve out the brown algae, but it seemed like the more they sieved out, the more momentum the algae gathered.

"We will have to go to Sally at VSI first and see if she has translated those pool instructions. The pool's out of bounds today kids," Colin stated, much to the disappointment of Ryan and Blaise.

"Do you want to come with us?" I asked, hoping they would decline, as I didn't fancy dragging two children around the centre of Valencia in the heat of the day.

"No, we want to stay here Ange," Ryan replied. "We'll play in our den until you come back."

"Are you sure you want to stay here? We may be gone some time," I said, mother worry setting in.

"No mum, we'll be OK here and I can get us something to eat from the fridge if we get hungry," Blaise added.

Colin assured me they'd be OK and my unease subsided.

"Keep in the play room and keep out of the sun," I warned.

"We will," they chorused, taking more croissants from the breadbasket.

Our plan was to drive to Villamarchante first and get the pool instructions from Sally. We could get the train from Riba Roja to Valencia, collect the bank cards, buy scart leads for the DVD and call at the supermarket on the way home. We also needed a good supply of chlorine for the pool. We dressed quickly, backed the car out through the gates and set off.

Fortunately, Sally had finished translating the pool instructions. It was a great relief, as they were much needed. We thanked her for her kindness and asked Alfredo if he had enjoyed his holiday in Argentina. He said he had particularly enjoyed wearing sweaters and winter coats. It had been a winter holiday and the weather had been cold. He thought it was wonderful to visit somewhere cold. We looked at him bemused and guessed that when all you had was day after day of relentless sun and heat; you hungered for a cold spell. We bade everyone at VSI farewell and rushed off to Riba Roja to catch the train to Valencia.

We arrived to find the railway workers on strike. However, there were still four or five trains running. The last train back was much earlier than we would have liked. We couldn't really change our plans, as it was our last day in Spain. It was the only day left for us to collect the bankcards. We bought our return tickets, which cost €5 for the two of us and waited for the train. I imagined a strike to mean that all trains were cancelled, a bit like a strike on the London underground. But, no, it was quite civilized, only four trains had been cancelled. The guard told us that the service was restricted, not stopped and that a country couldn't continue to be productive if everything came to a standstill. Oh that England would adopt the same philosophy I thought to myself!

"You must either get the ten past three, ten past four or ten past five train," a passer-by reminded us politely, as she stood alongside us on the platform.

Her spoken English was excellent. She explained that if we didn't, we could be stranded in Valencia for the night. The train pulled up at the platform and we thanked her for her assistance.

The train carriage was clean and there were plenty of seats to choose from. My thoughts returned to the last time I caught a train in London. I was travelling from London Victoria to West Malling. The train was running very late and was full to bursting by the time I'd got on. I had sat in a first class carriage so that my back wouldn't be twisted or squashed. The first class carriage, while offering a seat, was absolutely filthy, filled with old polystyrene coffee cups and crumpled paper sandwich bags that spewed half eaten sandwiches on to the floor. Graffiti covered both the interior and exterior of the carriage. The train for Valencia, in stark contrast, was clean and there was not a bit of graffiti to be seen anywhere. The train was running on time too. A female guard made her way slowly down the aisle towards us. The Spanish guard had blonde hair and a smiling, friendly face. She punched a hole in our tickets and wished us a good trip. Could you ever imagine that on the Ashford International train?

In order to pass the time, I decided to play 'snake' on my mobile telephone. My reflexes were very slow and I couldn't seem to score more than a few points before the snake bit its own tail and hissed. I hissed back at it each time it caught me out, much to the amusement of two toddlers who sat opposite me. Colin wasn't amused!

"Stop doing that!" he commanded. "It's embarrassing."

"I'm not at all embarrassed," I continued.

The two toddlers giggled and their mother smiled at me. I continued to hiss back until we arrived at Valencia. The train arrived precisely on time. I cheered and the two toddlers laughed and waved goodbye, their mum shepherding them down the aisle of the carriage.

Making our way through the station, Colin asked me to quicken my pace so that we could get to the bank before they closed for lunch. We would then have about forty minutes to get back for our train home.

The route to our bank was very simple, one straight road really and about a brisk walk of ten minutes. However, in 35 degrees, just putting one foot in front of the other was a major effort. Add to that a repairing slipped disc and a twisted sacroiliac joint and it all became a bit of a nightmare. I didn't even have time to look in the wonderful shops that we passed along the way. Finally we arrived at the hundred year old trees, magnificent specimens, right in the centre of Valencia. It was supposed to bring you good luck if you touched them and I was eagerly anticipating placing my hands around their massive trunks. Unfortunately, Colin figured we had walked too far along the road and we needed to make a left turn. Thank goodness for his excellent compass skills and his superb sense of direction. Doing as he suggested, we finally arrived at the CAM bank.

We entered and met the lady who attended our house signing. She gave us a warm greeting and spoke a few words of English to us. She produced our bankcards and pin numbers, asked for our signatures and then handed them over to us. She wished us good luck in our house and well for the future, before ushering us out of the doors.

Happy that we had caught the bank in time, we made our way back towards the station. Passing a motorbike shop, Colin suggested we call in. We looked at the motorcycle leathers, turning the price tags of several pairs. They were expensive by English standards and Colin said he could get them much cheaper in England. We left the shop and made our way to El Corte Ingles.

We entered El Corte Ingles at the rear entrance and walked up and down the aisles, happy to browse the different goods for sale. I looked at leather purses and leather bags while Colin made his way to the electrical department to look for DVD connectors. What I really wanted was a Spanish fan. I was frequently suffering from hot flushes and thought a fan would be very useful. I could carry it with me and use it to cool me down during a 'tropical moment.'

I thought carefully about the sort of fan I wanted. My selection process was simple. I wanted a fan no larger than my hand would hold comfortably. That meant it must measure 10" or less. It had to have a traditional Spanish scene or craftwork on it and it had to flick open and shut easily. If possible, I wanted one made out of wood, but I was open to buying a plastic one if the fan met the other requirements. And so began my quest for the perfect fan.

I delved into various compartments on the tabletops, picking one up after another and sizing up each one. I studied the painted scenes on them. There were ladies in long flowing Flamenco dresses, ladies on horseback and matadors with scarlet red capes. I flicked them open and shut several times. I passed each fan from one hand to the other. An eagle-eyed shop assistant studied me closely. I caught her eyeing me and sighed. Up and own the aisles I walked, picking up this fan and that, all the time searching for that perfect fan. At the end of the aisle in the last compartment, I noticed a pale wooden fan. I opened it, shut it, opened it, shut it and continued to flick it open and shut several times more. Colin reappeared without any leads for the DVD. He stood looking at his watch nervously. It was three o'clock and our train was due to leave in ten minutes!

"Eureka!" I called enthusiastically. "This is it Colin, this is perfect!"

"Well hurry up and buy it then," he said, looking at his watch again. "We'll have to run for the train at this rate."

I picked up the fan, made my way to the cash desk, paid for it and set off for the station like an Olympic walker.

"I hope we wont be stranded," I puffed, a little short of breath and struggling to keep up, my flip-flops hindering me at every step. We arrived at the station with three minutes to spare, looking like two red-faced Indians.

"We made it," I gasped.

"Yeah, only just though," Colin replied.

Pleased with ourselves, we looked for our train information on the platform notices. There was no train to Riba Roja listed. We found a guard and asked him which platform the train for Riba Roja was departing from. He told us that the train would not be departing until twenty past four. Colin and I managed a forced smile, thanked him for the information and strode indignantly towards the cafeteria. We needed something to drink. It was incredibly hot and we were parched with thirst. Colin ordered ice cold drinks and I sat down at one of the tables.

"I'm going back to El Corte Ingles to look for Scart Leads," Colin announced, taking a swig of his drink. "There are two stores and the last chap said the other store has a proper electrical department," he continued.

"Order me some food and I'll be back in a jiffy," he said, turning on his heel.

I watched him jog towards the exit sign and disappear from sight. I stood at the café bar counter and ordered two baguettes, willing Colin to find his Scart Leads quickly and return in time for the train.

The food arrived quickly. I tucked into my cheese salad baguette and slurped ice-cold lemonade. I glanced at the station clock in mild panic. It was now ten past four and Colin was nowhere to be seen. If he didn't show up soon, we would miss the train and be stranded at the station. It would cost a fortune to get a taxi home. I picked up my bag and exited the café to look for him. Suddenly I spotted him jogging through the station entrance.

"I got 'em!" he shouted happily, waving a plastic bag at me, "I got the leads Ange."

"Great Colin, now let's get on the train," I replied impatiently.

We boarded the train with one minute to spare! Colin was panting and red faced. Sweat beads formed on his brow.

"I'm really pleased with myself Ange. I asked for the Scart Leads in a combination of Spanish and English. I tried to describe what I was looking for and gestured with my hands. Suddenly, the man knew exactly what I wanted. You'll never guess what they are called in Spanish Ange."

"Well go on then, what are they called?" I responded wearily.

"Euro connectors!" piped Colin loudly. "How's your fan then?"

"Oh blimey, I forgot all about it Col," I responded, delving into my El Corte Ingles carrier bag.

"Here it is," I said, handing the fan over to him. "It's just perfect for me."

Colin studied the fan carefully. It was about 8" in length and was made from wood. It was embossed with a lace design. It flicked open and shut easily and was easy to use in either hand. Actually, the fan was a combination of wood and fabric but it was a very pretty design.

"It's very nice," Colin said, handing the fan back to me.

I flicked the fan open and began fanning myself furiously. I spent the journey home thinking about what to cook for our neighbours Francisco and Mercedes and closed my eyes, my head nodding in rhythm with the 'chug' of the train.

We arrived home laden with goodies. The children ran to greet us and helped ferry the food and other purchases inside.

"It's all hands to the deck now," I chirped to everyone. "Time to make dinner for eight!"

The children set the patio table with tortillas, potato wedges, pizza, nuts, bread and salad.

At nine o'clock, Francisco, his wife Mercedes and their daughters, Barbara and Lourdes, arrived to feast with us. We shook hands and kissed three times on the cheek in greeting. We sat around the large patio table, quite excited at the prospect of an evening with our Spanish neighbours.

Francisco looked splendid in his clean crisp trousers and shirt and his beautiful wife Mercedes looked spectacular in a denim mini skirt and top, a broad chartreuse hair band holding back her long dark hair. Barbara and Lourdes wore modern trousers and tops.

We, in contrast, looked like we had just come off the beach. I wore shorts and a T-shirts, Colin wore a football shirt and shorts and Blaise wore her new pink jeans, pink high heels and a 'Lola Bunny' top. She could hardly walk in the shoes and stooped forward in her efforts to balance. She tried so hard to look dignified, but obviously found it extremely difficult to walk in her new high heeled shoes. I was sure she would discard them before long. Ryan wore his new jeans and his Manchester United football shirt. He looked very 'grown up' and quite stylish. He had even put a generous amount of gel in his hair and spiked it!

The conversation flowed and we all communicated easily. Dinner was a very leisurely affair, and we were glad to see Francisco and his family help themselves to the food. Francisco asked us if we liked music and if we played any musical instruments. We told him Blaise played the piano a little but was somewhat shy of performing. Francisco said he played the guitar and that he would go and fetch his guitar and a small keyboard from their house so that he and Blaise could play for us.

Several minutes later we clapped for Blaise as she finished her tune on the piano. She had played a Christmas Carol but it was still lovely to watch her play. Francisco thanked Blaise and picked up his guitar. His fingers plucked the strings methodically and the melodious sound of Lennon and McCartney's 'Michelle' rang in the air. It sounded so beautiful that I almost cried. Francisco was undoubtedly a talented musician! It was such a moving experience, sitting under the stars in the warmth of the Jasmine scented air, listening to a Spanish guitar being expertly played by our Spanish neighbour. When Francisco had finished we clapped our hands loudly in appreciation.

We poured more drinks and chatted about the children and about 'Bona Gent.' Barbara and Lourdes went with Ryan and Blaise to play basketball at the back of the house and the evening passed quickly. All too soon, the evening ended and Francisco explained that they had to retire for the night because they were leaving early in the morning. We bade them goodnight and promised to keep in touch. We said we would see them again the following year when we came for our holiday and gave each of them a farewell kiss. We waved them off through the gates, pleased that the evening had gone so well. It had been a great success, worth all the effort we had put in.

"I'm going to connect the TV and DVD Ange. Can you manage to clear the table and stuff without me?" Colin asked.

"Of course we can, can't we kids?" I said, turning to Ryan and Blaise.

They groaned but collected the dirty dishes and glasses nonetheless.

"Mum, can we watch a DVD?" Blaise asked softly.

"I don't think we have any darling. But next time we come out, we will bring some with us. OK?"

"OK mum," Blaise said resigned to clearing up and going to bed.

"OK everyone, I have a surprise for you," Colin shouted from the lounge.

We all entered the lounge and sat down expectantly in front of the TV. To our utter surprise, Colin had bought a DVD player that had a dual language facility. He had also bought a DVD and surprised and delighted us all. It was 'Oliver!'

"Hurray, hurray!" Blaise and Ryan shouted, jumping up and down eagerly.

We settled down to watch the movie. I thought I would be the last one who wanted to watch a film. After all, I had put enough objections in the way when Colin first suggested we buy a TV and DVD. But sitting in our family group, I thoroughly enjoyed the film and we all joined in with the songs we knew. Finally at one o'clock in the morning, we made our way to our beds. Colin, being in an exceptionally good mood, started to sing ...

"Consider yourself at home,
Consider yourself one of the family,
We've taken to you so strong,
It's clear; we're going to get along!"
Consider yourself our friend,
Consider yourself part of the furniture,
We don't have a lot to share
Who cares, whatever we've got we share."

We all hummed the tune and filed into our bedrooms one by one. I dozed off with Blaise's soft voice in my ears as she sang the finale ...

"Consider yourself .... One of us!"

Peace descended upon our household. Ryan yawned and shouted goodnight to everyone.

"Goodnight Ryan!" we shouted and succumbed to peaceful sleep.

Chapter 20
When the Orange Blossoms

Wednesday 1 September 2004. I awoke early. I normally poured myself a drink and sat for a time outside on the patio. But today was not a 'usual' sort of day and I headed straight to the lounge. It was very hot again and I took time to enjoy the feel of the wonderfully cool floor tiles under my feet. I opened the front door as wide as I could. Taking a seat on the patio chair, I looked out over the swimming pool. I wondered when the huge green baubles hanging from the tree would turn orange. I tried to imagine what it would look like in the Turia Valley with millions of oranges hanging from the columns of orange trees. Would I ever see them as ripe fruit? I wasn't sure. Candice told me that they ripened in December and sweetened in the New Year.

A sharp pain shot down my right thigh and I winced with pain. I had probably trapped a nerve at some point during the night, perhaps caused by turning awkwardly in my sleep. I would have to take more painkillers to ease the gnawing sensation down my leg.

I wandered down to the pool in the warm Jasmine scented air and peered over the ledge. Large brown slime blobs had appeared all over the surface of the water. Colin would have to speak to Candice about it. I slowly walked the borders of our garden. The oriental iris, geraniums, rosemary and roses all seemed OK, if a little crisp in places. I ran my fingers along the smooth green spears of rosemary and lifted them to my nose. The pungent smell made my mouth water and I could almost taste a slice of succulent roast lamb. I slowly made my way back to the villa, ready to rouse everyone from slumber. It was packing up day and we would be leaving 'Bona Gent' very soon.

I prepared the breakfast solemnly and chided myself for feeling sorry for myself. After all, this was our house; we could come back any time we liked. Heck, we could even live here if we wanted to. I put the crockery and cutlery on the patio table and formed a 'packing up plan' in my mind as I went along.

"OK everyone, up and eat!" I shouted, as loudly as I could.

I peered over the fence towards Francisco and Mercedes' house. Their car had gone. They must have left very early. I had hoped we would see them once more before they left, even if it was only for a moment. Still, I had Francisco's card and we had promised to keep in touch by email.

I continued making my plans and placing food and drinks on the table. Ryan extended our Dutch awning; giving us much needed extra shade.

"Another hot one!" said Colin, as he poured fruit juice for everyone.

"Yes, it is. I wonder how long the warmth lasts here," I mused, trying to make conversation.

We ate in silence.

"It's sad that we've got to leave," Ryan said, reaching for a slice of melon.

"I guess we are all feeling a little sad today," I sighed. "But the good news is, this is our villa, our garden, our pool, our Spanish home and we can come here at any time we like. We'll be back before you know it," I chirped, trying my best to sound jolly.

"Why does time go quick when you are happy and slow when you aren't?" Blaise asked, scrunching up her nose.

"It always does that," added Ryan. "When you don't want time to go fast it does and when you do want it to go fast, like when you are waiting for something special or to go somewhere, it takes ages."

"Well, we've had a marvellous time here. We've seen a fiesta, seen the bulls run and watched a firework display. We've seen lots of different animals. I almost had my head blown off by a banger. We saw a Preying Mantis too," I stated, trying to remember all the things we had seen and done.

"And we saw the tiny Gecko drinking at the side of the pool," added Blaise.

"And we made friends with Probenta, whatever her name was, at the first villa," Ryan joined in.

"And I got a TV and DVD," added Colin.

"And you both got new outfits from the retail outlet at Bonaire," I said, remembering how Blaise had teetered on high heel shoes the previous evening.

"And we have really good neighbours don't we?" said Ryan.

"Barbara and Lourdes are really nice aren't they? They played basketball with us and although we couldn't speak Spanish, we all tried to be friends and it was good," said Blaise happily.

"And I got a TV and DVD," repeated Colin.

"We've eaten fresh figs from our very own fig tree; do you know how lucky we are to do that kids?" I sighed, remembering the sweet, sticky, purple fruit.

"Aw mum, remember the Melon Man," said Blaise cheekily.

"Hmmm, yes, we still have thirteen melons to dispose of. I gave Francisco two of them. What are we going to do with the rest?"

"Can't we take them home with us?" Ryan asked.

"Not thirteen of them Ryan," added Colin between mouthfuls of fresh melon, adding, "I can cut some up for the airport though."

"Good idea Colin," I replied, thinking of the deep plastic containers I had bought at the Carrefour.

"But we will have to give most of them away. We can leave some for Candice and perhaps we can take some to the English people who live in the villa at the end. Ange, are you going to take some fresh figs home with you?" Colin finished.

"I most certainly am Colin," I confirmed. "I also told Candice that I would give her some figs too. The rest will drop and probably rot but there's absolutely nothing I can do about that," I added, resigned to the fact that my bumper fig crop would go to waste.

"Well, we better get on with it then, time to pack up and go!"

We cleared the dirty breakfast pots away and Blaise stacked the dishwasher.

There was much tidying, packing, sweeping, mopping and bleaching to do. I packed all the perishable goods into plastic carrier bags for friends and neighbours. Beds were stripped of their sheets, the washing machine was loaded and all our personal belongings were stored and locked away.

The car was loaded. Colin packed the melon slices into plastic containers and put them in our hand luggage. We took a last look at our home, 'Bona Gent.' The Dutch awning had been wound in tight, the garden had been watered and the Jasmine smelt as sweet as ever, it's heavily scented star shaped flowers swirling on the ground like confetti at a wedding. The metal shutters were rolled down and all the outbuildings were locked. The metal gate to the pool area was closed and bolted.

Ryan and Blaise stood like sentries at either side of our double gates, waiting to lock them once Colin had reversed the car out. Colin started the engine and reversed the car through the gates into the road. The gates were locked and Ryan and Blaise climbed in the car. We drove past three villas to the English couple's home. Although I felt a little silly calling to say hello and goodbye in the same breath, I was sure they would understand and I was glad of the diversion. It quelled the feeling of sadness that had welled up inside me.

We rang the outside bell of a large white villa that stood on a huge corner plot. A large black dog ran to the gate. It barked and growled at us relentlessly. A young woman appeared and we introduced ourselves to her. She invited us in and we sat on the patio while she introduced us to the rest of her family. Her name was Anita, her husband's name was Peter and they had three children, Tasmin, Kieran and Reece. Anita's mum and dad lived with them too. Peter and Anita had just set up a business running a magazine called 'Lookforit.' Anita kindly offered us cool drinks while we sat under a huge canvas umbrella on her patio. She gave us a copy of the magazine and after chatting for about an hour, we excused ourselves. We had to leave or we would miss our flight home. We gave our perishable food to her and promised to look them up when we next came over. Anita's daughter, Tasmin, was the same age as Blaise and I hoped they would become friends. We said farewell and climbed back into our little white car. We faced a long drive back to Barcelona for our flight home. The car pulled away and Anita and her family waved us goodbye.

The mood in the car was very grim as we headed away from 'Bona Gent.' The children fell asleep quickly and night closed in. I was glad of the darkness as I shed tears, sorry to be leaving but overcome with emotion as to what we had achieved. Colin's eyes were focused firmly on the motorway as my tears fell like dew drops down my cheeks and onto my blouse. It had been a wonderful, if somewhat hectic holiday. Well, more than a holiday really. Colin and I had realized our dream. We had a home in Spain. After four years of thinking about it, talking about it, planning it and dreaming about it, we had finally done it. Tears spilled over my cheeks and dripped off the end of my nose. I fumbled for a tissue in my bag.

"Hormones?" nodded Colin sympathetically.

"Yes, I'm afraid so darling," I sniffled.

As the car passed the sign wishing us a safe journey from the Costa del Azahar, I remembered the first time we had visited, how we had fallen in love with the garden of Spain and the simple Spanish way of life in the Turia Valley. I remembered Moxy the dog, the orange groves that spread for miles, down as far as the seashore. I remembered our quest to try and find the beach at El Puig and our joy at finding the vast retail outlet at Bonaire. It had all been so wonderful. Our dream had come true. At long last we had made it happen. We had a house amongst the orange groves of Pedralba. I looked at my wonderful family, my whole being choked with emotion, my throat tight with swallowed tears. Colin squeezed my hand tenderly. He had supported me every step of the way. This was our beginning, here on the Orange Blossom Coast. This was it, a new start, our 'Orange Blossom Beginning.'

Printed in the United States
88138LV00010B/84/A

9 781425 965891